Legal Research: Step by Step

REVISED FOURTH EDITION

Margaret Kerr
JoAnn Kurtz
Arlene Blatt

 ▪ Toronto, Canada ▪ 2018

Emond Montgomery Publications Limited
1 Eglinton Avenue East, Suite 600
Toronto ON M4P 3A1
http://www.emond.ca/highered

Printed in Canada.
Reprinted June 2019.

We acknowledge the financial support of the Government of Canada.   Canadä

Emond Montgomery Publications has no responsibility for the persistence or accuracy of URLs for external or third-party Internet websites referred to in this publication, and does not guarantee that any content on such websites is, or will remain, accurate or appropriate.

Vice president, publishing: Anthony Rezek
Publisher: Lindsay Sutherland
Director, development and production: Kelly Dickson
Developmental and production editor: Natalie Berchem
Production supervisor: Laura Bast
Copy editor: Dawn Hunter
Typesetter: Pronk
Text designer: Tara Agnerian
Permissions editor: Alison Lloyd-Baker
Proofreader: Mikayla Castello
Indexer: Paula Pike
Cover image: iStock.com/Trout55

Library and Archives Canada Cataloguing in Publication

Kerr, Margaret Helen, 1954-, author
    Legal research : step by step / Margaret Kerr, JoAnn
    Kurtz, Arlene Blatt.

(Working with the law)
Includes bibliographical references and index.
ISBN 978-1-77255-327-7 (softcover)

    1. Legal research—Canada—Textbooks.   2. Textbooks.   I. Kurtz, JoAnn, 1951-,
author   II. Blatt, Arlene, author   III. Title.   IV. Series: Working with the law

KE250 K477 2018   340.072'071   C2017-906750-8
KF240 K477 2018

ISBN 978-1-77255-327-7

To Sarah and Gael.
To Ely, Max, Jacob, and Danny.
To Jeffrey, Jordan, and Matthew.

Brief Contents

Detailed Contents

PART III
THINKING ABOUT LEGAL RESEARCH

PART IV
WORKING WITH LEGAL RESEARCH SOURCES

13   Finding and Updating Cases

15   Legal Writing

APPENDIXES

Preface

This book is designed for students who have no previous experience of legal research. We demonstrate how to approach legal research by analyzing fact situations and identifying legal issues, and we provide detailed, practical guidance on how to use various resources—both online resources and traditional paper ones—to find solutions to legal issues. The many examples and exercises we have included will make this text very useful in the classroom.

Although the fourth edition of *Legal Research: Step by Step* was published recently, the nature of this textbook means it is important to maintain currency. Changes to Quicklaw (now called Lexis Advance Quicklaw) and the *Canadian Encyclopedic Digest* (CED), and requests from users of the book to update screenshots and search instructions, encouraged the publisher to prepare this revised fourth edition. The changes are restricted to Chapters 8 through 14:

Chapter 8: We updated the discussion about the CanLII database and added a information about the Lexis Advance Quicklaw database.

Chapter 9: There is an added discussion about *natural or plain language* searching.

Chapter 10: We have updated the text and figures on using the CED to reflect changes to the classification of the CED topic used in the research example.

Chapter 11: This chapter has new text and figures that reflect the changes to the classification of the topic in the CED, a new discussion about using a combination of browsing and searching to find information, and an updated discussion on how to find what you need by using *Halsbury's Laws of Canada* (part of the new Lexis Advance Quicklaw platform).

Chapter 12: Figures have been updated. We have revised the discussion about Westlaw's new way to search and KeyCite, added a discussion on how to find federal and provincial or territorial statutes and regulations by using Lexis Advance Quicklaw, and changed all text references from Quicklaw to Lexis Advance Quicklaw.

Chapter 13: You will find a revised discussion of how to search and KeyCite a case, statute, or regulation by using its name or citation in Westlaw, including a description of the new Find dropdown menu. We've also updated the discussion on finding and updating case law using Lexis Advance Quicklaw, and expanded the discussion on updating cases using CanLII. Several figures have been updated.

Chapter 14: Several figures have been updated.

These chapters also have updated chapter review questions and answers.

Author Arlene Blatt undertook the task of making the necessary revisions, and the other authors and Emond Publishing particularly want to thank her for her work.

The fourth edition improved upon the third in several significant respects. The chapters were reorganized and the structure was simplified to make the book easier to use: 21 chapters were condensed into 15. At the same time, the entire text was revised to reflect the growing availability and authority of computerized resources for legal research. We added a discussion of how to undertake effective keyword searches—an essential skill for anyone using online sources to find legal information. Updated screenshots and pictures were included in abundance to help students navigate secondary sources. We added a discussion of *Halsbury's Laws of Canada*. We also added a chapter, near the end of the book, that takes students through a research problem from beginning to end, step by step, giving them a practical occasion to use the paper and computerized sources discussed.

Following is a chapter-by-chapter account of the fourth edition's contents and features.

Chapter 1: The Basics of Legal Research

This chapter sets out the purpose and basic steps of legal research and identifies in general terms the categories of law, the sources of law, and the skills required to be an effective researcher.

Chapter 2: Statutes

This chapter expands the third edition's treatment of statutes. In addition to explaining why and how a legal researcher reads statutes and their provisions, we added substantive new contextual material concerning the nature of a statute, how statutes are created and published, and how to interpret statutory citations.

Chapter 3: Regulations

This chapter explains what regulations are, why and how we read them, and how they are cited. It includes material on how regulations are created and published.

Chapter 4: Cases

This chapter explains what cases are, how they are published, and why they are important. It includes a clear, detailed account of how they are structured, and explains how to properly read and cite them.

Chapter 5: How to Analyze a Fact Situation

This chapter develops the third edition's instructions for how to analyze a fact situation. It sets out the particular questions to be asked in identifying the legal issues, and it explains how to formulate the issues and write them down. An example enables students to practise analyzing a fact situation.

Chapter 6: Preparing for and Performing Research

Enlarging the third edition's discussion of this topic, this chapter includes a fuller account of binding law and persuasive law, with more comprehensive coverage of the court structures and chains of appeal in Canada and Ontario, respectively. A step-by-step account of the practical preparations necessary for legal research rounds out the theoretical discussion.

Chapter 7: Paper Research Sources

This chapter provides an overview of paper research sources, with a general account of what primary and secondary sources are available, where to find them, and how to work with them.

Chapter 8: Computerized Sources

This chapter explains the advantages and disadvantages of computerized legal research and offers an up-to-date overview of computerized research sources. It identifies and compares dedicated online sources and general ones, and it explains the differences between subscription services and free ones. It has been further updated in the revised fourth edition.

Chapter 9: Computerized Searches Using Keywords

New to the fourth edition, this chapter provides a focused discussion of how to use keywords in computerized legal research. It explains the role of legal knowledge in keyword searches, the various kinds of keyword searches, and the differences between plain language searches and Boolean searches, with a comprehensive account of the latter's principles. It has been further updated in the revised fourth edition.

Chapter 10: Legal Encyclopedias—Paper

This chapter discusses the legal encyclopedias that are available in print—the Canadian Encyclopedic Digest (CED) and *Halsbury's Laws of Canada* (Halsbury's)—and explains how they are organized and how to use them for legal research. It has been further updated in the revised fourth edition.

Chapter 11: Legal Encyclopedias—Computerized

This chapter, new to the fourth edition, provides a focused discussion of the CED and Halsbury's in their computerized forms, explaining how to gain access to them and how to search them: by browsing, by a plain language search, and by a Boolean terms and connectors search. It has been further updated in the revised fourth edition.

Chapter 12: Finding and Updating Statutes and Regulations

This chapter describes how to find and update statutes and regulations. Paper sources are discussed, but the emphasis in the fourth edition is on computerized sources—Justice Laws, Ontario e-Laws, the online versions of the CED and Halsbury's, Westlaw, Lexis Advance Quicklaw, and CanLII. The discussion reflects and incorporates the most current versions of these online resources. It has been further updated in the revised fourth edition.

Chapter 13: Finding and Updating Cases

This chapter explains how to use print and computerized sources to find and update cases, with instructions that reflect the expanding online coverage of case law. The discussion includes the most current versions of these online resources. It has been further updated in the revised fourth edition.

Chapter 14: A Sample Research Problem: From Start to Finish

New to the fourth edition, this chapter recaps the instructions of previous chapters and enables students to apply to a sample research problem their newly acquired facility with online and paper sources. It has been further updated in the revised fourth edition.

Chapter 15: Legal Writing

This chapter teaches students how to write memos of law and opinion letters, and it leaves them with some principles of good legal writing.

For their suggestions and feedback during the development of the fourth edition, we would like to thank Diana Collis (Fleming College) and Karen Schucher (Humber College).

About the Authors

Margaret H Kerr, BA, LLB, MA, PhD, has extensive teaching experience at Ontario community colleges and the bar admission course, has been both a legal research lawyer and a litigation lawyer, and since 2001 has run a commercial law practice. She is the co-author with JoAnn Kurtz of *Legal Research: Step by Step* (with Arlene Blatt), *The Canadian Small Business Kit for Dummies, Wills and Estates for Canadians for Dummies, Canadian Tort Law in a Nutshell* (with Laurence Olivo), *Make It Legal: What Every Canadian Entrepreneur Needs to Know About the Law, and Buying, Owning and Selling a Home in Canada*, among other books. Her doctorate is in medieval studies (legal history).

JoAnn Kurtz carried on a general practice with an emphasis on family law and real estate before joining Seneca College, where she is the program coordinator for the law clerk diploma program of the School of Legal and Public Administration. She has taught various topics, including contract law, family law, and residential tenant law and advocacy, and is the author or co-author of many general interest and academic texts. She attended New York University and holds a JD from Osgoode Hall Law School.

Arlene Blatt is a full-time professor in the School of Legal and Public Administration at Seneca College and teaches a variety of legal subjects to paralegal and law clerk students. She obtained her JD degree from Osgoode Hall Law School and is a member of the Ontario Bar. She has co-authored four Emond publications: *Advocacy for Paralegals, Residential Real Estate Transactions, Legal Entities and Relationships*, and *Legal Research: Step by Step*. She has also contributed a chapter on residential landlord and tenant law to an introductory legal textbook. Her areas of academic interest include landlord and tenant law, real estate law, and legal research.

PART I

Introduction to Legal Research

Every legal professional, whether lawyer, paralegal, or law clerk, will be called on from time to time, and perhaps frequently, to perform legal research. If you have to do it at all, it makes sense to do it competently. In fact, legal research is a skill that both lawyers and paralegals, under their respective rules of conduct, are required to have and to apply when they undertake matters on behalf of their clients.

Don't let anyone tell you that legal research is easy. But if you enjoy problem solving, legal research can be interesting—even fun.

Legal research is often taught as a series of exercises in using such resources as the *Canadian Abridgment* or LexisNexis Quicklaw (Quicklaw). However, there's not much point in working with resources if you don't know how to read and understand the primary sources to which the *Abridgment* or Quicklaw directs you—statutes, regulations, bylaws, and cases. Nor is there any point in working with resources if you don't know how to identify the issues you have to research.

The purpose of this book is to take you through the research process step by step so that you can

- identify an issue after hearing the story of a client's problem;
- identify and use the right research tools to find information about that issue;
- read and understand the sources to which the research tools point you;
- apply the law you find so that you can solve the client's problem; and
- write up the solution, in an opinion letter or memo of law.

The Basics of Legal Research

1

LEARNING OUTCOMES

After reading this chapter, you will understand:

- The purpose and the basic steps of legal research

- The categories of law

- The sources of law

- The difference between primary sources of law and secondary sources

- The differences between paper sources of law and computerized (electronic) sources

- What it takes to be a good legal researcher

Introduction

In this chapter, we take a look at the fundamentals of legal research. Research is something that legal professionals are constantly doing, whether it's strictly "legal" research—that is, finding out the law from statutes, regulations, bylaws, and cases— or various other kinds of research, such as finding out the correct legal name of a corporation, what county a town is located in, or whether there is a security lien on a chattel or a construction lien on real property.

The ability to find things out—in other words, to research—is therefore an essential skill for a legal professional.

We live in an information age: we are surrounded by information—in newspapers, books, magazines, journals, and directories; on television and the Internet. The information needed by a legal professional is available *somewhere*, but you have to know where and how to find it and be able to understand, evaluate, and apply it.

The Purpose and Basic Steps of Legal Research

All research, legal or otherwise, has the same purpose—to gather information that you don't yet know, or to confirm the accuracy of information you already have. All research, legal or otherwise, involves the same standard steps, whether you are using paper sources or computerized sources. These steps are as follows:

- identify the issue to be researched in order to solve a specific problem;
- identify and use the right research tools to guide you to information about that issue;
- find the sources to which the research tools point you;
- understand those sources; and
- apply the information you have found to answering a question or solving a problem.

In legal research, the information you don't have and are seeking is the law. For this reason, the research steps are a bit more specialized. You must

- identify a *legal issue* after hearing the story of a *client's* problem;
- familiarize yourself with, find, and work with specialized *legal research tools and sources*; and
- apply the *law* you find so that you can solve the *client's* problem.

A legal professional will engage in legal research to learn about the law, so that he or she can take action or advise a client how to proceed in a given situation. For example, consider the following situations, each involving a different area of law:

- A commercial lawyer researches case law to advise a client whether a contract she entered into is valid and whether the other party can be forced to perform his obligations under the contract.

- A family lawyer researches statute law to advise a client whether the foreign divorce he got is valid and whether he can marry again without committing bigamy.

- A tax lawyer researches statute law and regulations to find out whether a client's business expense is deductible for tax purposes.

- A paralegal or lawyer researches case law clarifying the rules of court concerning substituted service to prepare to appear on a motion.

- A paralegal researches statute law to advise a landlord client whether she has grounds to evict her residential tenant.

Categories of Law

No legal professional knows all the law all the time. But legal professionals have to know *enough* law to fit a client's problem into the proper category of law; they need to know where to begin to look for answers. To navigate your way through the vast amount of legal information available, you need to have some understanding of the categories of law.

The three broadest categories of law are substantive law, procedural law, and the law of evidence (see Figure 1.1). **Substantive law** defines legal rights and obligations. Legal rights may be enforced by way of legal proceedings, and substantive law also sets out defences to such proceedings. **Procedural law** sets out the process that a party must follow to enforce his or her rights in a court proceeding or to defend a proceeding. The **law of evidence** sets out the manner in which facts are introduced and proved in a trial or a proceeding.

Substantive law may be further divided into public law and private law. **Public law** governs the relationship between legal persons (individuals, partnerships, and corporations) and the state (federal, provincial, or municipal government), and it includes such areas as

- constitutional law,
- criminal law,
- tax law,
- immigration and refugee law,
- environmental law,
- child welfare, and
- municipal law.

substantive law
defines legal rights and obligations; legal rights may be enforced by way of legal proceedings, so substantive law also includes defences to legal proceedings

procedural law
sets out the process that a party must follow to enforce his/her/its rights in a court proceeding or to defend a proceeding

law of evidence
sets out the manner in which facts are introduced and proved in a trial or a proceeding

public law
governs the relationship between legal persons (individuals, partnerships, and corporations) and the state (federal, provincial, or municipal government), and includes such areas of law as municipal law, immigration and refugee law, environmental law, constitutional law, criminal law, tax law, and child welfare

Figure 1.1   Categories of Law

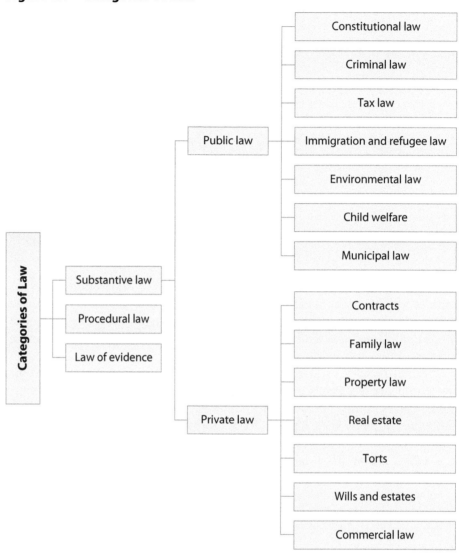

Private law governs the relationship between legal persons, and includes such areas as

- contracts,
- family law,
- property law,
- real estate,
- torts,
- wills and estates, and
- commercial law.

Sources of Law

Substantive, procedural, and evidentiary Canadian law are made up of a combination of

- statutes passed by either the federal Parliament or the provincial legislatures (the Canadian Constitution defines whether it is a federal or a provincial government that has the power to make laws in a particular area);
- regulations made either by the federal government or by a provincial government, pursuant to their respective statutes;
- bylaws made by a municipality pursuant to powers granted to it under the provincial *Municipal Act, 2001*; and
- decisions made by judges and adjudicators in court and tribunal proceedings (case law).

Primary Versus Secondary Sources

In legal research, we make a distinction between primary sources and secondary sources. **Primary sources** are the actual statutes, regulations, bylaws, and case decisions that create the law. **Secondary sources** are sources that summarize, discuss, or explain primary sources. They include:

- legal encyclopedias,
- digests of cases,
- indexes to statutes,
- textbooks, and
- articles.

primary sources
the statutes, regulations, bylaws, and case decisions that create the law

secondary sources
sources that summarize, discuss, or explain primary sources, and include legal encyclopedias, digests of cases, indexes to statutes, textbooks, and articles

When you perform legal research, you cannot rely on secondary sources alone. Secondary sources are the finding tools that help you gain an understanding of the law and direct you to the primary sources that actually create the law. You must then examine the primary sources to which you have been referred.

Paper Sources Versus Computerized Sources

Most primary and many secondary legal sources are available in both paper and computerized format. Statutes and regulations are bound into book format, and cases are collected in report series. When it comes to secondary sources, most legal texts are available only in book format, and many journal articles are published only in print. However, legal encyclopedias, case digests, and indexes to statutes are found in both print and computerized versions. Online versions of statutes, regulations, bylaws, and cases are available on free websites or through subscription services; and online services such as Quicklaw and WestlawNext Canada combine the finding features of a secondary source with direct access to the primary sources themselves.

While the current trend is to perform legal research using computerized sources alone, there are still some advantages to using paper sources. First, it is much easier to browse through paper sources and see how your research topic fits within the general area of law you are researching. Computerized sources, by comparison, will show you only what you asked to see. Second, computerized sources—in particular, the sources that provide statutes, regulations, and bylaws—do not extend very far into the past and therefore may not be able to show you the law that governed when the legal problem arose. If you want to see a version from before 2000, you may need to use paper sources.

What It Takes to Be a Good Legal Researcher

The legal research you perform will be relied on to give legal advice to a client or to initiate legal action. Your legal research must therefore be accurate. This means the following:

- Your final information must come from the most reliable sources—that is, primary sources.
- You must find *all* the relevant statutes, regulations, bylaws, and case decisions, and then make sure that the statutes, regulations, or bylaws have not been amended or repealed, and that the cases have not been overturned on appeal or by statute or regulation.
- You must understand the information you have found, and summarize or copy it correctly.

KEY TERMS

law of evidence, 5
primary sources, 7
private law, 6
procedural law, 5
public law, 5
secondary sources, 7
substantive law, 5

RESEARCH EXERCISE

This exercise will introduce you to the basic steps of research and allow you to develop some standard research skills.

Read the fact situation below and answer the questions that follow. Please feel free to use your creativity and powers of deduction! You are not being asked to consider questions of substantive law or procedure.

Fact Situation

Angelina Jolly was visiting Niagara Falls, Ontario. While she was driving near the falls, her car was struck by a car driven by Jennifer Annistone. Brad Pitts, a driver in another car, witnessed the incident; he gave his name and telephone number to Angelina before Angelina was taken by air ambulance to Toronto Slicendice Hospital. While Angelina was recuperating at the hospital, a nurse entered her room in the middle of the night and stole an extremely valuable ring.

After her release from the hospital, Angelina retained your law firm to bring two separate actions: one against Jennifer Annistone, for damages for her injuries and the cost of replacing her car; and one against the Slicendice Hospital for the theft of her ring.

There are some preliminary matters for your firm to consider. Read the questions below and suggest how you would go about finding the information required.

1. What is the monetary jurisdiction of the Ontario Superior Court of Justice? Of the Ontario Small Claims Court?

2. What is the filing fee for a claim in the Ontario Superior Court of Justice? In the Ontario Small Claims Court?

3. How can you find the location and telephone number of the Superior Court or Small Claims Court office where your firm will file the statement of claim?

4. You need to contact the witness, Brad Pitts. Unfortunately, Angelina lost his telephone number, but remembers that he lives in Los Angeles, California. How can you find Brad's telephone number?

5. Angelina is claiming that she suffered neurological injuries in the accident. If the action goes to trial, your firm will need an expert witness in the field of neurology to testify about the effects of Angelina's injuries on her ability to work. Where can you find an up-to-date list of all neurologists registered in your province?

6. Angelina has an insurance certificate valuing the stolen ring at US$23,950. In order to determine whether a legal action should be brought in Small Claims Court or Superior Court, you need to know the Canadian dollar equivalent of the US dollar amount at today's exchange rate. Where can you find this information?

7. Legal research brings to light the somewhat similar case of *Holmes v. Kidman*, and your firm would like to obtain the advice of the lawyer who was named in *Holmes* as counsel for the plaintiff. How can you find the lawyer's address and/or telephone number?

8. A court summons will have to be served personally on Angelina's hospital roommate, who was in the next bed when the nurse made off with Angelina's ring. Angelina happens to know the roommate's home telephone number, but not her street address. It doesn't seem like a good idea to alert the roommate to the summons by calling her. How can you use the roommate's telephone number to find out her address?

9. Your firm is a busy one and has matters besides Angelina's to deal with. Turning to your brimming inbox, you discover you have to send a package to the Banff Springs Hotel in Banff, Alberta, but the courier service won't accept the package without a postal code even though you have provided the rest of the address. How can you find the postal code without telephoning the hotel?

10. In another unrelated matter, you need to write to a member of Parliament on behalf of a client. How can you find out the name and address of your client's MP, the member for the Trinity-Spadina riding in Toronto?

PART II

Sources of Canadian Law

The fundamental sources of legal research are statutes, regulations, bylaws, and case law. Statutes are created by Parliament and the provincial legislatures; regulations are created by government departments; bylaws are created by municipalities under a delegated legislative power from the province; and case law is created by judges and adjudicators to explain their reasons for making a decision after hearing a case. A client who needs legal advice may be affected by one or more of these kinds of law. When you know what law governs the client's problem, you begin to know what can be done and what choices to give the client about how to proceed.

Statutes

2

LEARNING OUTCOMES

After reading this chapter, you will understand:

- What a statute is

- How statutes are created and published

- Why we read statutes

- How to read a statute

- How to read provisions within a statute

- How to cite a statute or statutory provision

- How to find the legislative history of a statute or statutory provision

- What a bylaw is, how bylaws are created, and how to research them

Introduction

Statutes are one of the four primary sources of law in Canada, as we mentioned in Chapter 1. Lawyers, paralegals, and law clerks need to know how to read, understand, and cite a statute. They should also know how statutes are created and published. The purpose of this chapter is to provide the basic background information about statutes that a legal researcher needs.

What Is a Statute?

statute
law created by Parliament
or a provincial legislature

Statutes—also known as legislation, acts of legislature, or, simply, acts—are written laws that have been created by the Parliament of Canada or by a provincial legislature. The Canadian Constitution, which is itself made up of two acts, determines whether it is within the power of Parliament or of a provincial legislature to create legislation about a particular subject matter. Statutes set out the law about a matter. For example, they may permit or they may require legal entities (individuals, partnerships, and corporations) to do things in certain circumstances, and *not* to do things in other circumstances. They may state the approved methods of doing things that are required or permitted. Statutes create penalties for not doing what is required, or for doing what is prohibited.

How Statutes Are Created

Federal Statutes

Statutes begin life as bills, which are, simply, proposed laws. Normally, the government (the federal political party in power) writes and puts forward bills, but any member of Parliament may bring forward a bill. (In the latter case, the bill would be known as a "private member's bill.") The bill goes through the following stages in the course of becoming a statute:

1. It is presented to the House of Commons for first reading, and then printed.
2. It is reintroduced for second reading, when the principles of the bill are debated and voted on; it may then be referred to a committee.
3. It is examined in committee, clause by clause, and then voted on. The committee reports back to the House, and may propose amendments to the bill.
4. As amended, it returns to the House for a third reading, debate, and vote. It passes with a simple majority (51 percent) of votes.
5. It then goes to the Senate, where it undergoes a process similar to the process in the House of Commons.
6. If the bill is passed by both the House and the Senate, royal assent is given (it is signed by the governor general, as the Queen's federal representative), and the bill is given a statute number. On receiving royal assent, the bill becomes law.

Provincial Statutes

In a provincial legislature, the creation of a statute from a bill follows much the same course as it does in Parliament, although the details vary, and there is no provincial equivalent of the Senate. The government (the provincial political party in power) writes and puts forward bills, but, again (as in Parliament), any member of the legislature may do the same. The ensuing development stages are the same:

1. The bill is placed before the legislature and read for the first time. (It is not debated.)

2. It receives a second reading in the legislature. The principles and purpose of the bill are discussed in detail, and there is some debate and a vote. Unless the bill is unanimously passed by the legislature, it then goes to a committee, which may propose amendments.

3. As amended, the bill receives a third reading in the legislature, and there is a final vote on it.

4. The bill passes with a simple majority (51 percent) of votes. If this happens, royal assent is given (the bill is signed by the lieutenant governor, as the Queen's provincial representative), and the bill is given a statute number. As in Parliament, the bill becomes law when it receives royal assent.

Coming into Force

You might think that after all the stages described above, a statute would come into force (that is, come into effect and start being applied) once it receives royal assent. Sometimes it does: if the statute specifically states that it comes into force on receiving royal assent, then all's done.

However, the statute may state in one of its provisions that it comes into force either (1) on a certain date, in which case the statute is in force once that date arrives or (2) upon "proclamation"—that is, on a date to be announced at a future time. The proclamation will usually be made in the *Gazette* (there are both federal and provincial gazettes), which is a government publication used to publish regulations and notices.

Amendment of a Statute

Sometimes a statute is amended to delete or revise existing sections, or to add new sections.

If a statute has been amended, the consolidated version of the statute incorporates all amendments. (For discussion of consolidated versions of statutes, see below.)

How Statutes Are Published

Statutes are published in print (paper) versions, and they are published electronically. In Ontario, s 15(1) of the *Legislation Act, 2006* provides that every act of the legislature shall be published both electronically (on the e-Laws website) and in print.

It is helpful to know how statutes are published in print, in order to understand statutory citations.

The Print Version of a Statute

Acts passed by Parliament or by the provincial legislatures in any year are collected in a series for that year. They appear in a bound annual volume that is designated by year. For example, SC 2012 (*Statutes of Canada, 2012*) contains only statutes passed in 2012. Statutes are given chapter numbers in the volume according to the order in which they were passed in that particular year.

Until recently, the annual statutes of the federal government and of some provincial governments were collected and revised every number of years. According to this system, all the statutes in force at the date of the revision are published in a format that incorporates any amendments that have been made to each statute since the previous revision.

The most recent federal revision was in 1985; the one before that was in 1970. Ontario statutes used to be revised every ten years, but that is no longer the case. The most recent revision of Ontario statutes was in 1990.

The Electronic Version of a Statute

Governments now maintain statutes electronically and publish them quickly on their official websites. The Ontario e-Laws site, for example, states that new source law (statute law) is usually published within two business days, while the federal Justice Laws website states that it is generally updated every two weeks. However, the electronic databases do not stretch back infinitely into the past. The federal Justice Laws website does not include any annual statutes enacted before 2001, although annual statutes published from 1998 to the present can be found in the electronic version of the *Canada Gazette*, Part III. For annual statutes before 1998, you must find a print version. The Ontario e-Laws website includes only annual statutes enacted on or after January 1, 2000.

The current trend is not to revise statutes at intervals but to consolidate them electronically on a continuing basis by incorporating amendments. The website will indicate how often the consolidation occurs; e-Laws, for example, has an e-Laws Consolidation Currency Date web page. However, for both provincial and federal statutes, you must check the beginning of the statute to determine its currency. Figure 2.1 shows the beginning of the *Dangerous Goods Transportation Act* on e-Laws.

Figure 2.1   Beginning of the Dangerous Goods Transportation Act

---

Dangerous Goods Transportation Act

R.S.O. 1990, CHAPTER D.1

Consolidation Period: From July 1, 2011 to the e-Laws currency date.

Last amendment: 2010, c. 16, Sched. 12, s. 1.

Why Read a Statute?

When a client seeks legal advice, you need to know what statutes apply to him, her, or it; and how he, she, or it has been or will be affected. For example, a woman in Ontario who has been charged with careless driving will be subject to the *Highway Traffic Act*. A man who wants a divorce will be subject to the federal *Divorce Act*. An Ontario corporation that wants to sell its shares to the public will be subject to the provincial *Securities Act*.

Warm-Up to Statutes

Statutes are not cuddly, and no one reads them for fun. We read them to determine what law applies to a client's problem.

In order to make the leap between the client's problem (a particular event or situation) and a statute (a rule or list of rules), a legal professional needs certain skills. These include the ability to do the following:

- logically sequence the facts of the client's problem;
- find the statute or the part of the statute (the rule) that is relevant to the client's problem;
- read and understand the statute, which includes working with defined terms within a statute; and
- apply the rule within the statute to the client's problem.

Below are some preliminary exercises to give you an opportunity to practise these skills.

1. Logically Sequencing Facts

Below is a list of rules. They are not in logical order. Arrange them in the logical order to determine what happens whenever Joe goes to the grocery store.

- Every time the grocery store guard stops a shoplifter, the guard calls the police.
- Every time a police officer chews gum, he or she spits it out on the sidewalk before getting into the police car.
- Every time someone shoplifts in the grocery store, the shoplifter is stopped by a store guard.
- Every time the police come to the grocery store, they complain to the store manager about all the sticky chewing gum on the sidewalk outside the door.
- Every time Joe goes to the grocery store, he shoplifts a package of chewing gum.
- Every time the police come to the grocery store, the manager gives each officer a free package of chewing gum.

2. Reading, Understanding, and Working with Defined Terms

Rob wants to send an invitation to meet on Saturday night to the group of friends he always meets at a bar on Friday nights. He has several mail-merge groups listing the friends he meets for different activities. The Friday-night-at-the-bar mail-merge group contains the following names: Anna Banana, Jelly Belly, Willoughby Wallaby, and Nicholas Knock. The Saturday-morning-run mail-merge group contains the following names: Roger Bannister, Carmelita Jeter, Usain Bolt, and Donovan Bailey. The Sunday afternoon baseball-and-beer mail-merge group contains the following names: Angela de los Angeles, Tex Ranger, Marlon Miami, and Rocky Colorado. If Rob uses the correct mail-merge group to email the invitation to meet on Saturday night, whom is he inviting?

3. Applying a Rule

Match each fact situation to the rule that applies to it, and then apply the rule to the facts.

Fact situations	Rules	Match fact situation to rule	Apply rule to fact situation
1. Fred takes his dog Suzy for a walk in the park.	A. Smoking is not allowed inside a bar.		
2. Joy wants to cut down a large tree in front of her house.	B. Dogs must be leashed in the park.		
3. George is having a drink with friends at the Tombstone Bar and wants to have a cigarette.	C. It is forbidden to cut down a tree without the permission of the city.		

How to Read a Statute

Most statutes are organized as follows:

long title
full, unabbreviated title of a statute

short title
abbreviated title of a statute

1. They are headed by a *chapter number*, and, when originally enacted, by a **long title** (the full name of the statute, beginning with "An Act respecting" or a similar phrasing). Either at the end or at the beginning of the statute, there may be a section that sets out the **short title** (beginning with "This Act may be cited as"). Use the short title when citing a statute. Lengthy statutes may include a table of contents setting out all the parts and sections of the statute.

2. Statutes may include a **preamble** or an initial section that sets out the purpose and main principles of the statute. The preamble usually begins with "Whereas."

3. Statutes are usually subdivided as follows:

I Part

1. Section

(1) Subsection

(a) Paragraph

(i) Subparagraph

Brief notes in the margins of a paper version of a statute next to or above a statutory provision may indicate what the section (and sometimes subsection) is about.

4. Statutes may have introductory sections that set out
   a. the *scope* of the statute (to what and to whom the statute applies);
   b. the definitions of words used in the statute;
   c. the officials who are responsible for administering the statute; and
   d. sometimes, other details about how the statute is to be administered.

5. The law itself is contained in the *body* of the statute. In some statutes, the body concludes with sections that create offences for disobeying the law and penalties.

6. Statutes end with **housekeeping provisions**, which can include the date when the statute will come into force and the right of officials who administer the statute to make regulations under the statute.

preamble
part of a statute that outlines its purpose and main principles

housekeeping provisions
sections that cover the details of statutes, such as the date of coming into force

The organization of a statute is illustrated in Figure 2.2, which reproduces some provisions from the Ontario *Residential Tenancies Act, 2006* (as first enacted). Note the following:

- The long title of the original statute is *An Act to revise the law governing residential tenancies.*
- The Act is quite lengthy—263 sections—and is divided into 19 parts.
- The purposes of the Act are set out in s 1.
- Definitions are found in s 2.
- A housekeeping provision—the power to make regulations—is found in s 241.
- The short title of the Act is set out in s 263, the statute's final provision.

In the later revised or consolidated versions of a statute, only the short title is used. Figure 2.3 shows the beginning of the current consolidated version of the Ontario statute. Note that the statute is now entitled simply the *Residential Tenancies Act, 2006.*

Figure 2.2 Selections from Ontario's Residential Tenancies Act, 2006

Français

Explanatory Note

CHAPTER 17

**An Act to revise
the law governing
residential tenancies**

Assented to June 22, 2006

Note: This Act amends or repeals more than one Act. For the legislative history of these Acts, see Public Statutes – Detailed Legislative History on www.e-Laws.gov.on.ca.

CONTENTS

**PART I
INTRODUCTION**

**PART II
TENANCY AGREEMENTS**

**PART III
RESPONSIBILITIES OF LANDLORDS**

Her Majesty, by and with the advice and consent of the Legislative Assembly of the Province of Ontario, enacts as follows:

**PART I
INTRODUCTION**

Purposes of Act

1. The purposes of this Act are to provide protection for residential tenants from unlawful rent increases and unlawful evictions, to establish a framework for the regulation of residential rents, to balance the rights and responsibilities of residential landlords and tenants and to provide for the adjudication of disputes and for other processes to informally resolve disputes.

Interpretation

2. (1) In this Act,

"Board" means the Landlord and Tenant Board; ("Commission de la location immobilière")

"care home" means a residential complex that is occupied or intended to be occupied by persons for the purpose of receiving care services, whether or not receiving the services is the primary purpose of the occupancy; ("maison de soins")

"care services" means, subject to the regulations, health care services, rehabilitative or therapeutic services or services that provide assistance with the activities of daily living; ("services en matière de soins")

"guideline", when used with respect to the charging of rent, means the guideline determined under section 120; ("taux légal")

"land lease community" means the land on which one or more occupied land lease homes are situate and includes the rental units and the land, structures, services and facilities of which the landlord retains possession and that are intended for the common use and enjoyment of the tenants of the landlord; ("zone résidentielle à baux fonciers")

"land lease home" means a dwelling, other than a mobile home, that is a permanent structure where the owner of the dwelling leases the land used or intended for use as the site for the dwelling; ("maison à bail foncier")

"landlord" includes,

(a) the owner of a rental unit or any other person who permits occupancy of a rental unit, other than a tenant who occupies a rental unit in a residential complex and who permits another person to also occupy the unit or any part of the unit,

(b) the heirs, assigns, personal representatives and successors in title of a person referred to in clause (a), and

(Figure 2.2 is concluded on the next page.)

Figure 2.2   Concluded

PART XVII
REGULATIONS

Regulations

241. (1) The Lieutenant Governor in Council may make regulations,

1. prescribing circumstances under which one or more rental units that form part of a residential complex, rather than the entire residential complex, are care homes for the purposes of the definition of "care home" in subsection 2 (1);

2. prescribing services that are to be included or not included in the definition of "care services" in subsection 2 (1);

3. prescribing charges not to be included in the definition of "municipal taxes and charges" in subsection 2 (1);

4. prescribing persons that are to be included or are not to be included in the definition of "tenant" in subsection 2 (1) and exempting any such persons from any provision of the Act specified in the regulation;

5. prescribing, for the purposes of the definition of "vital service" in subsection 2 (1), the part of each year during which heat is a vital service;

6. prescribing classes of accommodation for the purposes of clause 5 (n);

7. prescribing federal, provincial or municipal programs for the purpose of paragraph 3 of subsection 7 (1);

8. providing that specified provisions of this Act apply with respect to any specified housing project, housing program, rental unit, residential complex or other residential accommodation or any class of them;

9. exempting any housing project, housing program, rental unit, residential complex or other residential accommodation or any class of them from any provision of this Act;

10. prescribing grounds of an application for the purposes of clause 9 (1) (b);

11. respecting the rules for making findings for the purposes of subsection 9 (2);

12. prescribing for the purposes of section 22, paragraph 3 of subsection 29 (1) and subsection 31 (1),

   i. standards and criteria to be applied by the Board in determining if a landlord, superintendent or agent of a landlord has substantially interfered with the reasonable enjoyment of a rental unit or residential complex in carrying out maintenance, repairs or capital improvements to the unit or complex, and

   ii. criteria to be applied by the Board in determining whether to order an abatement of rent under subsection 31 (1) when a landlord, superintendent or agent of a landlord is found to have substantially interfered with the reasonable enjoyment of a rental unit or residential complex in carrying out maintenance, repairs or capital improvements to the unit or complex and rules for calculating the amount of the abatement;

Short title

263. The short title of this Act is the *Residential Tenancies Act, 2006*.

Figure 2.3   Start of the Current Consolidated Residential Tenancies Act

Residential Tenancies Act, 2006

S.O. 2006, CHAPTER 17

Historical version for the period June 1, 2014 to June 30, 2015.

Last amendment: 2013, c. 3, s. 20-56.

CONTENTS [–]

PART I
INTRODUCTION

PART II
TENANCY AGREEMENTS

How to Read a Statutory Provision

You are more likely to need to read one or more **provisions** (a section or subsection) in a statute than to read a whole statute. Thank your lucky stars!

In order to understand a statutory provision, begin by asking the following questions:

1. With what matters in general does the statute deal?
2. With what matters does this particular provision of the statute deal?
3. To whom is the particular section directed—for example, the general public, a corporation, a real estate agent, a spouse?
4. Does the provision
   a. order,
   b. prohibit, or
   c. permit

   something to be done? What? In what circumstances?
5. If there is an order or prohibition, how is it enforced?

Answering these questions will give you a general idea about the provision.

In order to understand a provision more particularly, you will need to break it down into its elements. Once you understand these, you will be able to identify all the important information in the provision—that is, identify the rules that you will apply to the client's fact situation.

Example

Section 265(1)(b) of the *Criminal Code*, RSC 1985, c C-46 defines a particular form of assault. As written in the statute, it looks like this:

> 265(1) A person commits an assault when …
>   (b) he attempts or threatens, by an act or a gesture, to apply force to another person, if he has, or causes that other person to believe on reasonable grounds that he has, present ability to effect his purpose.

Broken down into its separate elements, it looks like this:

A person
commits an assault when

(ONE OF THE FOLLOWING)

1. he attempts	2. he threatens
by an act	by an act
or a gesture	or a gesture
to apply force	to apply force
to another person	to another person

(PLUS ONE OF THE FOLLOWING)

1. if he has
   present ability
   to effect his purpose

2. if he causes
   that other person
   to believe on reasonable grounds
   that he has
   present ability
   to effect his purpose

If you break down a provision into its elements, you can use the breakdown as a checklist to compare with the client's fact situation. Each element must be accounted for in the facts of the client's situation if the statutory provision is to be applicable. For example, let's say the client (who has been charged with assault under s 265(1)(b)) yelled at and shook his fist at a cinema ticket seller, then threatened by a gesture to apply force to the ticket seller. When this happened, the ticket seller was locked safely inside a Plexiglas booth. Because of the locked Plexiglas booth, your client had no present ability to effect his purpose, and the ticket seller had no reasonable grounds to believe that the client had present ability. Therefore, the client has not committed assault as defined by s 265(1)(b).

A word of warning: When you copy out a statutory provision for research, never paraphrase it or put it into your own words. Quote the statute exactly, or you'll change its meaning. For example, if the statute says "any individual may apply" and you write "any person may apply," you will have changed its legal meaning. An "individual" excludes corporations, but a "person" usually includes corporations.

Sometimes you will have to research further to find out what each element of a statutory provision means. For example, what exactly is "present ability," referred to in s 265(1)(b)? Would the client have *present ability* to apply force to the ticket seller if the client were standing outside the locked booth with a tire iron in his hand? Or what are "reasonable grounds" for believing that the client has present ability? Would the ticket seller have *reasonable grounds* to believe that your client could get into the booth using only his bare hands? To answer these questions, you might have to look at another section of the statute for a definition, or you might have to look for cases that discuss these issues.

As well as breaking down a statutory provision into its elements in order to understand it, you may have to do the opposite and build up the elements by referring to other provisions. You may, for example, have to look in the definition section of the statute in order to understand the legal meaning of a word. For example, the *Change of Name Act*, RSO 1990, c C.7, s 4(3) says:

> 4(3) An application by a child requires the written consent of every person who has lawful custody of the child.

In order to know exactly who qualifies as a "child," you must look at s 1 of the Act, which contains definitions. There, "child" is defined as "a person under the age of eighteen years."

Building up a statutory provision can be more complex than that, however. Instead of adding the definition of a word, you may have to add other entire provisions. For example, s 108(1) of the *Canada Business Corporations Act*, RSC 1985, c C-44 reads as follows:

> 108(1) A director of a corporation ceases to hold office when the director
> (a) dies or resigns;
> (b) is removed in accordance with section 109; or
> (c) becomes disqualified under subsection 105(1).

So, in order to find out what s 108(1) *really* means, you have to refer to these other sections. Section 109(1) says:

> 109(1) Subject to paragraph 107(g), the shareholders of a corporation may by ordinary resolution at a special meeting remove any director or directors from office.

Section 105(1) says:

> 105(1) The following persons are disqualified from being a director of a corporation:
> (a) anyone who is less than eighteen years of age;
> (b) anyone who is of unsound mind and has been so found by a court in Canada or elsewhere;
> (c) a person who is not an individual; or
> (d) a person who has the status of bankrupt.

To understand s 108, you have to incorporate into it the sections it refers to. For example, this means reading s 108(1)(c) as follows:

> 108(1) A director of a corporation ceases to hold office when the director …
> (c) becomes disqualified under subsection 105(1).
>
> > 105(1) The following persons are disqualified from being a director of a corporation: …
> > (b) anyone who is of unsound mind and has been so found by a court in Canada or elsewhere; …
> > (d) a person who has the status of bankrupt.

Once you have built up a statutory provision by adding all the references, you have to break down your new creation into its elements in order to understand it properly. A built-up, broken-down s 108(1)(c) will look like this:

> 108(1)   A director of a corporation
> ceases to hold office
> when the director …
>
> (c)   becomes disqualified
> under subsection 105(1).

105(1) The following persons
are disqualified from being
a director of a corporation: …

(b) anyone who is of unsound mind
and has been so found by a court
in Canada or elsewhere; …

(d) a person who has the status of bankrupt.

Statutory Citations

The citation of a statute gives you essential information about the statute, including where to find it using print sources. A citation is made up of the following four components: the name of the statute, the volume title abbreviation, the chapter number, and the section number.*

Development Charges Act,	SO 1997,	c 27,	s 2
1	2	3	4
Business Corporations Act,	RSO 1990,	c B.16,	s 2

Note that the components are similar whether the statute is an annual one (the first example) or a revised one (the second example).

1. Name of the Statute

The short title of the statute is used, without the word "the." (The short title is usually found at the end of the statute and is prefaced by the words "This Act may be cited as.") The name of the statute is italicized and is followed by a comma. Sometimes the year is in the short title of the statute. In that case, include the year in the citation as follows: *Pharmacy Act, 1991*, SO 1991, c 36.

2. Volume Title Abbreviation

The volume title tells you the name of the statute series in which the statute appears, including the year of publication. When cited, the volume title is followed by a comma. Annual volumes are abbreviated as

- SC (*Statutes of Canada*), and
- SO (*Statutes of Ontario*).

---

* Please note that this book follows the style set out in the *Canadian Guide to Uniform Legal Citation*, 8th edition. The Guide, in contrast to many of the extracts you will encounter in this text, omits periods from references and citations, including statutory and case citations.

Revised volumes are abbreviated as

- RSC (*Revised Statutes of Canada*), and
- RSO (*Revised Statutes of Ontario*).

In the citation examples above, the *Development Charges Act* is shown as being published in the *Statutes of Ontario* for the year 1997, and the *Business Corporations Act* is shown as being published in the *Revised Statutes of Ontario*, 1990 revision.

The following are some additional examples of volume title abbreviations:

- SC 1989 (*Statutes of Canada* for 1989)
- SO 1993 (*Statutes of Ontario* for 1993)
- RSC 1985 (*Revised Statutes of Canada*, 1985 revision)
- RSO 1980 (*Revised Statutes of Ontario*, 1980 revision)

3. Chapter Number

The chapter number tells you the specific number assigned to the statute in the volume. In annual statute volumes, the statutes are put in chronological order and then numbered from 1 onward, using numbers only—for example, c 46.

In revised statute volumes, the statutes are first put in alphabetical order and then numbered (this is called an "alphanumeric")—e.g., c A.10, c B-16, or c C.32. The uppercase letter in an alphanumeric chapter number corresponds to the first letter of the title of the statute. So in "c C.32," the uppercase "C" means that the statute name begins with the letter "C"; the lowercase "c" just means "chapter number." The chapter number is followed by a comma if you are going to refer to a particular section (discussed below). Revised Ontario statutes use a period in the alphanumeric (c A.10). Revised federal statutes use a hyphen in the alphanumeric (c B-16).

4. Section Number

The section number tells you which particular provisions in the act are being referred to. The abbreviation "s" stands for section (e.g., s 2). The abbreviation "ss" stands for sections. If the reference is to a subsection of a section, the subsection appears in brackets—e.g., s 2(1).

Legislative History

legislative history
a citation to the previous revision of a provision followed by a citation to any statute that amended the provision; given at the end of each provision in a statute

In successive revisions of the *Statutes of Canada* or of a province, the same statute may appear under a different chapter number and the same statutory provision may appear under a different section number.

At the end of each provision in a statute, the **legislative history** (also known as a "historical footnote") of the provision is given. It contains a citation to the previous revision followed by a citation to any statute that amended the provision. So if you know the current section number of a provision, looking at the legislative history will permit you to find the section number of a provision in a previous revision. If the provision was newly created between revisions, the historical footnote will contain the citation for the amending statute.

For example, s 6(1) of the *Blind Persons' Rights Act*, RSO 1990, c B.7 reads as follows:

> **6.**—(1) Every person who is in contravention of section 2 is guilty of an offence and on conviction is liable to a fine not exceeding $5,000. R.S.O. 1980, c. 44, s. 6 (1); 1989, c. 72, s. 18, *part*.

The tag at the end of s 6(1) means that this section existed, also as s 6(1), in the RSO 1980 revision and was subsequently amended by *Statutes of Ontario, 1989*, chapter 72, section 18 (in part). If you look at chapter 72 of the annual Ontario statutes published in 1989 you will find the *Provincial Penalties Adjustment Act*. Section 18 of that Act amends the amount of the penalty in s 6(1) of the *Blind Persons' Rights Act* from $1,000 to $5,000.

Concording a Statute

It may be important, when you are reading a case that interprets a statutory provision, to find out whether the provision has been amended since the decision in the case was made. If the provision's wording in the current revision of the statute differs from its earlier wording, the case law interpreting the earlier version of the provision may not be useful in your research. If you need to find the current section number of a provision but only know the number in a previous revision, you will have to consult a concordance. Concordances align two adjacent revisions of a statute series.

This research may require print sources. Although the online version of the *Canadian Encyclopedic Digest (3d)* has a legislative concordance, it is arranged by topic rather than by name of statute, and it does not include all statutes.

For federal statutes, the *Revised Statutes of Canada, 1985* has a companion volume called *Table of the History and Disposal of Acts* (1995) that concords statutes enacted to December 1, 1988. Similar tables exist for the revisions of 1970 (in the Second Supplement to RSC 1970); 1952 (in the Appendixes volume of RSC 1952); 1927 (in the Appendixes volume of RSC 1927); 1906 (in the Appendixes volume of RSC 1906); and 1886 (in volume 2 of RSC 1886).

For Ontario statutes, use the *Canadian Encyclopedic Digest (3d)*'s *Ontario Statutes Concordance 1980-1990*; or look at Schedule B, "Table of Disposition," in the *Revised Statutes of Ontario, 1990*, volume 12 (Appendix).

Bylaws

Under provincial legislation (the Ontario *Municipal Act* for municipalities generally; and the *City of Toronto Act, 2006* for Toronto specifically), the province can delegate to a municipality the right to legislate on a prescribed range of matters. Section 10(2) of the Ontario *Municipal Act* lists these matters. They include the following: the health, safety, and well-being of persons; the protection of persons and property; animals; structures, including fences and signs; and business licensing. A city or municipality legislates by passing bylaws.

A **bylaw** comes into existence as follows:

bylaw
law made by a body (here, a municipal government) that is granted the power to do so by a legislature

1. The city council or municipal council makes a decision about a matter within its power, through a simple majority vote by council members. Matters are brought before council through reports and other communications from municipal officials and committees, and they are brought by individual council members. (The council can also delegate bylaw-making powers to others, such as community councils, agencies, and boards.)

2. Council's decision is confirmed by a bylaw enacted at the council meeting. Bylaws are numbered by the year and order of enactment. For example, Bylaw 2013-01 *or* Bylaw 01-2013 is the first bylaw enacted by council in 2013.

3. Some decisions of council are then turned over to the city solicitor or municipal solicitor to be drafted into a specific bylaw, particularly if they are decisions that will be frequently referred to, require enforcement, or amend existing bylaws. These draft bylaws are also known as *bills*. A bill has to be taken back to the council for enactment, again through a simple majority vote.

4. A bylaw is effective on the date it is enacted unless a different date is specified in the bylaw, in which case it is effective on that date.

5. In the City of Toronto, bylaws of general application are added to the *Municipal Code*. Each chapter of the Code is a bylaw in itself. The *Municipal Code* is updated after every City Council meeting. When consulting the Code, you must check the list of Recent Amendments for changes to Code chapters since the last update.

Figure 2.4 shows Chapter 903 of the Toronto *Municipal Code*.

Bylaws are often enforced through the provincial justice system, with the breach of a bylaw being a provincial offence. For example, municipal parking infractions can be prosecuted under the *Provincial Offences Act*. However, the province of Ontario under the *Provincial Offences Act* may enter into an agreement with a municipality to allow the municipality to perform court administration and to conduct prosecutions.

Many cities and municipalities in Ontario have some or all of their recent bylaws online in a searchable database. If you cannot find the bylaw you are looking for online, or if the website warns that the electronic version is not the official version, you will have to contact the City Clerk's Office or the municipal Clerk's Office or Clerk's Department to get a paper copy of the bylaw. Contact information for the Clerk is usually available on the municipality's website.

Figure 2.4   Chapter 903 of the Toronto Municipal Code

TORONTO MUNICIPAL CODE
CHAPTER 903, PARKING FOR PERSONS WITH DISABILITIES

<u>Schedule V, Exempted Provisions of By-laws and Municipal Codes of Former
Municipalities and the amalgamated City of Toronto for Permit Holders</u>

[HISTORY: Adopted by the Council of the City of Toronto 2007-04-24 by By-law No. 443-2007.[1] **Amendments noted where applicable.]**

GENERAL REFERENCES

Parking Authority - See Ch. 179.
Fire routes - See Ch. 880.
Parking machines - See Ch. 910.
Parking on private or municipal property - See Ch. 915.
Parking on residential front yards and boulevards - See Ch. 918.
Permit parking - See Ch. 925.
Temporary closing of highways - See Ch. 937.
Traffic and parking - See Ch. 950.
Highway Traffic Act - See R.S.O. 1990, c. H.8.
Planning Act - See R.S.O. 1990, c. P.13.
Repair and Storage Liens Act - See R.S.O. 1990, c. R.25.

ARTICLE I
On-Street and Off-Street Parking for Disabled Persons

§ 903-1. General definitions.

A term not defined in this section shall have the same meaning as the term has in the *Highway Traffic Act* and its associated regulations and its successors.

§ 903-2. Specific definitions

As used in this chapter, the following terms shall have the meanings indicated:

To find City of Toronto bylaws, you can

- search the post-amalgamation (1998) bylaws generally or the Toronto *Municipal Code* at <http://www.toronto.ca/legdocs/bylaws/lawsearch.htm>;
- search the By-law Status Register to track the amendment history of bylaws and the relationship between bylaws at <http://app.toronto.ca/BLSRWEB _Public/HomePage.do>;
- obtain a certified copy of a bylaw or a *Municipal Code* chapter for a fee at Toronto City Hall (100 Queen Street West, Toronto, Ontario, M5H 2N2) or the City of Toronto Archives (255 Spadina Road, Toronto, Ontario, M5R 2V3); or
- obtain copies of pre-amalgamation bylaws at the City of Toronto Archives.

To search the post-amalgamation (1998) bylaws generally, select "By-laws" from the "By-laws or code" drop-down menu, then choose a year from the "By-law year" drop-down menu. Enter a search term in the "Word or Phrase" field.

To search the Toronto Municipal Code, select "Toronto Code" from the "By-laws or code" drop-down menu, then enter a search term in the "Word or Phrase" field.

To search the By-law Status Register, select the "Search the Register" link, then follow the instructions on the resulting web page.

KEY TERMS

bylaw, 28
housekeeping provisions, 19
legislative history, 26
long title, 18
preamble, 19
provision, 22
short title, 18
statute, 14

EXERCISES

1. Break down the following statutory provisions into their separate elements.

   a. The *Criminal Code*, RSC 1985, c C-46, s 265 provides, in part, as follows:

   > 265(1) Any person commits an assault when ...
   >   (c) while openly wearing or carrying a weapon or an imitation thereof, he accosts or impedes another person or begs.

   b. The *Criminal Code*, RSC 1985, c C-46, s 265 provides, in part, as follows:

   > 265(1) Any person commits an assault when
   >   (a) without the consent of another person he applies force intentionally to that other person directly or indirectly; ...
   > (3) For the purposes of this section, no consent is obtained where the complainant submits or does not resist by reason of
   >   (a) the application of force to the complainant or to a person other than the complainant;
   >   (b) threats or fear of the application of force to the complainant or to a person other than the complainant;
   >   (c) fraud; or
   >   (d) the exercise of authority.

   c. The *Land Titles Act*, RSO 1990, c L.5, s 93, prior to its amendment in 1998, provided, in part, as follows:

   > 93(2) A charge that secures payment of money shall contain the amount of the principal sum that the charge secures, the rate of interest, and the periods of payment including the due date.

   d. The *Canada Evidence Act*, RSC 1985, c C-5, s 4 provides, in part, as follows:

   > 4(3) No husband is compellable to disclose any communication made to him by his wife during their marriage, and no wife is compellable to disclose any communication made to her by her husband during their marriage.

2. Read the following fact situations and answer the questions, using the applicable statutory provision from question 1.

   a. A mortgage (charge) made in Ontario in 1997 contains the following payment clauses. Does it meet the statutory requirements then in effect?

   > The amount of principal secured by this Charge/Mortgage of Land is Thirty Thousand ($30,000) dollars and the rate of interest chargeable thereon is Ten (10%) percent per annum calculated quarter-yearly not in advance.

Provided this Charge/Mortgage to be void on payment of Thirty Thousand ($30,000) dollars of lawful money of Canada with interest at Ten (10%) percent per annum as follows:

Five hundred ($500) dollars on account of the principal sum shall be payable on the 8th days of each of the months of May, August, and November in the year 1998 and the 8th days of each of the months of February, May, August, and November in the year 1999. The first payment of interest is to be computed from the 8th day of February 1998 upon the whole amount of principal hereby secured, to become payable on the 8th day of May 1998.

b. Richie and Maya lived together for years. During that time, he robbed several banks and told her the details of each robbery. Eventually, Richie and Maya decided to get married and had the ceremony performed at city hall. Unfortunately, as they were leaving the building, a police officer who had been called to the scene of one of the robberies bumped into them and recognized Richie. Two days later, Richie was in jail, charged with armed robbery. Should he worry that Maya will be forced to testify against him at his trial?

c. Do the following situations involve assault?

    i. Lisa and her husband, David, were having an argument. To emphasize a point, David threw a vase at the wall. He expected it to shatter, but the vase bounced off the wall and hit Lisa.

    ii. When their next-door neighbour dropped by to show off the karate moves she had just learned, Lisa's husband told the neighbour that she had his permission to demonstrate on Lisa. The neighbour whacked Lisa across the arm.

    iii. Lisa went to her doctor to set her broken arm. It was excruciatingly painful, far worse than she expected. The only reason she went through with it and didn't run screaming from the doctor's office was that she was afraid of ending up with a deformed arm.

    iv. Lisa later found out that the doctor who had set her arm was not licensed to practise medicine.

3. In each of the three examples that follow, you are shown the beginning of a statute and one of its provisions. Properly cite the statute and section number in each case.

    a.

Français

Provincial Offences Act

R.S.O. 1990, CHAPTER P.33

Consolidation Period: From May 1, 2017 to the e-Laws currency date.

Last amendment: 2017, c. 2, Sched. 2, s. 28.

Minimum age

94 No person shall be convicted of an offence committed while he or she was under twelve years of age. R.S.O. 1990, c. P.33, s. 94.

b.

Français

Courts of Justice Act

R.S.O. 1990, CHAPTER C.43

Composition of court
3 (1) The Court of Appeal shall consist of,

    (a) the Chief Justice of Ontario, who shall be president of the court;

    (b) the Associate Chief Justice of Ontario; and

    (c) fourteen other judges.

---

c.

Access to Information Act

R.S.C., 1985, c. A-1

An Act to extend the present laws of Canada that provide access to information under the control of the Government of Canada

---

ACCESS TO GOVERNMENT RECORDS

RIGHT OF ACCESS

Right to access to records

    4. (1) Subject to this Act, but notwithstanding any other Act of Parliament, every person who is

(*a*) a Canadian citizen, or

(*b*) a permanent resident within the meaning of subsection 2(1) of the _Immigration and Refugee Protection Act_,

has a right to and shall, on request, be given access to any record under the control of a government institution.

---

4. Consider the following citations, then answer the questions below with regard to each:

- _Film Classification Act, 2005_, SO 2005, c 17, s 4
- _Mortgages Act_, RSO 1990, c M.40, s 2(3)
- _Pension Act_, RSC 1985, c P-6
- _Language Skills Act_, SC 2013, c 36, s 2

    a. Is it an Ontario or a federal statute?

    b. Is it an annual or a revised statute?

    c. What are the chapter and section numbers (if any)?

Regulations

3

LEARNING OUTCOMES

After reading this chapter, you will understand:

- What a regulation is
- How regulations are created and published
- Why we read regulations
- How to read a regulation
- How to cite a regulation

Introduction

Regulations are the second primary source of law in Canada, and lawyers, paralegals, and law clerks must know how to read, understand, and cite a regulation. They should also know how regulations are created and published. This chapter provides such information.

What Is a Regulation?

regulations
rules made under the authority of a statute

enabling statute
statute that delegates the power to make regulations

Regulations, also called subordinate or delegated legislation, are rules made under the authority of an **enabling statute**. They are not passed by Parliament or a legislature; rather, they are implemented by the government as an administrative matter.

How Regulations Are Created

No regulation can be made without statutory authorization. For federal regulations, the enabling statute delegates the power to make regulations either to specific department and ministry officials or to the governor in council. For Ontario regulations, the enabling statute delegates the power to make regulations to the lieutenant governor in council. Both federal and provincial regulations are prepared by the government ministry responsible for the subject matter of the legislation. Because regulations do not need to be brought before Parliament or the legislature to be voted on, they can be created and amended by the government more quickly and easily than statutes can.

Regulations can come into force upon "filing," "registration," or "publication"; the wording differs in each jurisdiction. Federal regulations come into force on the day specified in the regulation or on the date of registration (recorded at the top of the text of the regulation). In Ontario, regulations come into force on the date on which they are filed, unless the regulation or its enabling statute provides otherwise.

How Regulations Are Published

Most federal regulations are required to be published in the *Canada Gazette*, Part II, within 23 days of registration. Since April 1, 2014, the *Canada Gazette* has been published electronically only.

Ontario regulations are published both electronically, on the e-Laws website, and in print in the *Ontario Gazette*.

In the past, regulations, like statutes, were revised or consolidated every number of years and published in a format that incorporated any amendments made since the previous revision. Federal regulations were last consolidated in print in 1978 in the *Consolidated Regulations of Canada*. Ontario regulations were last revised in print in 1990 in the *Revised Regulations of Ontario*. Both federal and Ontario regulations are now consolidated electronically on an ongoing basis.

Consolidated versions of federal regulations are available on the Justice Laws website of the federal Department of Justice: <http://laws-lois.justice.gc.ca>. Regulations are organized by name and are ordered alphabetically. Under the heading Laws, choose "Consolidated Regulations." Then, under the heading Regulations by Title, choose a letter to find all current consolidated regulations beginning with that letter. Find the regulation in the resulting list and select it. If you don't know the name of the regulation, you can search for the title of the statute pursuant to which it was made. The statutes themselves are ordered alphabetically. Under the heading Laws, choose "Consolidated Acts," and then click on the "R" next to the name of the statute to see all regulations made under a particular act. The "current-to" date of a regulation, as well as the date of its most recent amendment (if available), is shown in the header area of the regulation. The website also allows you to see previous versions of the regulation where they exist (select the "Previous Versions" link in the header area), but generally no further back than March 22, 2006.

Consolidated versions of Ontario regulations are available on the Ontario government's e-Laws website: <http://www.ontario.ca/laws>. Consolidated regulations are organized by the title of the statute under which they were made (again, the statutes are in alphabetical order). Choose the "Search or Browse Current Consolidated Law" link. Then, choose the letter that corresponds to first letter of the statute under which the regulation was made. Find the statute in the resulting list and select the plus sign preceding the statute name. A list of regulations under that statute will appear. Find the regulation in the resulting list and select it. At the beginning of each consolidated regulation, there is a notice of currency, which shows the consolidation period for the regulation. The consolidation period for most regulations is up-to-date to the "e-Laws currency date." Select the "e-Laws currency date" link in the notice of currency to see the e-Laws currency date for the regulation. (The government's goal is to provide up-to-date consolidated law within three business days of enactment of a new law or amendment of an existing law.)

In addition to consolidated versions of the regulations, the e-Laws website contains other things you will find useful if regulations research becomes an important part of your work. These include the following:

- All regulations as they read when filed, dating back to January 1, 2000. These are organized first by the year in which the regulation was filed and then by the name of the statute under which the regulation was made; the statutes are in alphabetical order.

- A "period in time" (PIT) database of current and historical versions of consolidated regulations, allowing the researcher to see the consolidated version of regulations as they read at different periods in time.

- A list of all the regulations that were filed during a specified year (dating back to 2000).

- The text of some revoked and spent regulations. (We know you're dying to ask, so here is the answer: A regulation can be revoked—that is, withdrawn—by a provision in the same regulation, in another regulation, or in a statute.) A regulation is "spent" when the regulation itself contains an expiration date and the date has passed, or when the authorizing statute is no longer in force, or when the regulation has become obsolete.

Why Read a Regulation?

Regulations are as important as statutes. Usually, the enabling statute deals with general principles and objectives, while the regulations under the statute are concerned with procedural and administrative aspects of the law; they provide details about how to carry out the enabling statute's overall purpose or objectives. In the case of **framework legislation**—a statute that provides an outline of the intended law and leaves the details to be worked out in the regulations—the regulations may appear more important than the statute.

If a statutory provision refers to a regulation, you will need to read the regulation in order to understand the full meaning of the provision. For example, s 2 of the Ontario *Food Safety and Quality Act, 2001* defines "deadstock" to mean "an animal that is specified in the regulations and that has died from a cause, other than slaughter." To determine whether or not an animal is deadstock within the meaning of the legislation, you must read the regulations.

Regulations are particularly important to those working in civil or criminal litigation because the rules of court are regulations made under the authority of the statute that creates the court system.

As with statutes, regulations require, prohibit, or permit certain actions and set out a method of doing what is required or permitted. They also create penalties for not doing what is required or for doing what is prohibited.

framework legislation
legislation that provides an outline of the intended law and leaves the details to be worked out in the regulations

How to Read a Regulation

The text of a regulation looks much like the text of a statute, although it may appear more detailed.

Figure 3.1 illustrates the first page of CRC, c 284, a regulation made under the *Canada Agricultural Products Act*, while Figure 3.2 illustrates O Reg 262/10, a regulation made under the *Retail Sales Tax Act*.

You read a regulatory provision the same way that you read a statutory provision. (So if you've been pining for a reason to reread Chapter 2, we've just given it to you.)

In order to understand fully a particular point of law, it may be necessary to read a regulation together with provisions of the statute under which it was made. You will have noticed, in looking at the two regulations shown in Figures 3.1 and 3.2, that the statute under which a regulation was made is clearly identified in the regulation itself.

Figure 3.1   First Page of a Federal Regulation (CRC, c 284)

CHAPTER 284	**CHAPITRE 284**
CANADA AGRICULTURAL PRODUCTS ACT	LOI SUR LES PRODUITS AGRICOLES AU CANADA
Egg Regulations	**Règlement sur les œufs**
REGULATIONS RESPECTING THE GRADING, PACKING, MARKING AND INSPECTION OF EGGS AND INTERNATIONAL AND INTERPROVINCIAL TRADE IN EGGS	RÈGLEMENT CONCERNANT LA CLASSIFICATION, L'EMBALLAGE, LE MARQUAGE ET L'INSPECTION DES ŒUFS, ET LE COMMERCE INTERNATIONAL ET INTERPROVINCIAL DES ŒUFS

<table>
<tr><td align="center">SHORT TITLE</td><td align="center">TITRE ABRÉGÉ</td></tr>
<tr><td>1. These Regulations may be cited as the Egg Regulations.</td><td>1. Le présent règlement peut être cité sous le titre : Règlement sur les œufs.</td></tr>
<tr><td align="center">INTERPRETATION</td><td align="center">INTERPRÉTATION</td></tr>
<tr><td>2. In these Regulations,</td><td>2. Dans le présent règlement,</td></tr>
<tr><td>"Act" means the Canada Agricultural Products Act; (Loi)</td><td>« additif alimentaire » S'entend au sens de l'article B.01.001 de la partie B du Règlement sur les aliments et drogues. (food additive)</td></tr>
<tr><td>"adulterated" [Repealed, SOR/2011-205, s. 1]</td><td>« Agence » L'Agence canadienne d'inspection des aliments constituée par l'article 3 de la Loi sur l'Agence canadienne d'inspection des aliments. (Agency)</td></tr>
<tr><td>"Agency" means the Canadian Food Inspection Agency established by section 3 of the Canadian Food Inspection Agency Act; (Agence)</td><td>« aliment » S'entend au sens de la Loi sur les aliments et drogues. (food)</td></tr>
<tr><td>"blood spot" means a small particle of blood on the yolk or in the albumen of an egg; (caillot sanguin)</td><td>« boîte » désigne un contenant pouvant contenir 15 douzaines d'œufs; (box)</td></tr>
<tr><td>"box" means a container made to contain 15 dozen eggs; (boîte)</td><td>« boîte à œufs » ou « carton » Contenant pouvant se fermer et destiné à contenir au plus 30 œufs dans des compartiments individuels. (carton)</td></tr>
<tr><td>"candling" means examining the interior condition of an egg by rotating or causing the egg to rotate in front of or over a light source that illuminates the contents of the egg; (mirage)</td><td>« caillot sanguin » désigne une petite tache de sang sur le jaune ou dans l'albumen d'un œuf; (blood spot)</td></tr>
<tr><td>"carton" means a container that is capable of being closed and that is made to contain not more than 30 eggs in separate compartments; (boîte à œufs ou carton)</td><td>« caisse » désigne un contenant pouvant contenir 30 douzaines d'œufs; (case)</td></tr>
<tr><td>"case" means a container made to contain 30 dozen eggs; (caisse)</td><td>« carton » [Abrogée, DORS/98-131, art. 1]</td></tr>
<tr><td>"code mark" [Repealed, SOR/2002-354, s. 1]</td><td>« code de l'exploitation du producteur » Combinaison de lettres, de symboles et de chiffres qui distingue les locaux du producteur d'où proviennent les œufs. (producer premises code)</td></tr>
<tr><td>"container" means any case, box, tray with an overwrap, carton, or other receptacle made to contain eggs; (contenant)</td><td>« code de producteur » [Abrogée, DORS/95-548, art. 2]</td></tr>
</table>

Figure 3.2   A Provincial Regulation (O Reg 262/10)

Retail Sales Tax Act
Loi sur la taxe de vente au détail

ONTARIO REGULATION 262/10

POINT OF SALE REBATES

Consolidation Period: From July 1, 2010 to the e-Laws currency date.

No amendments.

This Regulation is made in English only.

Definition
1. In this Regulation,

"Federal regulations" means the *Deduction for Provincial Rebate (GST/HST) Regulations*, SOR/2001-65 made under the *Excise Tax Act* (Canada). O. Reg. 262/10, s. 1.

Rebate for books
2. A book is qualifying property for the purposes of section 51 of the Act if it is property that is described in paragraph 1, 2, 3 or 4 of Schedule 1 to the Federal regulations. O. Reg. 262/10, s. 2.

Rebate for children's clothing, footwear and diapers
3. (1) Children's clothing is qualifying property for the purposes of section 51 of the Act if it is children's clothing as defined in section 1 of the Federal regulations and is included in Schedule 1 to those regulations. O. Reg. 262/10, s. 3 (1).

(2) Children's footwear is qualifying property for the purposes of section 51 of the Act if it children's footwear as defined in section 1 of the Federal regulations and is included in Schedule 1 to the Federal regulations. O. Reg. 262/10, s. 3 (2).

(3) A children's diaper is qualifying property for the purposes of section 51 of the Act if it is a children's diaper as defined in section 1 of the Federal regulations and is included in Schedule 1 to those regulations. O. Reg. 262/10, s. 3 (3).

Rebate for children's car seats and booster seats
4. A children's car seat or booster seat is qualifying property for the purposes of section 51 of the Act if it is a children's car seat as defined in section 1 of the Federal regulations and is included in Schedule 1 to those regulations. O. Reg. 262/10, s. 4.

Rebate for feminine hygiene products
5. A feminine hygiene product is qualifying property for the purposes of section 51 of the Act if it is a feminine hygiene product as defined in section 1 of the Federal regulations and is included in Schedule 1 to those regulations. O. Reg. 262/10, s. 5.

Rebate for prepared food and beverages
6. Prepared food and beverages are qualifying property for the purposes of section 51 of the Act if they are qualifying food and beverages as defined in section 1 of the Federal regulations and if the circumstances described in paragraph 11 of Schedule 1 to those regulations exist. O. Reg. 262/10, s. 6.

Rebate for newspapers
7. A newspaper is qualifying property for the purposes of section 51 of the Act if it is a qualifying newspaper as defined in section 1 of the Federal regulations and is included in Schedule 1 to those regulations. O. Reg. 262/10, s. 7.

Regulatory Citations

You must be able to read a regulatory citation correctly in order to find the text of the regulation, and you must be able to provide the correct citation of any regulation to which you refer when reporting your research.

Regulations are usually cited by year and number—the year in which the regulation was made, and the chronological number of the particular regulation in that year. The name of the regulation is typically not included in the citation. (That would be giving too much away. Regulations like to preserve a certain air of mystery.) Regulations of Canada are identified by "SOR," which stands for "Statutory Orders and Regulations." You may also see "SI," the abbreviation for "**Statutory Instrument**," which is a broader term than regulation, including, for example, rules of court. As an example, the citation for the federal regulation titled *Canada Student Loans Regulations*, which was made under the *Canada Student Loans Act*, is SOR/93-392. This tells us that it was the 392nd federal regulation filed in 1993. Provincial regulations are identified by an abbreviated name of the province plus "Reg" for Regulation. For example, the citation for the regulation *Driver Licence Examinations*, made under Ontario's *Highway Traffic Act*, is O Reg 341/94, indicating that it was the 341st Ontario regulation filed in 1994.

We noted above, under the heading "How Regulations Are Published," that regulations used to be periodically consolidated and published in print and that the last consolidation of federal regulations was made in 1978. It is cited as the *Consolidated Regulations of Canada, 1978* (CRC) and includes all regulations in force on December 31, 1977, each of which has its own chapter number. Cite a regulation from this 1978 consolidation as CRC plus chapter number. For example, the citation for the federal regulation *Certification of Countries Granting Equal Copyright Protection Notice* (made under the federal *Copyright Act*) is CRC, c 421.

The most recent consolidation of Ontario regulations took place in 1990, when all regulations then in force were incorporated into the *Revised Regulations of Ontario* (RRO) and assigned a number. Cite a regulation from the 1990 revision as RRO 1990 plus the regulation number. For example, the citation for the revised Ontario regulation titled *Speed Limits*, made under Ontario's *Highway Traffic Act*, is RRO 1990, Reg 619.

statutory instrument
general term that includes federal regulations

KEY TERMS

enabling statute, 34
framework legislation, 36
regulations, 34
statutory instrument, 39

EXERCISES

1. Correctly cite the following regulations:

a.

> **ONTARIO REGULATION 253/12**
>
> made under the
>
> **HIGHWAY TRAFFIC ACT**
>
> Made: September 5, 2012
> Filed: September 6, 2012
> Published on e-Laws: September 6, 2012
> Printed in The Ontario Gazette: September 22, 2012
>
> **AMENDING O. REG. 366/09**
>
> **(DISPLAY SCREENS AND HAND-HELD DEVICES)**

b.

> **Pension Benefits Act**
>
> **R.R.O. 1990, REGULATION 909**
>
> **GENERAL**

c.

> **Federal Child Support Guidelines**
>
> **SOR/97-175**
>
> DIVORCE ACT

d.

> **Designated Areas Firearms Order**
>
> **C.R.C., c. 430**
>
> CRIMINAL CODE

2. For each of the regulatory citations below, state (1) whether it is a federal or an Ontario regulation, and (2) where you would look for it.

   a. CRC, c 945

   b. O Reg 104/96

   c. CRC, c 870

   d. O Reg 864/93

3. Read the following regulatory and statutory provisions, then answer the questions that follow. You will need to start your answer by identifying which of the regulatory provisions is relevant to the situation described in the question. Then you will have to apply the regulatory law to the fact situation.

   Section 4 of O Reg 429/07, made under the authority of the *Accessibility for Ontarians with Disabilities Act, 2005* provides as follows:

   4(1) This section applies if goods or services are provided to members of the public or other third parties at premises owned or operated by the provider of the goods or services and if the public or third parties have access to the premises.

   (2) If a person with a disability is accompanied by a guide dog or other service animal, the provider of goods or services shall ensure that the person is permitted to enter the premises with the animal and to keep the animal with him or her unless the animal is otherwise excluded by law from the premises.

   (3) If a service animal is excluded by law from the premises, the provider of goods or services shall ensure that other measures are available to enable the person with a disability to obtain, use or benefit from the provider's goods or services.

   (4) If a person with a disability is accompanied by a support person, the provider of goods or services shall ensure that both persons are permitted to enter the premises together and that the person with a disability is not prevented from having access to the support person while on the premises.

   (5) The provider of goods or services may require a person with a disability to be accompanied by a support person when on the premises, but only if a support person is necessary to protect the health or safety of the person with a disability or the health or safety of others on the premises.

   (6) If an amount is payable by a person for admission to the premises or in connection with a person's presence at the premises, the provider of goods or services shall ensure that notice is given in advance about the amount, if any, payable in respect of the support person.

   (7) Every designated public sector organization and every other provider of goods or services that has at least 20 employees in Ontario shall prepare one or more documents describing its policies, practices and procedures with respect to the matters governed by this section and, upon request, shall give a copy of a document to any person.

   (8) In this section,

   "guide dog" means a guide dog as defined in section 1 of the *Blind Persons' Rights Act*;

   "service animal" means an animal described in subsection (9);

   "support person" means, in relation to a person with a disability, another person who accompanies him or her in order to help with communication, mobility, personal care or medical needs or with access to goods or services.

   (9) For the purposes of this section, an animal is a service animal for a person with a disability,

        (a) if it is readily apparent that the animal is used by the person for reasons relating to his or her disability; or

        (b) if the person provides a letter from a physician or nurse confirming that the person requires the animal for reasons relating to the disability.

The *Liquor Licence Act*, RSO 1990, c L.19, ss 30(1), 30(13)(a), and 31(1) and (2) state the following:

> 30(1) No person shall knowingly sell or supply liquor to a person under nineteen years of age. ...
>
> (13) This section does not apply,
>
> (a) to the supplying of liquor to a person under nineteen years of age in a residence as defined in section 31 or in a private place as defined in the regulations by a parent of the person or a person having lawful custody of the person. ...
>
> 31(1) In this section,
>
> "residence" means a place that is actually occupied and used as a dwelling, whether or not in common with other persons, including all premises used in conjunction with the place to which the general public is not invited or permitted access, and, if the place occupied and used as a dwelling is a tent, includes the land immediately adjacent to and used in conjunction with the tent.
>
> (2) No person shall have or consume liquor in any place other than,
>
> (a) a residence;
>
> (b) premises in respect of which a licence or permit is issued; or
>
> (c) a private place as defined in the regulations.

RRO 1990, Reg 718, ss 3(1), (2), and (3), made under the *Liquor Licence Act*, states the following:

> 3(1) For the purposes of clauses 30(13)(a) and 31(2)(c) of the Act,
>
> "private place" means a place, vehicle or boat described in this section.
>
> (2) An indoor place to which the public is not ordinarily invited or permitted is considered to be a private place except at the times when the public is invited or permitted access to it.
>
> (3) Despite subsection (2), an indoor place that is available for rental by members of the public for occasional use is not a private place.

Rule 3.01 of the *Rules of the Small Claims Court*, O Reg 258/98, made under the authority of the *Courts of Justice Act*, states the following:

RULE 3 TIME

Computation

> 3.01 If these rules or an order of the court prescribe a period of time for the taking of a step in a proceeding, the time shall be counted by excluding the first day and including the last day of the period; if the last day of the period of time falls on a holiday, the period ends on the next day that is not a holiday.

a. Your client, Sam Johnston, has epilepsy and recently acquired a service dog that is specially trained to alert him to an oncoming seizure. Must the dog wear a special collar or harness before the owner or manager of a clothing store is required to allow Sam and his dog into the store?

b. Rule 9.01 of the *Rules of the Small Claims Court* provides that a defendant who wishes to dispute a plaintiff's claim shall serve the plaintiff with a defence within 20 days of being served with the claim. Your client Johannes Barnes is served with a plaintiff's claim on the 4th day of the current month. What is the latest date by which Johannes must serve a defence?

c. Your client J.W. Hart, president and CEO of Hart Industries Inc., is having a party to which both adults and children will be invited. The client intends to serve champagne and would like to serve not only the adults but the older children (the 17- and 18-year-olds), too, with their parents' permission. The legal drinking age in Ontario is 19. The client wouldn't be consulting you if the party were being held in his own home, but he's concerned because the party is being held in a big tent on the grounds of a well-known public garden. A large area around the tent will be roped off to keep out uninvited people.

Can the client legally serve wine to anyone under 19 at the party? Explain, quoting the relevant statute and regulation.

Cases

4

LEARNING OUTCOMES

After reading this chapter, you will understand:

- What a case is
- Why we read a case
- How to read a case
- How cases are published
- How to cite a case

Introduction

Judicial decisions, known more informally as case law, are one of the four primary sources of Canadian law. As with statutes, bylaws, and regulations, legal professionals have to know how to read and understand a case. It is also helpful to understand how cases are published, and how to cite a case. This chapter provides such information.

What Is a Case?

A case is the record of a live legal proceeding, reduced in writing to the most important matters by the individual before whom the proceeding occurs. A legal proceeding may be a trial, an appeal, a motion, or a hearing.

Canada's court system is made up of courts and administrative tribunals. Both judges (presiding over courts) and adjudicators (chairing tribunals) have the authority to hear disputes and make decisions that affect the legal rights or obligations of the parties appearing before them.

The format of a case reflects what takes place during the proceeding. So we will approach the question of what a case is in a rather roundabout way, by first talking about what happens during a proceeding in the courtroom or hearing room.

The two main parts of a proceeding are the evidence and the legal argument. The parties present both of these to the judge or adjudicator; each side tells its version of the story and points out the law that tends to support its side of the dispute. In a civil trial, the parties are called the *plaintiff* and the *defendant*. In a criminal trial, the parties are called the Crown and the accused. In a motion or hearing, they may be called the *applicant* and the *respondent*. In an appeal, they are called the *appellant* and the *respondent*.

In a proceeding, the first thing the judge or adjudicator must do is listen to both sides' stories. In a trial or hearing, these stories are brought forward by witnesses, who give evidence on behalf of one party and are cross-examined by the other party (or parties). In motions and in some hearings, the evidence may be brought forward in writing—for example, by way of an individual's sworn statement plus a record of the other side's cross-examination of that individual. Once all the evidence has been presented, each party orally summarizes its view concerning the law that applies to the fact situation. Then the judge or adjudicator has to decide, between the conflicting stories of the parties, what he or she reasonably believes *actually* happened. In other words, the judge or adjudicator needs to establish the facts and then to choose the law that he or she believes is applicable to those facts.

In an appeal, which is an appellant's request to a higher court to overturn the decision of a lower court or tribunal, there are generally no witnesses to give evidence because the facts have already been determined by the trial judge or adjudicator. Instead, the appellant and respondent have each prepared a "factum" setting out a summary of the prior proceedings and the facts on which each is relying in the appeal. The court is provided with the transcript of the oral evidence from the trial or hearing. The factum also contains a statement of the relevant law on which the party is relying. The parties also have the opportunity to make oral argument about the law; the appellant's argument attempts to show that the trial judge or adjudicator made a mistake of some kind.

The judge or adjudicator ends the dispute by making a decision in favour of one side or the other and then telling the parties what happens next. For example, the judge might say, "I find for the defendant; case dismissed"; or, "The applicant has made out its case; therefore the application is allowed"; or "Appeal allowed. The matter is to be returned to the trial judge for a reassessment of damages." Finally, the judge or adjudicator provides his or her reasons for decision. Sometimes, he or she states the reasons orally at the end of the trial, hearing, or appeal. Sometimes, the reasons are "endorsed" on (written on the back of) the *record*—that is, the formal court document that serves (you might say) as the dispute's passport, and is provided to the judge or adjudicator at the proceeding. At other times, if the judge or adjudicator doesn't have time to give reasons or wants to organize them carefully, he or she will provide them in writing at a later date.

Once the reasons for decision have been distributed beyond the judge or adjudicator and the parties to the dispute, they are referred to as a "case."

Why Read a Case?

Case law research can tell you many things—such as whether a client has a cause of action to begin with and whether the action, if pursued, would succeed; how much a client could expect to be awarded in damages; and what evidence has to be presented at trial.

The law in a particular case is useful to your client in a particular situation only if

- the issues in the case and in the client's situation are similar,
- the facts in the case and in the client's situation are similar, and
- the case is binding (a court must follow the case) or at least persuasive (a court is not required to follow the case, but may follow it if it wishes) in your jurisdiction (see Chapter 6 for more detailed discussion of binding law and persuasive law).

If the issues and the facts are similar, and the case is at least a persuasive authority, the law in the case can be applied to your client's situation.

How to Read a Case

If you haven't read many cases, you may just see a shapeless mass of words when you look at one. But the truth is that all cases, however long or short, share a particular structure. Once you learn how to identify the different parts of a case, you will be able to use the case in research. Reasons for decision, which reflect the process that took place in the courtroom or hearing room, contain certain structural elements, and therefore cases contain them too. These elements are as follows:

- purpose,
- facts,

- issues,
- law,
- *ratio decidendi* (Latin for "reason for deciding"),
- decision, and
- disposition.

If there are several decision-makers, there may be several separate reasons for decision. This will be the case when several judges sit in appeal, as in a provincial or federal Court of Appeal, the Supreme Court of Canada, or the House of Lords in England. (Yes, when doing legal research you might well be tormented by foreign as well as Canadian case law.) Sometimes, separate reasons for decision reflect multiple opinions—both **majority opinions** and **dissenting** (or **minority**) **opinions**. It's easy enough to understand why there would be separate reasons from a dissenting judge. However, it also sometimes happens with majority decisions that several judges each set out their own separate reasons for reaching the same conclusion; and the reasons may differ—sometimes quite a lot. Then you end up with a case that is—for your purposes—several cases strung together under one name.

majority opinion
the opinion agreed upon by a majority of the appeal court judges

dissenting opinion
opinion written by an appeal court judge who did not agree with the majority opinion

minority opinion
see *dissenting opinion*

headnote
editor's explanation of the case, appearing at the head of the case

Headnote and Summary

Even before you get to the purpose of the case, you may find a short **headnote** at the beginning, inserted by the editor of the law report series or database. A headnote might start with "catch lines" (for example, "Malicious prosecution and false imprisonment—Defences—Lawful authority—Arrest by private citizen") before moving on to summarize the facts, issues, and *ratio decidendi* of the case, and then finishing with a list of the primary and secondary sources cited in the case (for example, other cases, statutes, regulations, and textbooks).

The headnote is useful in several ways. It tells you, before you commit time and energy to reading the case, whether the subject matter is relevant to your problem. Its early identification of the issues will help you to get a grip on the case before you delve further into it. (Try to grip the case rather than your hair. Tearing your hair out while reading a case will lead to premature baldness but will not help you otherwise.) A word of warning about headnotes, however: they are not always correct. Never rely on the headnote alone. Read the case yourself, and write your own summary of the case. Your own summary should not be paraphrased or in your own words; it should quote directly from the case itself.

Purpose

Why did this case come before the court or tribunal?

purpose
the nature of the proceedings

At the beginning of the case, after the headnote, there usually will be a short reference to the **purpose** (or nature) of the proceedings. This has been inserted by the editor of the law report series. It might say, for example, "Action for damages for negligence," "Motion for summary judgment," or "Appeal from a decision of the General Division." If no such reference appears, you'll find that judges and adjudicators usually begin their reasons with a brief mention of why the proceeding is before them.

Facts

What happened? In a trial or hearing, the facts are the events that led up to the moment when the cause of action came into existence. In an appeal, the decision under appeal is also treated as part of the facts.

Most judges set out the facts up front, in a single section at the beginning of their reasons. Irritatingly, some do not do this; instead, they scatter them throughout their reasons, usually placing them with the various issues to which they are relevant.

You want to focus on the facts that are relevant to the issues decided. But you will have to examine the issues and the law before you can decide which facts are relevant. Many cases—especially at the trial or hearing level—are long and contain much information that is not necessarily essential to understanding the issues.

Issues

What legal questions must the judge or adjudicator answer in order to decide the case?

The **issues** are the specific problems that the decision-maker must resolve in order to reach a decision. Often, they are set out in question form or introduced by the word "whether." Understanding the issues is key to understanding the case as a whole.

Once the decision-maker has identified an issue, he or she must consider all the elements that make up that issue, by

1. looking at the law connected with the issue to identify the legal rules involved, and then
2. looking at the particular facts of the matter to determine whether the requirements or conditions of any legal rules identified have been met.

For example, if the issue is "whether the defendant committed battery on the plaintiff," the judge has to examine the law to see what the legal test for battery is (what elements make up the tort of battery). Then the judge has to examine the facts to see whether the defendant's actions meet that test.

Students often find that identifying legal issues is the hardest part of legal research. You will find some help with that in Chapter 5, so don't despair yet. It takes practice to identify issues either in a case or in your own client's fact situation. Decision-makers sometimes seem unable themselves to identify the issues; they express opinions that are not directly concerned with the issues in the proceeding at hand. These excursions outside the proper issues are called *obiter dicta* (Latin for "words by the way") or simply *obiter*.

issues
specific problems that the judge or adjudicator must resolve to reach a decision

Law

What did the law say before this dispute came before the decision-maker?

After the decision-maker sets out the issues, he or she usually discusses the pre-existing law on each issue. Statutes, bylaws, regulations, other cases, and textbooks or journal articles may be quoted, cited, and relied on as authorities. Sometimes, if the law is well known, the decision-maker simply states the law without referring to any authority. He might say, for example, "A plaintiff must prove his or her case on the balance of probabilities."

lines of authority
sets of cases that share the same or similar viewpoint over a period of time

Because the opposing sides in a proceeding usually cite different **lines of authority** (sets of cases that share the same or a similar viewpoint over a period of time) to support their own side, the decision-maker may cite two or more cases, statutes, or texts that (apparently) give very different views of the law on a single issue. In this case, the decision-maker must choose which line of authority to follow before applying the law to the facts of the case and reaching a decision. Note which line of authority is chosen. Bingo! The law that the decision-maker chooses to follow is law for which you can cite the case for research.

If the case you are reading is an appeal, keep in mind that the law followed in dissenting reasons probably is not useful for you to cite.

Ratio Decidendi and Decision

What principle of law does the case stand for?

ratio decidendi
often simply called the *ratio*, a combined statement of the pre-existing principle of law on which the judge based the decision on an issue and its application to the facts of the particular case; Latin for "reason for deciding"

The **ratio decidendi** (or *ratio*) is a statement combining (1) the principle of law on which the judge is basing his or her decision on an issue and (2) the application of the principle to the facts of the particular case. The *ratio* is frequently introduced by words such as "here," "in this case," or "in my view," and is often short—a sentence or a brief paragraph. Bingo again! The *ratio decidendi* of a case is law for which you can cite the case when you are using it for research. If there is more than one issue, there will be more than one *ratio*.

If there are dissenting reasons in an appeal, the *ratio* in those reasons has no immediate value for your research, so you can ignore it. (Some day, that dissenting judge may be hailed as a visionary, but it isn't likely to be the day you're doing the research.)

But we're not done yet. The *ratio* for each issue must be followed by a *decision* for each issue. The decision itself—for example, "The applicant has not shown that it is entitled to the remedy requested," "The action in negligence must fail," or "The plaintiff has made out a good case in battery"—usually appears either at the beginning or at the end of the *ratio*.

Disposition

What is the procedural outcome of the proceeding?

disposition
judge's orders set out at the end of a case

Where do the parties stand when the dust settles? At the end of the case, the judge's or adjudicator's **disposition** or order(s) about the entire proceeding is set out—for example, "Judgment for the defendant," "Application allowed," "Motion for summary judgment granted," or "Appeal dismissed." The disposition usually includes an award of costs to the successful party and also may include administrative directions to the parties, such as an order that documents be filed by a certain date or a referral of the matter to another judicial official for an accounting.

Warm-Up Exercise: Reading a Case

Now that you know the structure of a case, you can try your hand at reading a case and extracting information from it.

For the case reproduced below (*Joly v Pelletier*), answer the following questions.

1. Identify the paragraph number or numbers in which you find each of the elements listed below. (In cases that have been edited, the editor often inserts paragraph numbers within square brackets for reference.)

   a. purpose

   b. facts

   c. issues

   d. law

   e. *ratio decidendi*

   f. decision

   g. disposition

2. Next, highlight in the paragraphs you identified in question 1 the text that most precisely expresses each of the elements you were looking for—that is,

   a. purpose

   b. facts

   c. issues

   d. law

   e. *ratio decidendi*

   f. decision

   g. disposition

3. Finally, using the excerpts you highlighted in question 2, summarize or condense (but don't paraphrase—don't put into your own words) the following:

   a. the facts

   b. the issues

   c. the law

Joly v Pelletier
Between
Rene Joly, and
R. Pelletier, Clive Livingstone Clarke, Henry Cussy et al.
And between
Rene Joly, and
Roland Pelletier, et al.
And between
Rene Joly, and
Shoppers Drugmart et al.
And between
Rene Joly, and
MDS Laboratories et al.
And between
Rene Joly, and
Wainbee Limited et al.
And between
Rene Joly, and
Royal College of Dental Surgeons of Ontario et al.
And between
Rene Joly, and
Pharma Plus Drugmarts et al.

[1999] OJ No 1728
Court File Nos 99-CV-166273 and 99-CV-167339
Ontario Superior Court of Justice
Epstein J
May 16, 1999.
(4 pp.)

Statutes, Regulations and Rules Cited:
Interpretation Act, s. 29.
Ontario *Rules of Civil Procedure*, Rules 1.02, 21.01(3)(b), 25.11.
Counsel:
No counsel mentioned.

[1] EPSTEIN J. (endorsement):—This endorsement relates to a series of motions brought on behalf of a number of the defendants in two related actions commenced in this Court by the plaintiff, Rene Joly. The moving parties seek orders striking out the Statements of Claim and thereby dismissing the actions on the grounds that the pleadings disclose no cause of action (rule 21.01(3)(b)) or are frivolous or vexatious or an abuse of the process of the Court (rule 25.11).

[2] Mr. Joly's claims in these two actions, and in several others not currently before me, all centre on his firm assertion that he is not a human being; rather a martian. As I understand them, the nature of his complaints against the numerous defendants who include a number of doctors, medical facilities

and government agencies is that they have conspired with the American government in its attempts to eliminate him and have otherwise taken various steps to interfere with his ability to establish himself and live freely as a martian.

[3] As indicated, there are two actions before me. At the beginning of the hearing Mr. Joly advised me that he has recently commenced a third action against, among others, the Central Intelligence Agency, President Clinton and the Honourable Anne McClellan for interfering with his D.N.A. test results that prove that he is, in fact, not human.

[4] Given the related issues in the three actions brought in this Court, I ordered that the three proceedings be consolidated. All parties consented to this order. An order will issue to this effect. Unfortunately, I failed to note the action number of the third action affected by this order.

[5] As another preliminary matter, I should indicate that given the unusual nature of the plaintiff's claims, a discussion took place at the beginning of argument as to whether I should order that a hearing be conducted pursuant to the provisions of rule 7 of the *Rules of Civil Procedure* for a determination as to whether the plaintiff was in a position properly to represent his interests on the motions or whether a litigation guardian should be appointed. As a result of this issue having been raised, I arranged for a reporter to record the proceedings and the plaintiff agreed to testify under oath and answer certain questions posed by Mr. Novak, counsel who appeared on behalf of a number of the defendants. At the conclusion of this form of hearing and having considered the submissions made, I determined that there was no reason to delay the argument of the motions. I made the observation that in every respect Mr. Joly properly conducted himself before the Court. He presented himself as polite, articulate, intelligent and appeared to understand completely the issues before the Court and the consequences should I grant the relief sought. There was nothing before me, other than the uniqueness of the pleadings in question, for me, on my own volition, to adjourn, pending a hearing to determine if Mr. Joly is under some form of disability. This observation, the fact that no one was really urging me to adjourn and the costs to all concerned of having these proceedings protracted, factored into my decision to proceed.

[6] Finally, I add that at the request of the parties, leave was granted to adduce evidence at the hearing. Both Mr. Novak and Mr. Joly presented evidence to the Court in support of their submissions.

[7] The crux of the various arguments advanced orally and in the written material is that Mr. Joly's claims disclose no cause of action and are otherwise frivolous, vexatious and an abuse of the process of the Court. It was also argued that the tort of conspiracy was not properly pleaded and that no damages have been identified or claimed. It was further pointed out that several of the defendants are not legal entities and are not capable of being sued.

[8] Mr. Joly, in a well prepared, thoughtful argument submitted that he had evidence of falsification of records and related wrongdoing. On the pivotal point of Mr. Joly's being in fact a martian Mr. Joly advised me that the only reason he was not now able to satisfy the Court that he is a martian, not a human, is due to the falsification of his D.N.A. test results by the Americans.

[9] The authorities relied upon by the moving parties are well known. On a motion to strike out a pleading, the Court must accept the facts as alleged in the Statement of Claim as proven unless they are patently ridiculous and incapable of proof and must read the Statement of Claim generously with allowance for inadequacies due to drafting deficiencies. See *Nash v. The Queen in Right of Ontario* (1995), 27 O.R. (3d) 1 (C.A.). Perhaps the leading case is that of *Carey Canada Inc. v. Hunt et al.* (1990), 74 D.L.R. (4th) 321 (S.C.C.) in which the test in Canada is described as assuming that the facts as stated in the Statement of Claim can be proved, the Court must be satisfied that it is "plain and obvious" that the plaintiff's statement of claim discloses no reasonable cause of action.

[10] Concerning rule 25.11, the Court will dismiss or stay an action as being frivolous, vexatious or abusive only in the clearest cases where it is plain and obvious the case cannot succeed. The decision in *Steiner v. Canada*, [1996] F.C.J. No. 1356 (Fed. T.D.) makes it clear that if a pleading does not present a rational argument, either on the evidence or in law, in support of the claim, and casts unreasonable aspersions [it] is frivolous.

[11] In my opinion there are at least two reasons why the two Statements of Claim in question ought to be struck and the actions dismissed.

1. Neither pleading discloses a cause of action. While conspiracy to do harm to someone is the basis of many actions in this Court there is a fundamental flaw in the position of Mr. Joly. Rule 1.03 defines plaintiff as "a person who commences an action." The *New Shorter Oxford English Dictionary* defines person as "an individual human being." Section 29 of the *Interpretation Act* provides that a person includes a corporation. It follows that if the plaintiff is not a person in that he is neither a human being nor a corporation, he cannot be a plaintiff as contemplated by the *Rules of Civil Procedure*. The entire basis of Mr. Joly's actions is that he is a martian, not a human being. There is certainly no suggestion that he is a corporation. I conclude therefore, that Mr. Joly, on his pleading as drafted, has no status before the Court.

2. In respect to the motions brought under rule 25.11 I am of the view that the test has been passed in the circumstances of this case. In other words, I am satisfied that the claims are frivolous and vexatious and constitute an abuse of the process of this Court. In addition to the fact that the tort of conspiracy has not been remotely properly pleaded, no damages have been claimed and many of the defendants are not even legal entities capable of being sued. More importantly, with all respect to Mr. Joly and his perception of reality, these actions are patently ridiculous and should not be allowed to continue as they utilize scarce public resources not to mention the time and money of the numerous defendants who have been forced to defend these actions.

[12] In the circumstances I have come to the conclusion that the moving parties are entitled to the relief requested. The Statements of Claim in both actions are struck and the actions are dismissed.

[13] The defendants are entitled to their costs of the actions but it would seem to be that the defence has likely incurred little if any costs in defending the actions. The moving parties are certainly entitled to their costs of the motions, if demanded. If the parties require any assistance with respect to the resolution of costs, they may arrange a conference call through the assistance of my secretary.

EPSTEIN J.

How Cases Are Published

It is helpful to understand how cases are published, in order to understand case citations.

Only some reasons for decision end up being published, or **reported**, in a law report series. The editor of the law report series will look to include cases that change or widen a legal principle or clarify an unsettled point of law, or that simply contain a good explanation or discussion of the law. The rest are **unreported**—not published in a law report series.

There are many different series of law reports. Some are organized by court level, such as the *Supreme Court Reports*, which contain only decisions of the Supreme Court of Canada. Others are organized by region or geographical area, such as the following: the *Ontario Reports*, which contain decisions of the Ontario courts; the *Western Weekly Reports*, which contain decisions from the western provinces; and the *Dominion Law Reports*, which contain decisions from all over Canada. Still others are organized by subject area, such as the *Reports of Family Law*, *Canadian Criminal Cases*, *Canadian Environmental Law Reports*, and the *Canadian Human Rights Reporter*, to name a few.

A case may be reported in more than one law report series. For example, an Ontario family law case that goes to the Supreme Court of Canada may be reported in the *Ontario Reports*, the *Supreme Court Reports*, and the *Reports of Family Law*. Nobody gets to call dibs on a case and prevent other law report series from including it, so there's little logic about what series will contain a case and a good deal of duplication between series. This is how law libraries come to have law report series stacked all the way up to the ceiling.

reported case
judge's decision and reasons about a case published in a law report series or a legal database

unreported case
case not published in a law report series

How to Cite a Case

To find the text of cases you want to read, you must understand how cases are identified or "cited." You must understand case citations.

A correct legal citation of a case consists of several parts as illustrated in the following examples, explained below:

1	2	3	4	5	6	7
Malette v Shulman	(1990),	67	DLR	(4th)	321	(Ont CA)
R v Mathieu,	[2008]	1	SCR		723	

1. Style of Cause

style of cause
portion of the citation
that sets out the names
of the parties; also
called a case name

The **style of cause** of the citation sets out the names of the parties (for individuals, last names only). The names of *all* the parties to the action are not always included in the citation. When some names are left out, the term "et al" is used; it means "and others." In a reported case, the editors of the law report series will have given the case a short style of cause as well as the complete one, if the latter is long. The words "indexed as" may appear before an abbreviated style of cause.

The names of the parties are separated by "*v*" (which is short for the Latin "versus," meaning "against," but spoken as "and" in civil cases and "against" in criminal cases). Undisclosed parties to a case—for example, minors—are identified by initials only. In Canada, the Crown (government) is in charge of prosecuting criminal cases. The Crown is represented by "*R*," which stands for *Regina* ("Queen") when the reigning monarch is a queen, and for *Rex* ("King") when the monarch is a king.

2. Year

The year in which the case is decided or published in a law report series follows the style of cause and will be enclosed in either round or square brackets.

Some law report series number their volumes sequentially no matter what the year, and it is not essential to know the year in which the case was reported in order to find it in the law report series. In that case, the year is enclosed in round brackets—( )—and is followed by a comma.

Other law report series start a new set of volume numbers each calendar year, and it is essential to know the year in order to find the case in the law report series. In this case, the year appears in square brackets—[ ]—and is preceded by a comma. For example, in each calendar year, the first volume of the *Supreme Court Reports* is volume 1. To find a case that is located in volume 1, you must know the year in which the case was reported to find the appropriate volume 1.

3. Law Report Volume Number

This number identifies the volume number of the law report series in which your case can be found. Some law report volumes are identified simply by volume number (as in the first example above), while others are identified also by the year in which the volume was published. More than one volume may be published in one year, as illustrated in the second example above. If the law report series starts a new sequence of volume numbers each year, then you must make sure you look for the volume number for the correct year. In the example of *R v Mathieu* above, you are looking for volume 1 for the year 2008.

4. Name of the Law Report Series

This part of the citation identifies the name of the law report series in which the case is reported. Abbreviations are generally used. In the example of *Malette v Shulman* above, "DLR" stands for the *Dominion Law Reports*. In the example of *R v Mathieu*, "SCR" stands for the *Supreme Court Reports*.

See Appendix A for a list of standard abbreviations covering the most commonly used law report series.

5. Law Report Series Number

Many reports do not continue past an arbitrary number of volumes. When the report reaches, for example, volume 75 or volume 100, that series ends and a new one begins. Subsequent editions are identified by 2d, 3d, 4th, and so on. If a series number is provided in a citation, be sure that you have the right series as well as the right volume number of the report. In the *Malette v Shulman* citation above, the case can be found in the 67th volume of the 4th series of the *Dominion Law Reports*.

6. Page Number

This number identifies the page number on which the case begins in the report volume. In a correct citation, no abbreviation such as p., pp., or pg. is used before the page number.

If the citation is followed by "at" plus a number, it means that the particular passage being referred to in the case appears on that numbered page. For example:

Hopp v Lepp, [1980] 2 SCR 192 **at 201**
Fucella v Ricker (1982), 35 OR (2d) 423 **at 426** (H Ct J)

7. Jurisdiction and Court

The abbreviation for jurisdiction and the level of court is found in round brackets following the page number on which the case begins. This information is omitted if the jurisdiction and/or court level is obvious from the name of the law report series.

If the citation refers to a law report series that includes cases for one province only, such as the *Ontario Reports* or the *British Columbia Reports*, only the level of court is set out. For example, the citation of a Court of Appeal case published in the *Ontario Reports* will end with "(CA)." The citation for the same case in the *Dominion Law Reports* (which publishes cases from across Canada) will end in "(Ont CA)."

If the citation refers to a law report series for one court only, the level of court will not be included in the citation. For example, the *Supreme Court Reports* cover only Supreme Court of Canada decisions. Therefore a citation for that law report series will omit both the jurisdiction and level of court, as illustrated in the examples of *R v Mathieu* and *Hopp v Lepp* above.

Sometimes, the name of the judge or judges who decided the case is included in the citation: for example, "(Ont CA—Robins J)." The "J" stands for judge or justice; it is not the initial of the judge's first name. "JJ" stands for justices and "JJA" stands for justices of an appeal court. "CJ" stands for chief justice. A judge's own initial is used only if it is necessary to distinguish between two judges with the same last name—for example, R.E. Holland J and J. Holland J.

Parallel Citations

We noted above that cases may be reported in more than one law report series. In that case, "parallel" citations may be given. A parallel citation tells you about other reports where the same case can be found. Parallel citations are separated by commas. Where there are parallel citations, the first citation is for the official law report series, if any. The *Supreme Court Reports* is an official series, as is the *Federal Court Reports*. "Official" means authorized by the court whose decisions are reported in the series. For example:

> *R v Carosella*, [1997] 1 SCR 80, 142 DLR (4th) 595, 112 CCC (3d) 289

This citation means that the case can be found in the *Supreme Court Reports*, the *Dominion Law Reports*, and *Canadian Criminal Cases*. You only need to look up the case in one of the law report series. Parallel citations are useful because not every private or public law library holds every law report series, and in a small library you may be lucky to find even one of the cited series.

Citation with Case History Included

If a case has been appealed to higher courts, the citation may include a complete appeal history or case history, informing you about the case's journey through the court system. For example:

> *Queen v Cognos Inc*, [1993] 1 SCR 87, rev'g (1990), 74 OR (2d) 176 (CA), aff'g (1987), 63 OR (2d) 389 (H Ct J)

This citation tells you that the 1993 Supreme Court of Canada decision reversed the 1990 decision from the Ontario Court of Appeal, but affirmed the 1987 decision of the Ontario High Court of Justice.

Neutral Citations

Canadian courts now assign neutral citations to judicial decisions. The neutral citation identifies only the case itself, and not where the case may be found in a publication. An example of a neutral citation is *R v Manning*, 2013 SCC 1.

1	**2**	**3**	**4**
R v Manning,	2013	SCC	1

The neutral citation consists of the following four elements:

1. the style of cause (names of the parties),
2. the year of the decision,
3. an abbreviation of the name of the court or tribunal that made the decision, and

4. a chronological number indicating the decision's place in the sequence of cases decided in that year.

If a case has a neutral citation, that citation is shown first, followed by the law report series citation. *R v Manning* was reported by the *Supreme Court Reports*. The complete citation for this case is therefore as follows: *R v Manning*, 2013 SCC 1, [2013] 1 SCR 3.

Electronic Database Citations

Computerized sources use their own case identifiers in their databases. You should use the computerized source's case identifier only when no law report series citation exists. If the case has not been published in print but has a neutral citation, use the neutral citation. Following are two examples of electronic database citations:

Neutral citation available	***Brown v Douglas***, **2010 BCSC 1059 (available on WLNC)** The words "available on WLNC" indicate that the case is available on the electronic database WestlawNext Canada.
No neutral citation available	***Bank of Nova Scotia v Visentin***, **[1996] OJ No 4563 (QL) (Ct J (Gen Div))** "QL" indicates that the case can be found on the electronic database LexisNexis Quicklaw. "OJ" (Ontario Judgments) indicates that this is a case from Ontario; however, the court level is not indicated, so "Ct J (Gen Div)" is needed at the end.

KEY TERMS

disposition, 50
dissenting opinion, 48
headnote, 48
issues, 49

lines of authority, 50
majority opinion, 48
minority opinion, 48
purpose, 48

ratio decidendi, 50
reported case, 55
style of cause, 56
unreported case, 55

EXERCISES

1. Read the following case and state the paragraph number(s) where you find the elements below. (If an element is not in a numbered paragraph, describe its location instead.)

- purpose,
- facts,
- issues,
- law,
- *ratio decidendi*,
- decision, and
- disposition.

Cyrenne v Moar

(1986), 2 RFL (3d) 414

Manitoba Court of Appeal, Monnin CJM, Huband, and Twaddle JJA

M.J. Bennett, for appellant.

C.N. Guberman, for respondent.
(No 193/86)
16th June 1986. The judgment of the court was delivered by

[1] MONNIN CJM (orally):—This is an appeal from a decision of Helper J. who dismissed the mother's application to strike out the access privileges granted to Mr. Cyrenne by a prior order of Simonsen J.

[2] We are of the view that it is not in the best interest of the child, Sonya Rose Moar, that access be given to Mr. Cyrenne. The original order most probably would not have been made if all the facts had been disclosed.

[3] We strike out the access rights granted to Mr. Cyrenne and will give more detailed reasons in due course.

[4] The matter of costs is reserved and will be dealt with in our extended reasons.

[5] 20th June 1986. Written reasons for judgment. The judgment of the court was delivered by

[6] HUBAND JA:—This court has decided that the visiting privileges accorded to John Cyrenne should end. What follows are my reasons for allowing the appeal of Annette Moar on 16th June 1986.

[7]   John Cyrenne is not the father of the child, Sonya, in whom he has taken such keen interest. John Cyrenne met Annette Moar in 1979 and had some form of relationship with her extending through to 1982. During part of 1981 and 1982 they maintained adjoining suites in the same dwelling house, and during that period of time the relationship seemed to have been at its closest.

[8]   Annette Moar was already the mother of a son who was born in 1974. The daughter, Sonya, was born on 19th June 1981. Initially John Cyrenne believed that he had fathered the child, but subsequent blood tests have confirmed that he is not the father of the child.

[9]   Believing the child to be his, John Cyrenne participated to some degree in the care of the baby, although he made no significant financial contribution. No doubt he developed a genuine fondness for the child.

[10]   In June 1982 John Cyrenne was sentenced to jail for six months, and the somewhat tenuous relationship between himself and Annette Moar began to crumble. When he was released from prison two months later, Annette Moar had moved to different accommodation. She began a new relationship with another man in the fall of 1982—a relationship which has persisted through to the present date. In October 1982 she told John Cyrenne that he was not the father of the child, Sonya, but John Cyrenne did not accept her statement at that time.

[11]   During 1983 John Cyrenne continued to visit the child from time to time, but with growing reluctance on the part of the mother and her new companion.

[12]   By the beginning of 1984 Annette Moar made it clear that she wanted John Cyrenne's visits with her daughter to end. His response was to seek custody or access by way of proceedings in court. On 22nd February 1984 he applied in the Provincial Court, Family Division, for custody of, or access to, the child. Annette Moar caused an answer to be filed asserting that John Cyrenne was not the father of the child, and on 27th February his application for custody or access was withdrawn.

[13]   A fresh application seeking custody or access was filed in the same court on 21st March 1984. This application also sought a declaration of parentage. The parties submitted to blood tests, and the results of those tests demonstrated that John Cyrenne was not the father of the child. Ultimately, this second application was discontinued on 6th December 1984.

[14]   But once again, a fresh action was commenced a few weeks later. This time a petition was filed in the Court of Queen's Bench on 17th December 1984, seeking access only, and relying upon s. 1.5 of the *Child Welfare Act* of Manitoba.

[15]   Annette Moar did not contest this petition. Later on she was to explain that she wilted under the bombardment of continuing applications and the constant harassment of John Cyrenne to gain access to the child. In any event, on 18th February 1985 John Cyrenne obtained an order from Simonsen J. in the Court of Queen's Bench granting him access to the child each Sunday from 10:00 a.m. to 7:00 p.m. While the order was made without

opposition from Annette Moar, it would appear that given the unusual nature of the order allowing access in favour of a person who is not a blood relation, Simonsen J. insisted upon some evidence before making the order. John Cyrenne testified and, since the petition was not opposed, the order was made.

[16] Problems with respect to the access arose almost immediately. About one month after the order was made, Annette Moar was seeking legal aid in order to move to set aside the access order, and within a further month John Cyrenne had instituted criminal contempt proceedings against Annette Moar for her disobedience of the access order. Attendances at Annette Moar's residence to exercise rights became confrontations. In June 1985 Annette Moar brought a motion in the Court of Queen's Bench seeking an order to vary the order of Simonsen J. by deleting the access privileges. John Cyrenne countered with a motion for an order of contempt against Annette Moar, and an order to vary the terms of the access order of Simonsen J. by "increasing the times of access." These two motions came before Schwartz J. of the Court of Queen's Bench in July 1985. In order to defuse the confrontations between the protagonists, Schwartz J. ordered an immediate variation to provide that some third party, other than John Cyrenne, attend to pick up the child. As to the merits of the motion and counter-motion, Schwartz J. ordered that they be dealt with by way of a trial in the fall of 1985.

[17] The trial commenced before Helper J. in November 1985. After two days of testimony the learned trial judge decided to order an assessment report from a family conciliation counsellor, and the testimony of the author of that report was heard on 26th April 1986. Helper J. delivered judgment on that same date. Helper J. did not vary the access as ordered by Simonsen J. approximately a year earlier.

[18] The learned trial judge seemed to believe that there must be proof of changed circumstances to justify a variation in the previous order of Simonsen J. She asked the rhetorical question, "What circumstances have changed since the pronouncement of the order to warrant any change in the existing order?" The learned trial judge went on to observe that animosity between John Cyrenne and Annette Moar both preceded and followed the order of Simonsen J. Helper J. found no significant change in circumstances to justify a variation.

[19] With respect, I do not think that proof of changed circumstances is essential. The order of Simonsen J. was made pursuant to s. 1.5 of the *Child Welfare Act*, S.M. 1974, c. C80. Section 1.5 was added by way of an amendment to the Act in 1983, and the provision reads as follows:

> 1.5. In exceptional circumstances, a court may make an order granting any person who has had or ought to have the opportunity to visit a child, the right to visit the child at such times and on such conditions as the court considers appropriate.

[20] The basis for varying an access order made under the *Child Welfare Act* is to be found in s. 21 of the *Family Maintenance Act*, C.C.S.M. c. F20, which reads as follows:

21. An order made under this Act or under [t]he *Wives' and Children's Maintenance Act* or under the *Family Maintenance Act*, being chapter 47 of the *Statutes of Manitoba*, 1977, or an order made under [t]he *Child Welfare Act* granting custody of, access to or maintenance for a child, may upon an application therefor be varied from time to time or discharged by the court making the order, if the court thinks it fit and just to do so, but no variation or discharge granted under this section shall be effective before the date on which the application therefor is made.

[21] The test for a variation or discharge would seem to be what is "fit and just" and unlike a variation to an order made under the *Divorce Act* of Canada, the variation or discharge does not hinge upon proof of changed circumstances.

[22] However, there is no need to dwell upon this difference between provincial and federal legislation, because using either test the appeal must be allowed. There were in fact changed circumstances between the granting of the access order by Simonsen J. and the trial before Helper J. The conflict between Annette Moar and John Cyrenne had escalated in intensity. Of greater significance, the passive toleration of access on the part of the mother had become firm and resolute opposition.

[23] This was not a case where Annette Moar had consented to access on a basis approaching an agreement. Non-opposition is not the same thing as active consent. As mother and guardian of the child, Annette Moar is entitled to say that she has changed her mind, and that John Cyrenne's visits with her child are no longer welcome. In a case of this kind, where the statute requires exceptional circumstances before the court may make an order of access, the opposition of the mother is enormously significant. She has the responsibility of rearing the child, and the child has the right to be reared by her. Her opinion as to who should visit with the child and under what circumstances deserves very great consideration. When non-opposition turns to defiant hostility, the circumstances have clearly altered.

[24] Further, I think it is "fit and just" that access be denied. The case of *Lapp v. Dupuis* (1985), 45 R.F.L. (2d) 28, 31 Man. R. (2d) 261, was a decision by this court dealing with similar circumstances. The petitioner had a brief romantic interest in the mother of the child, which was not reciprocated. The petitioner became good friends with the mother, however, and from that relationship he developed an interest in her 5-month-old child. That interest continued over a period of a few years, and for approximately a year and one half the petitioner served as principal babysitter for the child. As time went by, the mother entered into a relationship with another man. There was animosity between the petitioner and the mother's new friend. When the mother insisted that the petitioner's visits cease, the petitioner applied for access, and the application was firmly opposed by the mother of the child. This court decided that an association emerging out of a babysitting arrangement, albeit over a lengthy period of time, was insufficient to establish the "exceptional circumstances" required under s. 1.5 of the *Child Welfare Act*. In that case, as in the present case, the petitioner had a genuine interest in the child, and his

visits were not disagreeable from the standpoint of the child. But the court concluded that an access order in favour of someone who is not a blood relation should be set aside in face of the opposition of the mother who wished to exercise responsible control over the destiny of her child and herself. As in the *Lapp v. Dupuis* case, a fit and just disposition is to cancel the access privileges.

[25] In my opinion, it was appropriate for the learned trial judge to vary the order of Simonsen J. and, given the evidence presented before her, she should have done so by deleting access.

[26] I am mindful of the argument on behalf of John Cyrenne that the paramount consideration is the best interests of the child. The very wording of s. 1.5 of the *Child Welfare Act*, however, suggests that it will only be under rare circumstances that court-ordered visits of a non-relative will be considered to be in the child's best interests, at least where there is opposition by the parent or parents. As noted in the case of *Lapp v. Dupuis*, the parents' attitude is not to be relegated to a parity with all other surrounding circumstances in determining what is best for the child. While not determinative, the parents' position is of prime importance in making the determination of best interests. I have no hesitation in this case in concluding that the access awarded to John Cyrenne is not in the child's best interests.

[27] For some period of time leading up to the date of the appeal hearing, Annette Moar was defiant of the order for access in favour of John Cyrenne. Under the circumstances, while her appeal is allowed, it is allowed without costs.

Appeal allowed;
access terminated.

2. Now we're going to take off your training wheels and let you summarize a case by yourself. (But if you feel a little shaky without your training wheels, proceed through this exercise following the pattern set out above in the Warm-Up Exercise that used the *Joly v Pelletier* case.)

Read the following case, and set out the following:

- purpose
- facts
- issues
- law
- *ratio decidendi*
- decision
- disposition

Dyck v Manitoba Snowmobile Association

[1985] 1 SCR 589

Ronald James Dyck   *Appellant*;

and

Manitoba Snowmobile Association Inc.   *Respondents.*
and Reginald Wood

1985: March 28, 29; 1985: May 23.

Present: Dickson CJ and Beetz, Estey, McIntyre, Wilson, Le Dain and La Forest JJ.

1. The Court—This is an appeal from the Court of Appeal of Manitoba in which it dismissed an appeal from a judgment of Kroft J. in which he dismissed the appellant's action in negligence against both respondents to recover damages for injuries suffered by the appellant in the course of a snowmobile race.

2. The facts are fully set forth in the judgments in the courts below and require only a brief summary here. The appellant, Dyck, on February 23, 1975, suffered serious injuries while taking part in a snowmobile race at Beausejour, Manitoba sanctioned by the respondent Snowmobile Association. Dyck was a member of the Association whose rules, which Dyck had read, purported to release the Association from all liability for injuries suffered by entrants in races sanctioned by it. The competition membership application signed by Dyck also purported to release the Association from such liability. These documents made no express mention of injuries resulting from the negligence of the Association or its servants but the entry form for the race, also signed by Dyck, expressly set forth his agreement to save harmless and keep indemnified the Association, its organizers, agents, officials, servants and representatives from all liability, howsoever caused, in connection with taking part in the race "notwithstanding that the same may have been contributed to or occasioned by [their] negligence."

3. The accident occurred when Dyck's snowmobile collided with the respondent Wood who was responsible for signalling the finish of the race. In doing this, Wood, following his usual practice, moved well onto the track to signal the driver, being around the middle of the track when Dyck collided with him. This caused Dyck to strike the outside wall of the track from which he suffered the injuries that gave rise to this action.

4. Kroft J. found that Dyck and Wood were both negligent and would have found Wood and, through the principle of vicarious liability, the Association responsible for one-third of the damages resulting to Dyck from his injuries. He, however, excluded the respondent Association from liability on the basis of the waiver of liability clause in the entry form of which, he found, Dyck had full notice. On the evidence, he further held that the clause applied to release Wood as well as the Association from liability.

5. The Court of Appeal disagreed with Kroft J. regarding responsibility for the accident, holding that the accident resulted solely from the negligence of

Wood. It, however, dismissed the appeal because of the operation of the waiver clause in the entry form Dyck had signed. It agreed with Kroft J. that this clause applied to Wood as well as to the Association.

6. We agree for the reasons given by Mr. Justice Huband on behalf of the Court of Appeal that, in the context in which it was signed, the waiver clause in the entry form exonerated the Association from liability for the accident, and that Wood is also exonerated because the Association was acting as his agent in obtaining the waiver.

7. On this appeal it was argued on behalf of Dyck that the waiver clause was worded in the form of an indemnity rather than a release. However, the context clearly reveals that a release is what the parties had in mind. Indeed at one point it is referred to in the entry form as a waiver of claim and the earlier waiver clauses underline that this was the parties' intention.

8. Counsel for the appellant also attempted to avoid the effect of the waiver clause on various grounds ultimately based on the thesis that it was unfair, unreasonable and inapplicable to the accident. One such ground was that the conduct of Wood in standing where he did on the track constituted negligence of a kind that was radically different from anything reasonable men could have contemplated. But surely this was precisely the type of negligence contemplated by the exclusion clause. This is underscored by the evidence which reveals that Wood's actions, though found to be negligent by the trial judge and the Court of Appeal, are not regarded as unusual by persons involved in snowmobile racing.

9. The appellant's argument on fundamental breach, however, went beyond one of mere construction of the contract and rather merged with his thesis that the waiver clause was unreasonable. Whether the doctrine of fundamental breach is confined to questions of construction, or whether it involves the power of a court to declare that certain contractual arrangements are so manifestly unfair and unreasonable as to be unenforceable, it is unnecessary to consider. The central fact is that a waiver clause of the kind in issue in the present case does not appear to be unreasonable. The appellant knew, or should have known, that snowmobile racing is a dangerous sport and he voluntarily participated in it. Though the Association had the control of snowmobile racing, this is hardly akin to the situations where the doctrine of fundamental breach has seen its widest extension, namely, where a commercial firm supplies to the public ordinary items of trade and from a commercial point of view dictates the terms on which consumers are to obtain these goods. The Association here is a voluntary body that organizes for the benefit of its members and the public a sporting activity that carries with it well-known and obvious dangers.

10. Nor does the relationship of Dyck and the Association fall within the class of cases, notable among which are contracts made on dissolution of marriage, where the differences between the bargaining strength of the parties is such that the courts will hold a transaction unconscionable and so unenforceable where the stronger party has taken unfair advantage of the

other. The appellant freely joined and participated in activities organized by an association. The Association neither exercised pressure on the appellant nor unfairly took advantage of social or economic pressures on him to get him to participate in its activities. As already mentioned, the races carried with them inherent dangers of which the appellant should have been aware and it was in no way unreasonable for an organization like the Association to seek to protect itself against liability from suit for damages arising out of such dangers. It follows from this that there are no grounds of public policy on which the waiver clause should be struck down, an issue also raised on behalf of the appellant.

11. In light of the foregoing, it becomes unnecessary to discuss the issues of negligence and contributory negligence or other questions raised by the parties. The appeal is dismissed with costs.

Appeal dismissed with costs.

3. Read the following fact situation and then, using the case law you examined in question 1, answer the question that follows.

A babysitter in Manitoba became very fond of the little girl she looked after, and the child adored the babysitter. The parents decided to hire a live-in nanny and let the baby-sitter go, but the babysitter still came each afternoon to visit the child. After a while it became clear that these visits were making it difficult for the nanny to establish a good relationship with the child. The parents told the babysitter that she could no longer visit the child. The babysitter has come to you for advice. She would like to apply to the court for access.

Would the babysitter's application for access be likely to succeed? Explain, quoting the relevant law.

ANSWERS TO WARM-UP EXERCISE

1. The paragraph numbers are as follows:

   a. Paragraph 1 (purpose)

   b. Paragraphs 2, 3 (facts)

   c. Paragraph 7 (issues)

   d. Paragraphs 9, 10, 11 (law)

   e. Paragraph 11 (*ratio decidendi*)

   f. Paragraph 11 (decision)

   g. Paragraph 12 (disposition)

2. The texts are as follows:

   a. The *purpose*:

   The moving parties seek orders striking out the Statements of Claim and thereby dismissing the actions on the grounds that the pleadings disclose no cause of action (rule 21.01(3)(b)) or are frivolous or vexatious or an abuse of the process of the Court (rule 25.11). [Paragraph 1]

b. The *facts*:

Mr. Joly's claims … that he is not a human being; rather a martian. … The numerous defendants … have conspired with the American government in its attempts to eliminate him and have otherwise taken various steps to interfere with his ability to establish himself and live freely as a martian. [Paragraph 2]

Mr. Joly … has recently commenced a third action against, among others, the Central Intelligence Agency, President Clinton and the Honourable Anne McClellan for interfering with his D.N.A. test results that prove that he is, in fact, not human. [Paragraph 3]

c. The *issues*:

The crux of the various arguments advanced orally and in the written material is that Mr. Joly's claims disclose no cause of action and are otherwise frivolous, vexatious and an abuse of the process of the Court. It was also argued that the tort of conspiracy was not properly pleaded and that no damages have been identified or claimed. It was further pointed out that several of the defendants are not legal entities and are not capable of being sued. [Paragraph 7]

d. The *law*:

On a motion to strike out a pleading, the Court must accept the facts as alleged in the Statement of Claim as proven unless they are patently ridiculous and incapable of proof and must read the Statement of Claim generously with allowance for inadequacies due to drafting deficiencies. See *Nash v. The Queen in Right of Ontario* (1995), 27 O.R. (3d) 1 (C.A.). Perhaps the leading case is that of *Carey Canada Inc. v. Hunt et al.* (1990), 74 D.L.R. (4th) 321 (S.C.C.) in which the test in Canada is described as assuming that the facts as stated in the Statement of Claim can be proved, the Court must be satisfied that it is "plain and obvious" that the plaintiff's statement of claim discloses no reasonable cause of action. [Paragraph 9]

Concerning rule 25.11, the Court will dismiss or stay an action as being frivolous, vexatious or abusive only in the clearest cases where it is plain and obvious the case cannot succeed. The decision in *Steiner v. Canada*, [1996] F.C.J. No. 1356 (Fed. T.D.) makes it clear that if a pleading does not present a rational argument, either on the evidence or in law, in support of the claim, and casts unreasonable aspersions is frivolous. [Paragraph 10]

Rule 1.03 defines plaintiff as "a person who commences an action." The *New Shorter Oxford English Dictionary* defines person as "an individual human being." Section 29 of the Interpretation Act provides that a person includes a corporation. [Paragraph 11]

e. The *ratio decidendi*:

… if the plaintiff is not a person in that he is neither a human being nor a corporation, he cannot be a plaintiff as contemplated by the *Rules of Civil Procedure*. … these actions are patently ridiculous and should not be allowed to continue as they utilize scarce public resources not to mention the time and money of the numerous defendants who have been forced to defend these actions. [Paragraph 11]

f. The *decision*:

Neither pleading discloses a cause of action. ... The entire basis of Mr. Joly's actions is that he is a martian, not a human being. There is certainly no suggestion that he is a corporation. I conclude therefore, that Mr. Joly, on his pleading as drafted, has no status before the Court. [Paragraph 11]

g. The *disposition*:

In the circumstances I have come to the conclusion that the moving parties are entitled to the relief requested. The Statements of Claim in both actions are struck and the actions are dismissed. [Paragraph 12]

3. Summaries of the excerpts from question 2 are provided below.

a. The *facts*:

Plaintiff claims to be a martian and not a human. [Paragraph 2]

Plaintiff claims that the defendants conspired to interfere with his ability to establish himself and live freely as a martian. [Paragraph 2]

b. The *issues*:

Whether pleadings should be struck and claims thereby dismissed if pleadings disclose no reasonable cause of action or if they are frivolous, vexatious, or an abuse of the process of the court. [Paragraph 7]

c. The *law*:

Assuming that the facts as stated in the Statement of Claim can be proved, the Court must be satisfied that it is "plain and obvious" that the plaintiff's statement of claim discloses no reasonable cause of action. [Paragraph 9]

The Court will dismiss or stay an action as being frivolous, vexatious or abusive only in the clearest cases where it is plain and obvious the case cannot succeed. ... if a pleading does not present a rational argument, either on the evidence or in law, in support of the claim, and casts unreasonable aspersions [it] is frivolous. [Paragraph 10]

PART III

Thinking About Legal Research

Sometimes, legal research merely means finding a particular statute, regulation, or case. Analysis of facts and issues may not be necessary. At other times, however, you must perform legal research that involves a stated fact situation. When this happens, going to the library or turning on the computer to look for cases and statutes is *not* the first thing to do. The first thing to do is *think*: to analyze the given facts in order to identify the relevant issues; to get your bearings in the applicable law; and to determine the tools you'll need to do the research.

Many of the exercises in this book can be done in the classroom and so are necessarily quite general in nature. Eventually, you will have to go to a law library or will have access to a computer with a link to law databases. When the time comes to do hands-on research using primary and secondary sources, your instructor will provide exercises that require you to find out what the law actually is at the time that you are doing the exercises.

How to Analyze a Fact Situation

5

LEARNING OUTCOMES

After reading this chapter, you will understand:

- The need to examine a client's fact situation in order to identify the issues involved in it

- What issues are, and why you need to solve them in order to give a client legal advice

- The steps involved in examining a fact situation

Introduction

You will rarely perform legal research for the sheer pleasure of it. (*Hmm … I've got some spare time today. I think I'd like to learn about the writ of withernam!*) Instead, your interest in researching something will be triggered when a client comes to you or your firm seeking advice about a legal problem arising out of a fact situation.

This chapter teaches you the steps involved in examining a fact situation. You will start your research by examining the fact situation in order to identify the issues that arise from it. **Issues** are the specific problems that you must solve in order to provide a client with a solution to a problem posed by the entire fact situation. The steps involved in examining the fact situation are as follows:

issue
the specific problem that you must solve in order to provide a client with a solution to a problem posed by the entire fact situation

1. identify, on a preliminary basis, the issues arising from the facts,
2. formulate those issues,
3. consider whether there are any hidden issues—issues not immediately obvious on hearing the fact situation, and
4. identify the need for further information.

Identify the Issues on a Preliminary Basis

Identifying issues is not easy. The following questions may help you to decide what issues arise out of a given set of facts.

What Does the Client Want?

Legal research starts with a client's request for advice. The request may be direct, in the form of a specific question from the client, such as the following: "Can a landlord enter a tenant's apartment when the tenant is not home?" Or the request may come to you from the lawyer who has been working with the client; she may ask for your help in preparing an answer for the client. In this case, the lawyer's instruction to you might be as follows: "I'd like you to hunt down a case that says that an unborn child has no legal status in Canadian courts."

The request may be less direct, and come in the form of a statement of what the client wants. For example, the client may state that he or she wants something: to receive financial compensation for an injury; to get out of having to pay damages for his or her own breach of contract; to register a mortgage on a property; or to patent an invention.

What Are the Relevant Facts?

Before you can identify the issues, you must first determine the facts behind the client's problem—the who, what, where, and when. To accomplish this, you get the client to tell the story of what happened—the full, true version, if possible. The client's story may not be told in any logical order and will probably include many irrelevant facts. Start by putting the facts into a logical order. Chronological order usually works best.

Then try to eliminate the irrelevant facts. If a particular fact does not change the legal outcome of the story, then it is irrelevant. If it does change the outcome, then it is relevant.

What Is the Area of Law?

The next step is determining what the area of law is. From the facts and from the client's request for advice, you will be able at least to venture a guess about the area of law involved.

First, identify the problem by general area—for example, criminal law, tort, contract law, family law, or real property. If you are unsure, try this: identify keywords in the fact situation and find them in the keyword index of the *Canadian Encyclopedic Digest* (CED), discussed in Chapters 10 and 11. For example, in a fact situation involving the eviction of your client from her apartment, the keyword "eviction" will lead you to the CED's "Landlord and Tenant" title.

Next, by refining your examination of the fact situation, look for more specific keywords. Identify the problem more particularly: if the general area is contract law, is the specific area breach of contract or assignment of a contract? If the general area is family law, is the specific area divorce or custody?

Finally, narrow the area of law even further. Within the area of custody, for example, is the particular area of law the child's best interests or the jurisdiction of a court to hear the matter? The more specifically and narrowly you identify the area of law you need to investigate, the more quickly and easily you will find the answers you need.

What Is the Objective of Your Research?

The objective of your research may be different from what the client is asking for. Clients may *want* things that are not legally possible or that do not provide the best solution to the problem. The issue—the problem to be solved—may not be the one that the client has identified. Your real goal may be to find the best legal means by which the client can resolve his or her problem.

Once you think you have identified a good solution, you will need to examine it carefully in light of the fact situation to make sure that it is really applicable.

Are There Any Hidden Issues?

The obvious issues can be hard enough to find, let alone the hidden ones. But hidden issues need to be kept in mind. Ask yourself the following questions:

- *Are there any special procedural requirements?* For example, is there a limitation period that may expire shortly? Are there any statutes or regulations governing procedure in the court or tribunal with jurisdiction over the issue? Is the correct jurisdiction federal or provincial?

- *Who, in law, are the parties involved?* Issues may arise out of the parties' legal status. For example, are they natural persons, corporations, adults, minors, spouses, mentally incompetent persons, the Crown, or agents rather than principals?

Formulate the Issues

Write down the issues you have identified, starting with the word "whether."

Examples

- whether a person who is not a parent of a child may apply for custody of that child;
- whether the limitation period for medical malpractice begins to run from the date of the medical procedure;
- whether a landlord can evict a tenant who has a dog, when the lease contains a no-pet provision;
- whether a defence of consent may exist in an action for assault.

Identify the Need for Further Information

After you have made a preliminary identification of the issues (by following the steps set out above, under the heading "Identify the Issues on a Preliminary Basis"), you may realize that you need more information before you can do your research. For example, you may need more facts in order to decide whether a cause of action has arisen, or you may need to know the legal status of all parties involved in the problem.

Example: Analyzing a Fact Situation

Sixteen-year-old Elwood Blues went into the Kwik-e-Mart, a convenience store close to his home. He walked all around the store looking for his favourite brand of cookies. He didn't find what he was looking for and was about to leave the store when he found his way blocked by the clerk, a husky man named Steve Barnes. Barnes said, "You put something into your pocket!" Elwood replied, "No, I didn't." "We'll see about that!" Barnes said. Barnes then told Elwood that he was making a citizen's arrest, called the police, and told Elwood that he couldn't leave the store until the police got there. Barnes stayed in front of the door until the police arrived, blocking the store's only exit. When the police arrived, Barnes told the officer, "I think this boy shoplifted something from my store and put it into his pocket." The police officer asked Elwood for his side of the story. Elwood said, "I didn't take anything. See?" and emptied his pockets. There was nothing belonging to the store in his pockets, so the police officer told Elwood he was free to go. Elwood left. Elwood and his parents have now come to your firm because they want to know whether Elwood can sue the store for every nickel it's got for the way he was treated.

- What does the client want?
  - The client wants to know whether he can sue the store for financial compensation.

- What are the relevant facts?
  - The store clerk suspected Elwood of shoplifting.
  - The store clerk prevented Elwood from leaving the store until the police arrived.
  - Elwood had not shoplifted.
- What is the area of law?
  - General area—tort law
  - Specific area—false imprisonment
- What keywords helped you identify the area of law?
  - "shoplifted"
  - "citizen's arrest"
  - "blocking the store's only exit"
- What is the objective of your research?
  - To determine whether Elwood has a cause of action in tort law, specifically for false imprisonment.
- Are there any hidden issues?
  - Can a sixteen-year-old start a lawsuit?
  - Who is/are the defendants—Steve Barnes or Kwik-e-Mart or both?
  - What sort of business entity is Kwik-e-Mart?
  - If damages are awarded in favour of Elwood, how much are they likely to be? Will the amount make it worth the trouble of a lawsuit? Is there some other course of action that Elwood and his parents could take that would satisfy their need for justice or retribution, such as demanding an apology from the store clerk?
- Formulate the issues:
  - Whether there was false imprisonment.
  - Whether a store clerk (a citizen, not a peace officer) can arrest a customer whom he suspects of committing a crime, but who has not in fact committed a crime.
  - Whether substantial damages will be awarded where a wrongful detention was of short duration and the detainee was not treated abusively.
- Do you need any further information?
  - What is Steve Barnes's relationship to Kwik-e-Mart? Is he the owner, or an employee, or even just a friend helping out?
  - Is Kwik-e-Mart a sole proprietorship? A partnership? A corporation?
  - Is any store surveillance video available?

KEY TERM

issue, 74

EXERCISES

1. Analyze the following fact situation. You need a basic understanding of tort law to do this exercise.

   The client, Marcello Phinias, has instructed your firm to bring an action for malicious prosecution against the local police. One night last week, he was celebrating his 21st birthday with friends at a suburban strip club. The friends didn't have a lot to drink, but they became quite lively in the club and were asked to leave. In the parking lot, they talked to each other for a while and then left in their own cars. Marcello was the last to leave.

   As he was getting into his car, a man suddenly appeared and told him to step away from the car. Marcello asked the man who he was. The man, who was wearing jeans and a T-shirt, told Marcello that he was a police officer, showed him a police badge, and asked him to accompany him to his car—not a marked police car—which was close by. The man told Marcello to sit in the back seat while he checked his driver's licence and vehicle licence. The man proceeded to do so, using a cellphone to run the checks.

   Marcello says that at one point the man said something like, "A bunch of us are just out here having a good time with Stan. Yeah, he's retiring, and we have to deal with some gang." At another point, the man said to the person on the phone, "It's my day off, can't you hurry it up?"

   Marcello says that he and his friends have never been in trouble with the law, and that he was picked on just because he's young, not because he was doing anything wrong. He tells you he was forced to sit in the man's car for about ten minutes before he was told he could go.

   a. What does the client want?

   b. What are the relevant facts?

   c. What is the area of law?

      i. General area

      ii. Specific area

   d. What keywords helped you identify the area?

   e. What is the objective of your research?

   f. Formulate the issue(s).

   g. Are there any hidden issues?

   h. Do you need any further information?

2. Analyze the following fact situation. You need a basic understanding of contract law to do this exercise.

   The client, a Canadian charity called the World United Fund (the Fund), has come to your firm with a problem. It recently ran a $1 million campaign to get donations to build a school in a poor country. Mrs. Euphemia Welsher promised to give $100,000; when the Fund had the entire $1 million in hand except for Mrs. Welsher's donation, it publicly declared the campaign successfully ended, and hired an architect to draw up the plans for the school. Mrs. Welsher then told the Fund that she intends to give the money to a home for cats in New York City, where she lives (except for two months in the summer when she resides in Canada). The client wants to know whether it can sue Mrs. Welsher and get the money she promised to pay.

a. What does the client want?

b. What are the relevant facts?

c. What is the area of law?

    i. General area

    ii. Specific area

d. What keywords helped you identify the area?

e. What is the objective of your research?

f. Formulate the issue(s).

g. Are there any hidden issues?

h. Do you need any further information?

3. Analyze the following fact situation. You will need to refer to the statute law that follows the fact situation.

Last year, Jose Murano signed a lease for a fixed term of one year, for a two-bedroom apartment in London, Ontario. The term of the lease is expiring at the end of next month. The other day, Jose came home to find a For Rent sign for his apartment posted on the lawn outside the building. When Jose asked the landlord what was happening, the landlord explained that because Jose's fixed-term tenancy was expiring soon, the landlord was trying to find a new tenant. Jose told the landlord that he has no intention of moving out at the end of his fixed-term lease. Jose has come to you for advice. Does he have to move out?

The *Residential Tenancies Act, 2006*, SO 2006, c 17 provides as follows:

> 38(1) If a tenancy agreement for a fixed term ends and has not been renewed or terminated, the landlord and tenant shall be deemed to have renewed it as a monthly tenancy agreement containing the same terms and conditions that are in the expired tenancy agreement and subject to any increases in rent charged in accordance with this Act.

a. What does the client want?

b. What are the relevant facts?

c. What is the area of law?

    i. General area

    ii. Specific area

d. What keywords helped you identify the area?

e. What is the objective of your research?

f. Formulate the issue(s).

g. Are there any hidden issues?

h. Do you need any further information?

Preparing for and Performing Research

6

LEARNING OUTCOMES

After reading this chapter, you will understand:

- What binding law and persuasive law are

- The importance of binding case law for legal researchers

- The chain of appeal in Canada that creates binding case law

- How binding case law and the chain of appeal work in the Ontario court system

- The practical steps involved in starting research— orienting yourself in the law, finding and updating the primary sources of law, and taking notes

- How to apply found law to the fact situation

Introduction

After you have analyzed a given fact situation and identified the legal issue(s) involved, you will be nearly ready to proceed with your research. Your goal now is to find the law that applies to the fact situation.

You will first need to do some preparatory work. To prepare for and perform legal research effectively, you need to know about binding law—what it is and what makes it binding. It is an important topic. Binding law, if you manage to find it, can compel a judge to decide a claim in your client's favour.

This chapter begins on a theoretical note. After defining binding law and persuasive law, we consider the sources of binding case law and explain which courts' decisions bind other courts in the Canadian legal system. We do the same, in greater detail, for the Ontario courts, providing a layout of the court structure, a jurisdictional breakdown, and an account of the appeal system. Having pummelled you with the theoretical background, we then proceed to more practical aspects of preparation: how to orient yourself in the law, how to find and update the primary sources of law, and how to keep track of the information you find.

Binding Law and Persuasive Law

binding law
law that must be followed by a court

persuasive law
law that a court is not required to follow, but may follow if it wishes (usually case law)

tribunals
agencies, boards, and commissions that make decisions under regulatory or legislative schemes

binding decision
existing decision that a judge or master must follow if the facts and/or issues in that case and in the case before the court are sufficiently similar

master
judge-like officer who decides certain procedural matters in the superior courts of some provinces

Binding law is law that must be followed by a particular court. It could be statute law, regulatory law, and/or case law. **Persuasive law** is case law that a particular court or **tribunal** is not legally required to follow but is permitted to follow—as long as it doesn't conflict with binding law.

When you research, you look first for binding law in favour of the client. After that, you look for persuasive law in the client's favour. You also want to know about binding law and persuasive law that go *against* the client. Why on earth would you want to know that? This knowledge will help you understand what opposition you face, so that you can take steps to neutralize it.

How do you neutralize law that goes against your client? Unfavourable case law can be "distinguished" in argument, meaning that the legal representative can try to persuade the judge that the facts in the present case are so different from those in cases cited by the opposing side that those cases are inapplicable and irrelevant.

Binding Statutes and Regulations

Federally enacted statutes and regulations bind the courts in all provinces and territories. Provincially or territorially enacted statute law and regulations bind the courts in the province or territory of enactment only.

Binding Case Law

A **binding decision** is a decision, made in a past case, that a judge or **master** must follow if the facts and/or issues in the earlier case and in the case before the court are sufficiently similar. What forces a decision-maker to follow a previous decision and not strike out on his or her own? It is **stare decisis** (Latin for "to stand by things decided")—the principle that similar cases should be decided in a similar fashion.

The theory underlying *stare decisis* is that it is pointless for a decision-maker not to follow a decision made by a court higher in the **chain of appeal**; if the decision-maker's non-conforming decision is appealed, it will be reversed. Most judges don't want to be known as "that guy who's always getting struck down on appeal." In short, a decision-maker is bound by a decision of another court if the earlier decision comes from a court higher up in the chain of appeal.

Note that the only part of a binding case that is actually binding is the *ratio decidendi*, which, as we said in Chapter 4, is the principle of law on which the judge is basing his or her decision on an issue, as applied to the facts of the particular case.

Multiple Ratios

In a case on appeal, where there is a majority opinion and a dissenting opinion (a different decision by a minority of the appeal judges), only the majority *ratio* is binding. If there is more than one majority opinion, there will, of course, be more than one *ratio* and then you can take your pick. If the case is reasonably well known, there will probably be one opinion that has emerged as the definitive one, and then you should stick with it.

Take, for example, *Donoghue v Stevenson*, [1932] AC 562. This was the famous English snail-in-the-ginger-beer-bottle case that expanded the law of torts. There were five judges in the House of Lords hearing the case. Every single one of them wrote a decision, and three wrote majority opinions. But the only decision that anybody quotes, or even remembers, is Lord Atkin's: "Who, then, in law is my neighbour?"

Persuasive Case Law

Persuasive case law comes from several sources. Judges, masters, and other decision-makers may be *persuaded* by decisions in cases from various courts inside and outside the province or territory, if these cases deal with facts and issues similar to those of the case at hand, and the decisions are well written.

Dissenting opinions are sometimes treated with great respect and have persuasive value, especially when expressed by judges on the highest courts—the Supreme Court in Canada and the United States, and the House of Lords in England. The same is true of **obiter dicta**. Well-thought-out dissents and *obiter dicta* may indicate the future direction of the law.

Binding Case Law and the Chain of Appeal in Canada: A General Overview

The Supreme Court

A decision of the Supreme Court of Canada binds every court in Canada, other than the Supreme Court itself. (However, the court will not depart from its previous decisions without strong reasons.) The Supreme Court of Canada is an appellate court,

stare decisis
principle that similar cases should be decided in a similar fashion; Latin for "to stand by things decided"

chain of appeal
path through the court system that an appeal must follow in accordance with the statutes governing the applicable courts

obiter dicta
statements made by a court in its reasons for judgment that may be of interest but that are inessential to the decision and therefore have no binding authority; Latin for "words by the way"

but there is no automatic right of appeal to it. An appellant must first seek and obtain **leave** (permission) to appeal, which is granted only if the case involves an issue of public importance or a significant issue of law (or mixed law and fact) that the court feels deserves its consideration.

When all positions in the Supreme Court of Canada are filled, nine judges hear cases. As you might expect, some cases have a lot of different opinions in them. And—as you also might expect—Supreme Court of Canada opinions tend to be long. Until 1949, a decision of the Supreme Court of Canada could be appealed to the Privy Council in Britain. The Privy Council was what the House of Lords was called when fulfilling its role of hearing an appeal from a British colony or former colony. Its decisions bound the Supreme Court of Canada and all Canadian courts below. From time to time, you may run into a Privy Council case in your research.

Provincial and Territorial Courts

A decision of a provincial or territorial *Court of Appeal*, the highest level of court in a province or territory, binds every court in that province or territory. Though it does not bind the Court of Appeal itself, the Court of Appeal will follow its earlier decision unless there are good reasons not to. Where there are conflicting Court of Appeal decisions on an issue, lower courts usually follow the most recent decision. A Court of Appeal decision does not bind courts outside the province or territory, but it is persuasive in other jurisdictions.

A decision of the *superior court*, the second-highest level of court in a province or territory, may be considered binding on a *provincial or territorial court*, the third-highest level of court in a province or territory. (Note that provincial or territorial courts are sometimes called "inferior" courts to distinguish them from the courts of appeal or the superior courts.) A decision of the superior court is not binding on other judges of the superior court but ought to be followed by them in the absence of a compelling reason not to. A superior court decision may be persuasive to judges in other provinces or territories. The superior courts of the provinces and territories are listed below. Unlike provincial courts of appeal, which are always called the "Court of Appeal," superior courts go by a multitude of names:

- Court of Queen's Bench (Alberta)
- Supreme Court (British Columbia)
- Court of Queen's Bench (Manitoba)
- Court of Queen's Bench (New Brunswick)
- Supreme Court—Trial Division (Newfoundland)
- Supreme Court (Northwest Territories)
- Supreme Court (Nova Scotia)
- Court of Justice (Nunavut)
- Superior Court of Justice (Ontario)
- Supreme Court (Prince Edward Island)
- Superior Court (Quebec)

- Court of Queen's Bench (Saskatchewan)
- Supreme Court (Yukon Territory)

A master's decision is not binding on judges of any court in the province or territory but is persuasive to other masters (but probably not to masters outside that province or territory).

A decision of a provincial or territorial court is not binding on, but is persuasive to, other judges of provincial or territorial courts (particularly those of that province or territory).

Quebec and Other Jurisdictions

Decisions from Quebec courts are rarely cited in the courts of the other provinces and territories. This is because Quebec follows the French civil law system, with the *Civil Code of Québec*, while the other provinces and territories follow the English common law system.

Decisions from common law jurisdictions outside Canada, such as the United States or England (after 1949), are not binding on Canadian courts. Whether they are persuasive depends on whether the law of the foreign jurisdiction is similar to the law in the particular Canadian jurisdiction. Be careful about using modern English cases: some of what is still common law in Canada is now statute law in England, and English case law in those areas will not be useful in Canadian courts.

Binding Case Law and the Chain of Appeal in Ontario

Now let's look more closely at binding case law and the chain of appeal in Ontario. When it comes to legal research, it's not enough to know generally about the chain of appeal in Canada. If you are researching Ontario case law, you need to know specifically about the appeal process in Ontario; its chain of appeal is not as straightforward as our discussion of Canada's chain of appeal may have led you to believe. In fact the appeal process, when you look at it more closely, is complex and at times downright confusing.

The Ontario Court System

The structure of the Ontario court system is shown in Figure 6.1. The Court of Appeal for Ontario sits at the top. Beneath it are the Superior Court of Justice (itself made up of four branches) and the Ontario Court of Justice (formerly known as the Provincial Court). (The Superior Court of Justice and the Ontario Court of Justice together compose the Court of Ontario.) Below these court levels are administrative boards and tribunals.

THE COURT OF ONTARIO

◇ **The Superior Court of Justice**

The Superior Court of Justice has four branches:

1. the trial division,
2. the Divisional Court,
3. the Family Court, and
4. the Small Claims Court.

As the province's superior court of record (a "court of record" being, according to some ancient classification scheme, one whose proceedings are recorded), the *trial division* has general jurisdiction over both civil matters (personal injury; monetary and property claims involving amounts over $25,000; wills and estates; bankruptcy and insolvency) and criminal matters (all indictable offences, but in practice only the most serious ones, such as murder, manslaughter, sexual assault, and drug trafficking). It also hears claims under the *Residential Tenancies Act, 2006* if the tenant is not in possession of the rental unit and the amount in dispute exceeds $25,000. (If the tenant *is* in possession, then the Landlord and Tenant Board has exclusive jurisdiction over these claims.)

The *Divisional Court* only has a review and appellate function; no trials take place there.

The *Family Court* exists only in certain parts of the province. Where it does exist, it has jurisdiction over all family law claims.

In parts of the province where the Family Court does not exist, the trial division of the Superior Court has sole jurisdiction in family law claims involving divorce and the division of marital property. In these parts of the province, the trial division shares jurisdiction (with the Ontario Court of Justice) over other kinds of family law claims: spousal support, and child support, custody, and access where no claims for divorce or property division are involved.

The *Small Claims Court* has jurisdiction over civil claims up to $25,000 in value.

Figure 6.1   The Ontario Court System

◇ **Ontario Court of Justice**

The Ontario Court of Justice has jurisdiction over a grab bag of matters:

- criminal matters (the less serious indictable offences, summary conviction offences, and young offender offences),
- provincial matters (offences under provincial statutes, such as the *Highway Traffic Act*),
- municipal matters (bylaw offences), and
- certain family matters (in parts of the province where the Family Court of the Superior Court of Justice does not exist)—namely, adoption, child welfare, and child custody and support in the absence of a claim for divorce or division of marital property.

ADMINISTRATIVE BOARDS AND TRIBUNALS

There are several hundred tribunals in Ontario—agencies, boards, and commissions that make decisions under regulatory or legislative schemes. (You can find a list at <http://www.pas.gov.on.ca/scripts/en/boardslist.asp>.) These tribunals include, for example, the Child and Family Services Review Board, the Consent and Capacity Board, the Human Rights Tribunal, the Landlord and Tenant Board, and the Workplace Safety and Insurance Appeals Tribunal.

Appeal Paths in Ontario

The general layout of the Ontario courts, as shown above, is not what's important when you're wondering whether a decision of one court is binding on another court. The chain of appeal looks different from the court structure.

As in all provinces and territories, decisions of the Supreme Court of Canada bind all Ontario courts.

Decisions of the Court of Appeal for Ontario bind all lower courts in the province. In the Court of Appeal, there is always a panel of three or five judges. This means that there may be multiple opinions for you, as a researcher, to worry about.

The Superior Court of Justice's trial division has an appellate function as well as a trial function. It hears appeals

- from masters' **interlocutory orders** (orders that relate to the process rather than to the substance of the matter under litigation);
- of certain cost assessments in the Superior Court of Justice;
- from orders of the Ontario Court of Justice in both criminal and family matters; and
- from orders made under various statutes.

The Divisional Court of the Superior Court of Justice hears appeals

1. from the Superior Court of Justice's civil trial division, in the case of
   - final orders (orders that end the matter under litigation) of judges concerning money or property with a value of less than $50,000,

interlocutory orders
orders that relate to the process rather than to the substance of the matter under litigation

- interlocutory orders of judges (leave to appeal required), and
- final orders of masters;

2. from the Family Court, in the case of final orders without leave and interlocutory orders with leave (except where the order was made under the federal *Divorce Act*—in that case, the appeal goes straight to the Court of Appeal);

3. from the Small Claims Court, in the case of final orders where the amount in dispute exceeds the jurisdiction of the Small Claims Court; and

4. of the decisions of certain tribunals, in accordance with the statute creating the tribunal.

There is usually a panel of three judges in the Divisional Court of the Superior Court of Justice.

You will be relieved to know that the Family Court, the Small Claims Court, and the Ontario Court of Justice do not hear appeals. Decisions of the Small Claims Court and the Ontario Court of Justice cannot bind other courts, although decisions of the Family Court of the Superior Court of Justice are, at the least, persuasive in family matters heard in the Ontario Court of Justice.

ADDED COMPLICATIONS

What makes the Ontario chain of appeal still more bewildering for the researcher is that the province's court system has only looked as it does in Figure 6.1 since 1999, when it was reformed. Your legal research into Ontario case law will at times bring you to cases from courts whose names are no longer in use. From 1881 until 1984, for instance, the superior court of record was called "the Supreme Court of Ontario" and its trial division was called "the High Court of Justice." From 1984 until 1999, the superior court of record was called "the Ontario Court of Justice (General Division)." Cases from these older, differently named courts have the same binding or persuasive effect as cases from the present civil and criminal trial division of the Superior Court of Justice. There also used to be another court level in Ontario, below the superior court, called "the County Court." County Court decisions may be considered persuasive in the Superior Court of Justice and the Ontario Court of Justice.

You have a growing suspicion that it is not perfectly simple to tell whether a particular court is bound by another court's decision and that you may sometimes need to do legal research to determine the appeal path from that court. Congratulations! Not only are you completely correct in your suspicion, but you are also starting to think like a researcher! When you don't know whether one Ontario court is bound by another court's decision, you may need to examine certain provincial legislation: the *Courts of Justice Act*, RSO 1990, c C.43, and, depending on the nature of the client's fact situation, one or more of the *Rules of Civil Procedure* (RRO 1990, Reg 194), the *Rules of the Small Claims Court* (O Reg 258/98), or the *Family Law Rules* (O Reg 114/99). (You may by now also wish to re-examine your choice of career ... is it too late to switch to the plumbing program?)

To find the appeal path for a tribunal rather than a court, you will need to consult the statute that created the tribunal. But we have some good news for you in this regard. You don't have to figure out what court decisions are binding on a tribunal! None of them are. Yes, you read that correctly. All case law is only persuasive to a tribunal—even Supreme Court of Canada cases.

Practical Preparations for Research

We've now come to the end of our theoretical groundwork and are ready to talk about the practical preparations for researching a subject.

Orient Yourself in the Law

When researching an area of law that you know nothing or very little about, it is best to start by finding a general statement or overview of the law concerning the issues you have identified. Don't focus on your pre-identified issue too quickly. Instead, scan the law to check whether you have identified the issue correctly or whether there is another way of looking at the problem to be solved. This approach should provide you with a summary of the law in the field, and also point you to the statutes, regulations, and cases that have created the principles of law applicable to the problem you need to solve. You may find that the answer has already been lined up for you, and all you have to do is update (see below for a discussion of updating and noting up).

You can find a general statement of the law in a secondary source (either in paper or computerized form). Specific secondary sources are discussed in detail in the chapters that follow. Here, for now, is a general list:

- legal encyclopedias;
- textbooks;
- loose-leaf services (texts that are updated on a continuing basis);
- articles, including conference and seminar materials;
- digests of cases; and
- indexes to statutes or cases.

Another way to get a general sense of the relevant law is to talk to a person who is knowledgeable about that particular area of law that concerns you.

Find the Primary Sources of Law

The secondary sources will lead you to the primary sources—the statutes, the bylaws, the regulations (if any), and the case law—that govern the issue(s) you are researching. Remember that you are searching for binding and persuasive law in favour of a client (and also the binding and persuasive law that goes against the client, so that you will know what you are up against).

Update the Primary Sources of Law

The law is always changing. For this reason, you must always **update** any statute, regulation, or case you find; you need to make sure it is still good law. Statutes and regulations found in computerized sources are generally up to date. However, you still need to determine whether there has been any case law explaining or interpreting them—or even striking them or some of their provisions down. (Yes, this happens! Sometimes law is an exciting battle between the courts and the legislatures.)

When researching case law, you must update to make sure that the case has not been overturned on appeal or that the legal principles have not been reversed or altered by subsequent cases. Previous cases are often **judicially considered** (that is, discussed or interpreted) by judges in their decisions, so you should also check cases judicially considered, to see whether a case you've found has been followed, ignored, or criticized. The entire process described in this paragraph is known as **noting up** a case.

Updating and noting up are discussed in detail in subsequent chapters.

Take Notes

As you look through primary and secondary sources, take notes. You should have notes on the following:

1. *Information that seems relevant or interesting.* Take down, for example, the citation of the case and a short description of what is useful about the case. *Hint*: A sense of *déjà vu* as you look for new information may indicate that you have exhausted the topic.

2. *The sources you have looked through.* Take careful note of the name and the edition of your source and the latest date of publication.

   After you have spent an hour or two on a particular text, statute, or website, you may think that it will be burned into your brain and that you will never forget either when you looked at it or how much of it you looked at. But you will forget it. This is especially true if your research has been interrupted. If you return to research on a subject after a hiatus of two or three weeks, you will not remember exactly which sources you already have covered thoroughly. Noting carefully what you have done and the date you did it will help you to avoid doing the same research twice.

Applying Found Law to the Fact Situation

After you have found, read, and understood the primary law that applies to your client's fact situation, you should be able to determine the answers to the issues you identified—and therefore the likely outcome of your client's case.

But perhaps (heaven forbid!) your research has not gone smoothly and answers are not lining up for you. What then?

Review Your Analysis of the Fact Situation

Once you have looked at the primary law and compared it with the fact situation, you may find that the issues you identified on a preliminary basis were incorrect; or you may find that you need more information from the client; or you may discover unexpected procedural problems. If you find yourself in one of these positions, you need to re-analyze the fact situation.

If Necessary, Research the Subject Again

If your preliminary identification of the issues was faulty or if you receive new information to add to the fact situation, you may need to re-research the subject.

KEY TERMS

binding decision, 82

binding law, 82

chain of appeal, 83

interlocutory orders, 87

judicially considered, 90

leave, 84

master, 82

noting up, 90

obiter dicta, 83

persuasive law, 82

stare decisis, 83

tribunals, 82

update, 90

EXERCISE

As set out in the table below, you have an upcoming proceeding in court ("Court X") and have found a case (*ABC v DEF*) that looks relevant and helpful to your client's matter. You want to cite the case before the decision-maker in Court X. Drawing on the discussion in this chapter, indicate in each case (in the spaces provided in the third column) whether *ABC v DEF* is binding on, persuasive to, or inapplicable to Court X's decision-maker.

Court X (and type of proceeding)	Court that decided *ABC v DEF*	Binding, persuasive, or inapplicable?
Ontario Court of Justice (summary conviction charge)	Ontario Court of Justice (General Division)	
Small Claims Court (claim for $13,000)	Ontario Court of Justice	
Family Court of the Superior Court of Justice (division of marital property)	Supreme Court of Canada	
Superior Court of Justice—trial division (final order of a master)	Divisional Court	
Divisional Court (appeal from a final order of a judge of the Superior Court of Justice [trial division])	British Columbia Court of Appeal	
Court of Appeal for Ontario (appeal from an order made under the *Divorce Act*)	Family Court of the Superior Court of Justice	
Supreme Court of Canada (appeal from the Court of Appeal for Ontario)	Supreme Court of Canada	

Working with Legal Research Sources

In Part IV, we discuss the various print and computerized legal research sources. There are usually several different sources you can use to find answers to your research questions, but you probably won't have access to all of them at the same time. Law books are expensive, and many of the computerized sources are available only through costly subscriptions. For that reason, all but the largest law libraries have very limited resources. That's why you need to know something about every available print and computerized source—so that when you sit down to start researching, you will know how to use whatever tools are available to you.

Paper Research Sources

7

LEARNING OUTCOMES

After reading this chapter, you will understand:

- Where to find primary and secondary sources of law in print

- How user's guides, tables of contents, and indexes can help you research paper versions of primary and secondary sources of law

- What secondary sources exist in print to help you initiate your research

- What finding tools (that is, specialized secondary sources) exist in print to help you locate statutes, regulations, and cases on a particular subject

- What paper sources are available to help you update statutes, regulations, and cases

Introduction

Despite the great increase in electronic research sources, there are still many paper sources available. Sometimes you will find it either convenient or necessary to consult them. These paper sources, divided into two broad categories of primary and secondary sources, are as follows:

1. Primary sources:
   - statutes
   - regulations
   - bylaws
   - cases
2. Secondary sources:
   - legal encyclopedias
   - subject-specific textbooks
   - subject-specific journal articles
   - finding and updating tools
     - indexes
     - **statute citators**
     - case digests
     - **case citators**
     - collections of words and phrases judicially defined
     - *Canadian Current Law—Legislation* (enables tracking of the progress of bills and recent developments in statutes and regulations)

This chapter will describe these research sources and how to use them.

statute citator
tool that updates a statute and lists cases that consider the statute generally or a particular section of the statute

case citator
tool that updates a case and lists other cases that have considered or mentioned the case

Working with Paper Sources

Every source takes a little effort to understand. In order to research efficiently, take some time to become familiar with a source before you start using it. Useful tools for this purpose include

- user's guides,
- tables of contents, and
- indexes.

User's Guides

user's guide
information in a research source about how to use that source

Most research sources (but generally not textbooks and journals) incorporate a **user's guide** or at least some information about how to use the source. In a single-volume source, the user's guide is usually found at the beginning of the volume. In a multiple-volume source, the user's guide may be found in the first volume of the source or in a separate volume. If you have not used a particular source before, it's a good idea to read the user's guide before you start.

Tables of Contents

Most research sources also contain a **table of contents**. This is a listing of the chapters or article titles in the order in which they appear in the source, along with the page numbers where each chapter or article starts. The table of contents of a single-volume source is usually found at the beginning of the volume, after the title page. Each volume of a multi-volume source usually contains a table of contents for that volume. In addition, there may be a table of contents in a separate volume for the entire multi-volume source. Topics in a legal encyclopedia will generally be dealt with alphabetically across the entire source, with each volume dealing with topics whose names start with a particular letter (or letters) of the alphabet.

A table of contents provides a quick overview of the content and organization of the source. Some tables of contents are quite detailed and provide not only chapter names, but also a breakdown of the subjects covered in each chapter, in the order in which they are covered. Reading a detailed table of contents will therefore give you a sense of the major topics within a particular subject area and how they fit together.

A book containing the text of cases will have a **table of cases**, instead of a table of contents, at the beginning of the volume. This table will list the cases contained in the volume, either in the order in which the cases appear in the volume or in alphabetical order.

Indexes

Most research sources also contain an **index**. This is a detailed list, in alphabetical order, of the matters covered in the source and the pages on which each entry appears. An index often provides more detailed information about the contents of the source than the table of contents does. It is designed to help the reader quickly find information about a specific topic or concept in all of its locations throughout the source.

Indexes for primary sources usually provide the following coverage:

- In a statute book, a book of regulations, or a book of bylaws, the index may broadly cover the subject matter contained in the statutes, regulations, or bylaws. An index may not be useful if your research question is not general but focuses on a specific provision.

- In a book of cases, the index will usually cover quite specifically the issues addressed in the cases—and so can be very useful. A case may be indexed under more than one heading if the court addressed more than one issue in the case.

Indexes for secondary sources usually provide the following coverage:

- In a legal encyclopedia or textbook, the index will cover specifically and in some detail the topics covered in the volume or volumes.

- A journal, whether single-issue or annual, may or may not contain an index.

table of contents
listing of chapters or article titles in a source together with the page numbers where each chapter or article starts

table of cases
list of all cases that are cited in a book

index
alphabetical, detailed list of names, places, and subjects discussed in a source and the pages on which each entry appears

The index of a single-volume source is usually found at the end of the volume. Each volume of a multi-volume source, such as a legal encyclopedia, usually contains an index. In addition, there may be an index for the entire multi-volume source.

Table of Contents or Index—How Do You Choose?

If you are looking in a legal encyclopedia or textbook for information on a particular subject, start by looking at the table of contents. If there is a chapter dealing with your subject, turn to it.

If the subject you are looking for is not listed in the table of contents, then look for the subject in the index. Even if the subject you are looking for is in the table of contents, you should also use the index if you are looking for specific, detailed information on a subject.

Secondary Sources of General Application

The law that you are looking for when you research will be found in the primary sources—statutes, regulations, bylaws, and/or cases. These primary sources are not at all user-friendly, however. As we said in Chapter 6, it is usually wise to start your research with secondary sources, using them to gain an understanding of the law and direct you to the primary sources. So first look in the following:

- legal encyclopedias, such as the *Canadian Encyclopedic Digest* and *Halsbury's Laws of Canada*;
- textbooks on the subject; and
- journal articles on the subject.

Legal encyclopedias are usually kept in the general reference area of a library. To find a textbook on a particular subject, you will have to consult the library's catalogue (the card file or an online catalogue), looking under the subject—for example, "Debtor–Creditor Relations" or "Municipal Law." Or you can look in the *Index to Canadian Legal Literature* of Carswell's *Canadian Abridgment*. To find a journal article, consult the *Index to Canadian Legal Literature*.

These various sources are discussed more fully in Chapters 9, 10, and 11.

Specialized Secondary Sources— Finding Tools

finding tools
secondary sources that refer you to primary sources of law

Finding tools are more specialized sources that you can use to locate specific statutes, regulations, bylaws, and cases.

Searching for Statutes on a Particular Subject

The finding tools designed to locate statutes on a particular subject include a table of statutes.

Finding statutes is discussed in more detail in Chapter 12.

Searching for Regulations on a Particular Subject

There are also specialized sources designed to help you locate regulations on a particular subject. These finding tools include

- Carswell's *Canada Regulations Index*, and
- Carswell's *Ontario Regulations Service*.

Finding regulations is also discussed in more detail in Chapter 12.

Searching for Specific Cases

Legal encyclopedias and textbooks will often refer you to only the leading cases on a particular subject. You may need to find additional cases. If so, you will need to use specialized sources designed specifically for this task. These finding tools include the following:

- *Canadian Abridgment Case Digests*, which you will use to look for cases dealing with specific subjects;
- *Canadian Statute Citations* (part of the *Canadian Abridgment*) or other statute citators, which you will use to look for cases that interpret statutory provisions;
- *Words & Phrases Judicially Defined in Canadian Courts and Tribunals* (also part of the *Canadian Abridgment*), which you will use to look for cases in which a word or phrase that has appeared in a primary source of law has been interpreted or commented on by a judge;
- *Consolidated Table of Cases* or the *Canadian Case Citations* (also part of the *Canadian Abridgment*), which you will use to look for a case if you have only a partial or incorrect citation; and
- digest services and legal newspapers for unreported cases.

Finding cases is discussed in more detail in Chapter 13.

Updating Tools

Once you find relevant primary sources of law, you must make sure that the statutes and regulations have not been amended or repealed and that the cases have not been overturned on appeal or the legal principles in them altered by subsequent cases. You do this by using secondary sources that we call **updating tools**.

It is unlikely that you will ever have to update statutes or regulations using paper sources (unless the Apocalypse arrives and the Internet breaks down). Just in case, however, the following paper sources will be there to help you update statutes:

- statute citators;
- *Canadian Current Law—Legislation*, including monthly softcover issues (part of the *Canadian Abridgment*); and
- tables of public statutes.

These updating tools are discussed more fully in Chapter 12.

updating tools
sources that update primary sources of law

The following paper sources will help you update regulations:

- Carswell's *Ontario Regulations Service* or *Canadian Current Law—Legislation* under "Regulations" (Ontario) for Ontario regulations; and
- Carswell's *Canada Regulations Index* or *Canadian Current Law—Legislation* under "Regulations" for federal regulations.

These updating tools are discussed more fully in Chapter 12.

It's also possible you may have to use paper sources to update cases. The following sources will assist you with that:

- *Consolidated Table of Cases* (part of the *Canadian Abridgment*); and
- *Canadian Case Citations* (part of the *Canadian Abridgment*).

These updating tools are discussed more fully in Chapter 13.

KEY TERMS

EXERCISES

1. Your law firm has been retained by a woman who recently separated from a man with whom she cohabited for five years. She wants to know whether she is entitled to spousal support, and you have been asked to conduct some preliminary legal research on the subject.

   a. What paper source(s) should you consult to find a general statement of the law?

   b. Assume that the general statement of the law mentions the *Family Law Act*. What paper source(s) would you use to help you find the statute?

   c. What paper source(s) would you use to find cases that interpret the *Family Law Act*?

   d. What paper source(s) would you use to update the cases that interpret the *Family Law Act*?

2. Your law firm has been retained by a corporation that wishes to expand into providing school bus services. You have been asked to provide some preliminary information about the licensing of drivers and of vehicles to be used for the purpose.

   a. What paper source(s) should you consult to find a general statement of the law?

   b. Assume that the general statement of the law mentions O Reg 340/94. What paper source(s) would you use to help you find the regulation?

   c. What paper source(s) would you use to find and update cases that interpret an Ontario regulation?

   d. The lawyer directing your work remembers that she recently read an article that was almost exactly on topic, and she wants you to find it. What paper source(s) should you consult to find the article?

Computerized Sources

8

LEARNING OUTCOMES

After reading this chapter, you will understand:

- The differences between subscription (pay-for-use) online sources of legal information and free online sources

- The differences between dedicated online sources for legal research and general online sources

- The advantages and disadvantages of computerized legal research

- The main *dedicated* online sources of legal information and how these sources are organized

- The differences between primary sources, general secondary sources, and specialized secondary sources, and the role of each in legal research

- The updating tools for computerized legal research

- The main *general* online sources of legal information—search engines, websites with law-related information, legal research sites, general legal sites, and bookmark lists

Introduction

When you conduct legal research using computerized sources, your purpose is exactly the same as it is when using paper sources—to find primary law, in the form of statutes, regulations, bylaws, and/or cases, that is relevant to the legal problem you need to solve. In this chapter, we begin examining how to use computerized sources to search efficiently and effectively for law.

Computerized sources come in two forms: (1) free and (2) subscription (that is, pay-for-use). These two forms both come in two "strengths"—dedicated to legal research, and of general application. In this chapter, we're going to focus on the following:

- dedicated legal research sources, both free and subscription, for
  - primary sources,
  - secondary sources,
  - finding tools, and
  - updating tools; and
- general sources of legal information on the Internet, all free, such as
  - search engines, and
  - websites containing law-related information, including sites about legal research.

After a general discussion of computerized research, we will look at the various kinds of computerized research sources. These sources are discussed in more detail in Chapters 11, 12, and 13.

Working with Computerized Sources: Pros and Cons

Don't assume that, just because you are now working with a computer, sources miraculously become easy to use. They don't. Computerized sources do allow you to find answers faster, but this applies to all answers, wrong ones as well as right ones. Computer sources allow you to find more material more easily than print sources do—irrelevant as well as relevant material.

What we're delicately hinting at is that online legal research, for all its benefits, has limitations. Although you may find, within minutes or even seconds, precisely the statute, regulation, or case you are seeking, you're just as likely to find yourself engulfed by information that will take you the rest of your life to read and an eternity to comprehend. Researching on the Internet, you can find enormous amounts of information, legal and otherwise, without much trouble. This is the Internet's strength as a research tool but also its weakness. The sheer volume of material that comes back from a search request can be overwhelming, far too much to sift through and evaluate.

Another problem with the Internet as a research tool is that the information may not be organized. With the paper sources we have discussed, human editors have organized the information in some way, whether by topic or chronologically. When you work with paper sources, you can begin to retrieve information by browsing through an index or a table of contents.

Computerized sources, by comparison, may or may not be edited. Information in all computerized sources is stored in databases. Only if the source is edited will there be a table of contents for you to use. If the source is not edited, its information is stored randomly and you can retrieve it only by searching through the database for specific words. It has been said that doing Web research is like using a library in which all the books have been dumped on the floor.

Internet sources can (and often do) change quickly and without notice—in appearance, organization, function, even name. For example, since the last edition of this book, the *Best Guide to Canadian Legal Research* has changed its name to the *Canadian Legal Research and Writing Guide* and is now being run by CanLII. As the movie critic Roger Ebert said, "Doing research on the Web is like using a library assembled piecemeal by packrats and vandalized nightly." Just when you've become comfortable using a source, you'll go to it one day and discover it looks completely different and its tools work in a different way. For that reason, you need to be aware, when you see images of web pages in this book, that we have included them more as illustrations than as permanently accurate representations of that source.

Computerized research can be time-consuming, too. You must familiarize yourself with the source websites (whether free or subscription). You must learn the particular search syntax used by whatever search engine is driving the site. If you use an incorrect search syntax, you may miss relevant documents or retrieve many irrelevant ones. To make your research easier, most websites have a Help function. To make your research more difficult, the appearance and function of these websites change regularly. To add insult to injury, response times to searches can be slow if you are researching during periods of heavy Internet traffic or if you are downloading large files.

Dedicated Online Sources: Subscription (Pay-for-Use) and Free

The basic instruments of legal research, as we have seen, are the following:

- primary sources,
- general secondary sources,
- finding tools, and
- updating tools.

With the dedicated online sources, these instruments tend to be blended, offering both primary source materials and secondary source ones, as well as search functions that serve as finding tools and updating tools. Lexis Advance Quicklaw (Quicklaw) and WestlawNext Canada are the two main subscription sources in Canada. Each comprises a number of databases, some with primary source content and others with secondary source content. Each also has search features that serve the function of finding tools and updating tools.

Quicklaw's databases include the following categories:

- court and tribunal cases—primary sources,
- case summaries and digests—secondary sources,
- legislation—primary sources,
- drafting materials—secondary sources,
- dictionaries—finding tool,
- secondary materials (texts, law reviews and journals, legal encyclopedias, NetLetter articles)—secondary sources,
- *Halsbury's Laws of Canada*—secondary source, and
- Case Citators—finding tool.

The Quicklaw databases are accessible using pre-search and post-search filters. You can select your desired content type before running your search, and this will limit your search results to that content only. Alternatively, you can run your search across all Quicklaw content and then narrow your search results to your desired content type using the post-search filters.

Quicklaw also contains the QuickCITE updating tool.

WestlawNext Canada's databases include the following:

- cases—primary sources,
- legislation—primary sources,
- articles, newsletters, and journals—secondary sources,
- the *Canadian Abridgment Digests*—finding tool,
- *Canadian Encyclopedic Digest*—secondary source,
- *Index to Canadian Legal Literature*—finding tool,
- Words and Phrases—finding tool, and
- Case Citators—finding tool.

As with Quicklaw, the contents of the WestlawNext Canada databases are accessible using either pre-search or post-search filters. Some of the databases in the list above also contain tables of contents, which can be browsed. WestlawNext Canada also contains the KeyCite Canada updating tool.

Let's turn now to the free dedicated legal resources on the Internet. The Canadian Legal Information Institute website, or CanLII (<http://www.canlii.org>), along with its sister website, CanLII Connects (<http://canliiconnects.org>), is the main one in Canada. CanLII is a non-profit organization managed by the Federation of Law Societies of Canada, the goal of which is to make Canadian law accessible to Internet users at no charge.

The CanLII website provides access to close to 2,000,000 court judgments and tribunal decisions from all Canadian jurisdictions—federal, provincial, and territorial—contained in nearly 300 case law databases, and to statutes and regulations of the federal government and each of the provinces and territories.

The newer CanLII Connects website was created to make access to legal commentary on Canadian court decisions faster and easier.

The contents of the databases on both sites are accessible through a search feature that serves as a finding tool.

General Secondary Sources

Despite putting primary sources at the top of each of the lists above, we are going to begin the discussion with secondary sources. Your basic research purpose, whether you are consulting print or online sources, is to find binding primary law (in the form of statutes, regulations, bylaws, and/or cases) that is relevant to the legal problem you need to solve. However, we don't recommend that you start your research with primary sources. That's because statutes, regulations, bylaws, and cases are no more user-friendly in computerized form than they are in paper form. Unless you know exactly what you're looking for, it is usually wise to start your computerized research with secondary sources. They will give you a preliminary understanding of the law in a given area, and they will direct you to the primary sources. (We will address primary sources below, after we discuss secondary sources.)

It is best, then, to start your online research with

- a legal encyclopedia, such as the *Canadian Encyclopedic Digest* (available through WestlawNext Canada) or *Halsbury's Laws of Canada* (available through Quicklaw);
- textbooks on the subject (some of which are available on WestlawNext Canada); and
- journal articles, news reports, and legal commentary on the subject (available through WestlawNext Canada and Quicklaw, and, in the case of legal commentary, on CanLII Connects).

On free-access websites dedicated to law, such as CanLII and CanLII Connects, discussed above, and other free-access websites, discussed below, legal encyclopedias and textbooks are not available at all, and access to journal articles is quite limited. You may find some journal articles on library sites and find case commentary on CanLII Connects, but not on CanLII or government sites.

Specialized Secondary Sources—Finding Tools

Legal encyclopedias, textbooks, and articles refer you only to the leading cases on a particular subject. When you want to find additional cases, there are computerized finding-tool sources designed specifically to help you. The main ones are the Finding

Tools available on WestlawNext Canada (which include Canadian Abridgment Digests and Words & Phrases) and the search templates of Quicklaw, both of which can be used to find

- cases dealing with a specific subject or legal issue,
- cases that have interpreted a statute or a section of a statute,
- cases in which a word or phrase is judicially considered,
- cases for which you have only a partial or incorrect citation (searching under these circumstances is called "treasure hunting"), and
- unreported cases.

There are other computerized finding tools that are not stand-alone sources. Rather, they are incorporated directly into the primary source websites. Government statute websites, court websites, the CanLII website, WestlawNext Canada, and Quicklaw all include a search feature. Finding relevant statutes and regulations using computerized sources is discussed in more detail in Chapter 12. Finding relevant cases using computerized sources is discussed in more detail in Chapter 13.

Primary Sources

Now we're ready to talk about primary sources of law. Finding tools will give you the citations of relevant statutes, regulations, bylaws, and cases, and sometimes a summary of their content. You must then go to these primary sources, read them, and understand what they say.

Statutes, regulations, bylaws, and many cases are available on the Internet. You can find statutes on free-access websites such as the following:

- federal (Justice Laws: <http://laws-lois.justice.gc.ca>) and provincial government websites for statutes and regulations—the online equivalents of the *Revised Statutes of Canada*, *Statutes of Canada*, *Canada Gazette*, *Revised Statutes of Ontario*, *Statutes of Ontario*, and *Ontario Gazette*
  - Ontario (e-Laws: <http://www.ontario.ca/laws>), Nova Scotia (Office of the Legislative Council: <http://nslegislature.ca/legc/index.htm>), British Columbia (BC Laws: <http://www.bclaws.ca/>), Quebec (LégisQuébec: <http://legisquebec.gouv.qc.ca/en/>), and Alberta (Laws Online/Catalogue: <http://www.qp.alberta.ca/Laws_Online.cfm>)
- CanLII

You can also find statutes and regulations on pay-for-use subscription services, including WestlawNext Canada and Quicklaw. However, the federal and provincial or territorial government websites are the most reliable sources. (Websites that provide access to statutes and regulations are discussed in more detail in Chapter 12.)

You can find cases on pay-for-use subscription services such as WestlawNext Canada and Quicklaw, as well as on free-access websites such as the following:

- various court websites—for example, the Supreme Court of Canada website (<http://www.scc-csc.gc.ca>) and the Court of Appeal for Ontario website (<http://www.ontariocourts.ca/coa/en>)—which provide access to the text of case reports, though *only* for cases decided by that court; and
- CanLII.

Websites that provide access to cases are discussed in more detail in Chapter 13.

Updating Tools

After you have found the statutes, regulations, and/or cases that are relevant to the legal problem you need to solve, you must make sure that the statutes and regulations have not been amended or repealed and that the cases have not been overturned on appeal and their legal principles changed by subsequent cases. To do this, you use secondary sources called "updating tools."

We have some good news for you when it comes to statutes and regulations. (Good news is a rare commodity in this book, we know.) On both the federal Justice Laws and the Ontario e-Laws sites, statutes and regulations are consolidated on a continuing basis. Amendments are incorporated into the statute itself within a few business days of their becoming law. So there is usually no need to update statutes and regulations as you would if you were using paper sources.

Cases, however, must still be updated, and the following computerized sources will help you do so:

- Quicklaw's QuickCITE, and
- WestlawNext Canada's KeyCite Canada.

These updating tools are discussed more fully in Chapter 13.

General Sources on the Internet—All Free

In addition to the dedicated legal sources discussed above, some free general sources on the Internet may come in handy when you are conducting legal research. These sources include search engines and websites that contain law-related information.

Search Engines

A **search engine** is an Internet site with a program that searches a database of Web documents or websites to match keywords that you supply. There are general search engines and specialized legal search engines.

Google (<https://www.google.ca>) is the search engine that everyone knows about and automatically turns to. Catherine Best, who developed the Canadian Legal Research and Writing Guide website, recommended Google because it has the

search engine
website with a computer program that searches a database of Web documents or websites to match supplied keywords

largest database of indexed pages; it also ranks its results, so that better-quality sites appear first. Apart from Google, there are the following search engines:

- Bing, at <http://www.bing.com>,
- Lycos, at <http://www.lycos.com>, and
- Yahoo, at <https://ca.yahoo.com>.

The main specialized legal search engines are the following:

- FindLaw, at <http://www.findlaw.com>. This Canadian site provides free legal information and includes a directory of lawyers and law firms.
- PublicLegal, at <http://www.ilrg.com>. This American site is run by the Internet Legal Research Group. It can find law-related sites in 238 countries, islands, and territories, including Canada, but its emphasis is on the United States.

Websites Containing Law-Related Information

There are a number of websites specifically about law, and many websites not specifically about law contain law-related information.

Government Sites

In addition to their statute sites, the federal, provincial, and territorial governments maintain websites that contain useful information for lawyers, law clerks, and paralegals.

GOVERNMENT OF CANADA

The main government of Canada site (<http://www.canada.ca>) provides information about government services for Canadians, non-Canadians, and Canadian businesses. It also provides information about the structure of the federal government, as well as links to federal departments and agencies, provincial and territorial governments, and municipalities.

Some other government of Canada websites that provide law-related information are the following:

- Statistics Canada (<http://www.statcan.gc.ca>) for statistics, including the consumer price index, population rates, and unemployment rates;
- Canada Revenue Agency (<http://www.cra-arc.gc.ca>) for income tax and GST/HST information and forms; and
- Innovation, Science and Economic Development Canada (<http://www.ic.gc.ca/eic/site/icgc.nsf/eng/h_07064.html>) for information related to business.

GOVERNMENT OF ONTARIO

The main government of Ontario site (<http://www.ontario.ca>) provides a complete services and offices directory, including all tribunals, boards, and agencies; a government of Ontario telephone directory; and links to specific ministries.

Other government of Ontario websites that provide law-related information are the following:

- Ministry of the Attorney General (<http://www.attorneygeneral.jus.gov.on.ca>) for information about such matters as going to court, getting a lawyer, handling family law matters, and using Small Claims Court; and
- Ontario Courts (<http://www.ontariocourts.ca>) for links to the Court of Appeal for Ontario, Superior Court of Justice, and Ontario Court of Justice.

OTHER PROVINCIAL GOVERNMENTS AND TERRITORIAL GOVERNMENTS

Each province and territory has a website similar to the government of Ontario website. You can find them individually—for example, by doing a Google search for "[name of province] government."

MUNICIPAL GOVERNMENTS

All major Canadian cities have their own websites with information about matters such as bylaws and contact information for city administrators. You can find a city's website by doing a Google search for "city of [name of city]."

Legal Research Sites

A number of websites contain information about legal research, including the following:

- The Canadian Legal Research and Writing Guide, at <http://legalresearch.org>. Developed by Catherine Best when she was a research lawyer and adjunct professor with the University of British Columbia Faculty of Law, this site (now run by CanLII) is an excellent source of information about legal research and contains links to legal sources.
- Bora Laskin Law Library, at <http://library.law.utoronto.ca>. Run by the University of Toronto Faculty of Law, this site contains guides to legal research, community legal information, and links to legal resources.
- William R. Lederman Law Library, at <http://library.queensu.ca/law>. Run by the Queen's University Faculty of Law, this site contains a comprehensive legal research manual.

General Legal Sites

Various law-related organizations maintain websites with access to information about the law. These organizations include the following:

- LawCentral Canada, at <http://www.lawcentralcanada.ca>. A website of the Centre for Public Legal Education Alberta, this site provides access to public legal education articles.
- Canadian Legal FAQs, at <http://www.law-faqs.org>. Also a website of the Centre for Public Legal Education Alberta, this site provides answers to commonly asked legal questions.

Most large law firms maintain websites that provide access to publications on legal topics written by members of their firms. The following are examples:

- Davies Ward Phillips & Vineberg, at <http://www.dwpv.com>;
- Gowlings, at <http://www.gowlings.com>;
- McCarthy Tétrault, at <http://www.mccarthy.ca>; and
- Torys, at <http://www.torys.com>.

You can access a comprehensive list of Canadian law firms, organized by practice area, by going to the Canadian Law List website at <http://www.canadianlawlist.com>.

Concerns When Using Free-Access Internet Sources

As Catherine Best said, "There is no guarantee that information posted on the Internet for free access is comprehensive, current, or reliable." When you use free-access websites, you must ask yourself the following questions:

- Who has written or edited the content for the website? Look for the author's or editor's name, credentials, and contact address.
- Is the site affiliated with a known, law-based organization?
- Is the site associated with an impartial organization or with a political or advocacy group? Does the site show a bias?
- How current is the information on the site? How often is the site updated?

You can generally rely on information found on sites maintained by

- governments,
- universities,
- law schools, and
- courts.

KEY TERM

search engine, 109

EXERCISES

1. Your law firm has been retained by a woman who has recently separated from a man with whom she cohabited for five years. She wants to know whether she is entitled to spousal support, and you have been asked to conduct some preliminary legal research on the subject.

   a. What computerized source(s) should you consult to find a general statement of the law?

   b. Assume that the general statement of the law mentions the *Family Law Act*. What computerized source(s) would you use to find the statute?

   c. What computerized source(s) would you use to find cases that interpret the *Family Law Act*?

   d. What computerized source(s) would you use to update the cases that interpret the *Family Law Act*?

2. Your law firm has been retained by a corporation that wishes to expand into providing school bus services. You have been asked to provide some preliminary information about licensing of drivers and vehicles to be used for the purpose.

   a. What computerized source(s) should you consult to find a general statement of the law?

   b. Assume that the general statement of the law mentions O Reg 340/94. What computerized source(s) would you use to find the regulation?

   c. What computerized source(s) would you use to find and update cases that interpret an Ontario regulation?

   d. The lawyer directing your work remembers that she recently read an article that was almost exactly on topic and wants you to find it. What computerized source(s) should you consult to find the article?

Computer Searches Using Keywords

9

LEARNING OUTCOMES

After reading this chapter, you will understand:

- What keywords are and why you need them for effective online legal research

- The role of legal knowledge and analysis in keyword searches

- How to choose keywords

- The difference between plain (or natural) language keyword searches and Boolean keyword searches

- The principles and techniques involved in Boolean keyword searches

- How to develop a Boolean search

- How to use an unfamiliar computerized source

Introduction

Computerized research sources will provide you with more or less the same information as paper sources. However, the methods of accessing the information using a computer are different from the methods used for paper sources.

Information in paper sources is edited and organized, usually by topic. This enables a researcher to use an index or a table of contents to locate information. When you work with paper sources, you must analyze the facts of your legal research problem to identify categories of law and/or legal concepts that may be relevant. You then use those categories and concepts to locate the information—statutes, regulations, or court decisions—you are looking for in an index or table of contents.

When you work with computerized sources, you likewise need to analyze the facts of your legal research problem and identify categories of law and legal concepts. Here, though, you do so to identify **keywords** that are likely to appear in the statutes, regulations, or court decisions that deal with your problem. When you conduct a keyword search, you will get only what you ask for. This is an important point. With print sources, you are able to see your subject in the context of adjacent or surrounding topics that may prove helpful and relevant to your search. This is not the case with computerized sources, where the quality of your research will depend on how well you choose your keywords.

keywords
words with which researchers search computerized sources for information stored randomly in databases

Searching by Keyword

Computerized sources are composed of databases in which information is stored randomly. A researcher "asks" the computer to locate information in the database by searching for words or combinations of words that we call keywords. A computerized search is a request for all documents that contain requested keywords. When the researcher enters the keywords, the computer searches the entire database for appropriate matches.

The Role of Legal Knowledge and Analysis in Keyword Searches

When you do computerized legal research, you are asking the computer to find cases that are relevant to your particular legal issue. You identify and enter keywords, and the computer searches the database for statutes, regulations, or court decisions that contain them. To choose the keywords that will guide the computer's search successfully, you must have some idea of the words that are likely to be found in a court's or tribunal's decision in a case, or in a statute or regulation that deals with your issue. You must know enough about the law to identify the legal issue(s) involved, and you must be familiar enough with the wording of statutes and the language of cases to be able to choose useful keywords.

The first step in this process is to situate your legal problem within the relevant area of the law. Every area of law has certain terms and expressions that are commonly used. You must know enough about the area of law you are researching to know what these terms and expressions are. They will be your keywords. If you use inappropriate keywords, you risk retrieving far too many documents and/or missing what you are looking for entirely. (And yes, you can do both at the same time!) Once you have entered your keywords and retrieved some statutes, regulations, and/or cases, you must review them to decide whether they are relevant to the issue you are researching. This will tell you how well you selected your keywords.

Here's an example. A client wants to sue her doctor. She went to the doctor because she had a broken arm, and the incompetent doctor made the break worse. You have to conduct a keyword search for relevant cases. If you don't know the relevant area of the law, your choice of keywords is limited to *arm*, *broken*, and *doctor*. A search using these terms will retrieve every case that contains those words, regardless of the area of law the case deals with. You'll get criminal cases about assault victims with broken arms who were examined by the doctor, and you'll even get product liability cases about broken armrests in doctored automobiles. If you know that the area of law is tort law, you can be more specific and add terms such as *medical malpractice* or *negligence* to your keyword search. This will reduce the number of unwanted cases that you retrieve.

Example: Knowledge and Analysis

How do you choose appropriate keywords? Consider the following fact situation and the questions and answers that follow:

> Marsha Steward had a party at her cottage, Loon Hill, in Muskoka. During the party, one of her guests slipped on the staircase leading from the dock to the cottage. In keeping with the theme of her party—"Decorating with Butter"—Marsha had placed butter carvings of Ontario birds all along the stairs. Unfortunately, the carvings melted in the heat, making the staircase slippery. The guest has sued Marsha, and Marsha wonders whether she will be held liable. She would like you to give her some advice. You decide you will research relevant case law.

- What area of law does this case involve?
  - Tort law.
- What kind of tort decisions are you looking for?
  - Cases dealing with negligence generally, but in particular with occupier's liability.
- What words might you expect to find in a decision about occupier's liability? Think of all the synonyms and variations of each term.
  - occupier's liability;
  - negligent, negligence, negligently;
  - duty of care;
  - owner, homeowner, occupier;
  - guest, invitee; and
  - slip, fall, trip.

Coming Up with Keywords

When researching online, you are asking the computer to search for statutes, regulations, or case decisions containing keywords you have chosen. You have to guess what words the documents you're looking for might contain. To choose useful keywords, try thinking about common words or phrases used within this area of law. You need to draw on your general knowledge of law or, if that doesn't get you far enough, on research you have done using secondary sources.

Usually there are several possible keywords you can try. Take a case of drunk driving, for example. *Drunk driving* is also known as *impaired driving, operating a motor vehicle while impaired,* or *driving over 80* (that is, driving with over 80 milligrams of alcohol per 100 millilitres of blood in your system). If you choose just one keyword or phrase—let's say *impaired driving*—you will not retrieve any of the cases that have referred to the matter as *operating a motor vehicle while impaired* or *driving over 80*. You increase your chances of getting the most accurate results when you search using a range of keywords.

To return to the fact situation of medical malpractice in the setting of a broken arm, you might start off with the keywords *doctor, medical malpractice,* and *broken arm*. However, the computer will search only for these specific words or phrases. It will not find a case that may prove useful to you that uses words such as *physician* or *surgeon* instead of *doctor,* or *negligence* instead of *malpractice*. So you want to search for cases that contain the word *doctor, physician,* or *surgeon* plus the word *arm, radius,* or *ulna* plus the words *medical malpractice, negligence, negligent,* or *negligently*. You need to look for all these synonyms because it is impossible to know in advance whether a particular written decision spoke of a *doctor* who was *negligent* in splinting a *radius* or of *medical malpractice* involving a *surgeon* who did not set an *arm* properly.

Types of Keyword Searches

For the legal researcher using computerized sources, there are two kinds of keyword searches:

1. the **plain or natural language search**, and
2. the **Boolean search**.

Plain or Natural Language Searches

A person using a plain or natural language search doesn't require much in the way of training. He or she just types a question or sentence (or even a few descriptive words!) into the search field, using ordinary English. The following are examples of plain or natural language searches:

"Are wild migratory birds protected in Canada?"
"wild migratory birds protected Canada"

These searches are interpreted in a far more flexible manner than Boolean searches.

plain or natural language search
method of searching a computerized source by means of a question, a sentence, or descriptive words, without using special syntax such as connectors and truncation symbols

Boolean search
method of searching that is based on principles of logic and that requires the use of keywords together with specific syntax

The computer looks for documents that best match the search, and it presents the searcher with a number of documents, ranking highest the one that most closely matches the words entered in the search. Plain or natural language searching is much like using Google to find information and, as is the case with Google, searches will generate a large number of results. These results can be easily narrowed down by using post-search filters.

Not all computerized sources are equipped for plain or natural language searches. Two that are so equipped are Lexis Advance Quicklaw and WestlawNext Canada. Lexis Advance Quicklaw calls them "natural language" searches, while WestlawNext Canada calls them "plain language" searches. Both Lexis Advance Quicklaw and WestlawNext Canada default to natural or plain language searches and offer multiple post-search filters to help you narrow and refine your search results.

Boolean Searches

In a Boolean search (named for a British mathematician, George Boole), the computer hunts through thousands of documents to locate requested combinations of words or phrases. The need to search this way arises from the fact that, as we discussed above, information is not arranged in a database by subject; the only way the computer can locate a document is to locate words within it. Boolean searches are more likely than plain language searches to find a specific document you are looking for.

Boolean Connectors

When you conduct a Boolean search using keywords, it is not enough simply to come up with the correct keywords. You must also think about how those words appear in combination. Do you want to see case decisions that contain *any* one of your keywords, decisions that have *some* of your keywords *but not* others, or only those decisions that contain *all* your keywords?

Boolean searching is based on principles concerning the logical relationship among search terms. Boolean searching uses three basic connectors:

- OR,
- AND, and
- NOT.

These connectors allow you to direct the computer to search for (1) any of your keywords, (2) some of your keywords but not others, or (3) all your keywords.

THE OR CONNECTOR

The OR connector directs the computer to search for documents that contain any or all terms you enter. For example, if you're looking for information about incarceration, you can search for two terms, *jail* OR *prison*. This search will retrieve documents in which at least one of the search terms is present—documents with either *jail* or *prison* or both in them. In Figure 9.1, the shaded circle with the word *jail* represents all the documents that contain the word *jail*; the shaded circle with the word *prison* represents all the documents that contain the word *prison*; and the shaded overlap area represents all the documents that contain both *jail* and *prison*. An OR search will retrieve all these documents.

Figure 9.1   OR Search with Two Terms

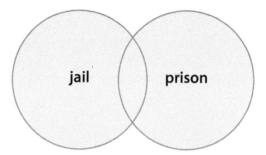

The OR connector is most commonly used to search for different ways of saying the same thing. The more terms or concepts combined in a search with the OR connector, the more documents the search will retrieve. For example, you can search for *jail* OR *prison* OR *penitentiary*, as illustrated in Figure 9.2. This search will retrieve documents that contain any or all of the three words.

Figure 9.2   OR Search with Three Terms

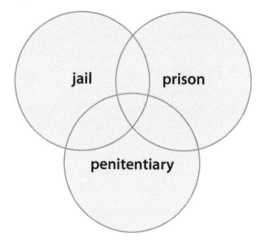

THE AND CONNECTOR

The AND connector directs the computer to search only for documents that contain all search terms. For example, if you're interested in researching the relationship between alcohol and abuse, you would search *alcohol* AND *abuse*.

This search will retrieve only documents in which *both* of the search terms are present. In Figure 9.3, this is represented by the shaded area in which the two circles overlap. The search will not retrieve documents containing only *alcohol* or only *abuse*.

Figure 9.3   AND Search with Two Terms

Figure 9.4   AND Search with Three Terms

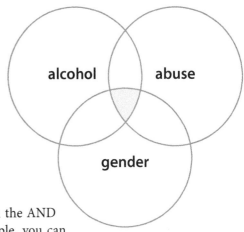

The more terms or concepts you combine in a search with the AND connector, the fewer documents you will retrieve. For example, you can search for *alcohol* AND *abuse* AND *gender*, as illustrated in Figure 9.4. This search will retrieve only documents that contain all three terms.

THE NOT CONNECTOR

The NOT connector is used when you want to retrieve documents that include one term, but not if the documents also include a second term. For example, if you want to see information about support, but want to avoid seeing anything about interim support, you would search *support* NOT *interim*. The search will retrieve documents in which *only* the word *support* is present. In Figure 9.5, the circle on the left represents all the documents that include the word *support*. The area of overlap represents documents that include the words *support* and *interim*. The shaded area represents the documents that contain the word *support* but not the word *interim*.

Figure 9.5   NOT Search

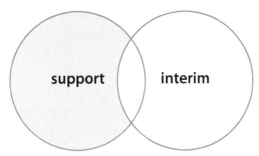

The NOT connector excludes documents from your search results. You must be careful when using the NOT connector because the term you are searching for may be present in relevant documents that also contain the word you want to avoid.

SEARCHING FOR A PHRASE

None of the Boolean connectors discussed above will retrieve documents containing a phrase—that is, a series of words in a given order. To search for an exact phrase, most computerized sources require you to enclose the phrase in quotation marks. For example, if you search for "child support" you will retrieve only documents that contain that specific phrase.

The following table summarizes the use of the connectors discussed so far:

Search	Explanation
rent OR arrears	Searches for documents that contain the word *rent*, the word *arrears*, or both words. As long as at least one word is present, the document will be found.
rent AND arrears	Searches for documents that contain both the word *rent* and the word *arrears*. If only one of the words appears, the document will not be found.
rent NOT arrears	Searches for documents that contain the word *rent*, but not if they also contain the word *arrears*. If a document mentions rent and also mentions arrears, the document will not be found.
"rent arrears"	Searches for documents that contain the exact phrase "rent arrears." If there are any words in between these two words, such as in "the rent is in arrears," the document will not be found.

More Advanced Boolean Searching

Once you have the hang of the simple Boolean searches described above, you can move on to somewhat more complicated search methods.

PROXIMITY CONNECTORS

To make sure that your Boolean search retrieves cases that are really about your topic, you may need to specify that certain words be close together.

If you are looking for cases on sexual harassment, for example, you can ask for cases where *sexual* and *harassment* both appear by joining the two words with the AND connector. A search query for *sexual* AND *harassment* will bring up cases where both words appear in the case. However, those words may appear anywhere in the document and may not be related to each other. For example, you may retrieve a case in which there was a criminal sexual assault on a victim who also claimed there was harassment by the investigating police officers. You can retrieve cases where *sexual* and *harassment* are joined as a phrase by putting the phrase in quotation marks: "sexual harassment." However, this will exclude relevant cases that don't contain that phrase but instead contain the phrase "sexual assault and harassment."

Proximity connectors allow you to ask for documents where the words are not necessarily beside each other in a phrase, but appear reasonably close to each other in the document—for example, within five or ten words of each other, or within the same paragraph. This ensures that the terms will be close enough to remain related but not so close that you exclude relevant cases that might include a few extra words within a phrase.

Proximity connectors are expressed by the formula /*n*. You replace the letter *n* with a number specifying how far apart your keywords must be from each other. For example, the phrase "rent /5 arrears" will find documents where the words *rent* and *arrears* are up to five words apart from each other in any order. This search will find documents containing all the following phrases:

Last month's rent was in arrears
Tenant owes arrears of rent in the amount of $2000
This month's rent is now in arrears

But a Boolean search using "rent /5 arrears" will not find a document that contains the following phrase: "The tenant is in arrears because she did not pay her rent." With that phrase, there are more than five words between the two keywords *rent* and *arrears*.

When choosing a value for *n*, think about how close together you want your keywords to appear. To see your words reasonably close together (but not as a phrase) choose "/5." To see them within the same sentence, choose "/10" to "/15." To see them within the same paragraph choose "/25" to "/50."

It is possible to use multiple proximity connectors in the same search. If you use multiple /*n* connectors with the same value, the connectors generally operate from left to right in a search. If they have different values, the smaller numbers operate first. For example, the search "landlord /10 eviction /10 arrears" will find documents that contain the word *landlord* within ten words of the word *eviction*, and then find that result within ten words of the word *arrears*. By contrast, the search "landlord /10 eviction /5 arrears" first finds documents in which the word *eviction* appears within five words of the word *arrears*, and then finds that result within ten words of the word *landlord*.

Two other proximity connectors are available: the "/p" connector and the "/s" connector. Use the /p connector between words when you want to find documents in which the words appear in the same paragraph of a document. Use the /s connector between words when you want to find documents in which the words appear in the same sentence.

SUBSTITUTION AND TRUNCATION

Most computerized sources use substitution and truncation symbols (sometimes referred to as "expanders" or "root expanders") to make the job of searching for all possible terms a little easier.

◇ Substitution

substitution symbol
symbol that replaces a single variable letter in keywords that may be spelled more than one way

Because your keywords may be spelled in more than one way (for example, *offence* and *offense*), you can ask the computer to search for the word spelled either way by using a **substitution symbol**—for example, "***" (that is, an asterisk)—for the variable letter in the word. To ask the computer to search for both *offence* and *offense*, you would use the keyword *offen*e*.

◇ Truncation

truncation symbol
symbol used in a computerized search to find all possible endings of a root word

Because your keywords may have different endings (*dismiss, dismissing, dismissed, and dismissal*), you can ask the computer for all these words by using the **truncation symbol**, which is "!" (an exclamation mark). If you want *dismiss* with its different endings, you would type in *dismiss!* Note that most sources will, by default, search both the singular and plural form of a word, so there is no need to add a truncation symbol to a word when you are looking for its plural form only.

CONNECTOR PRIORITY

When undertaking computerized legal research, you will often need to combine connectors to develop the most effective Boolean search for information. If you are using multiple Boolean and/or proximity connectors, you must determine in what order your search will be processed. Depending on connector priority, searches can be processed in different ways. For example, consider the following Boolean search: "child /5 support AND divorce OR separation."

If a computerized source processes this search from left to right, it will first find documents in which the word *child* appears within five words of *support*, and then combine the result with all documents containing the word *divorce*. It will then combine that result with all documents containing the word *separation*. If, however, the source processes this search based on its default connector priority, the search may be processed differently. For example, it could find documents in which the word *child* appears within five words of *support* as one result, then find documents containing the word *divorce* or *separation*, or both, as another result, and then find all documents that contain both of these results.

If you are not sure of a source's connector priority, or if you want to change its connector priority, use parentheses to force the order of processing you need. Connectors within parentheses will have priority over and operate before connectors outside the parentheses.

For example, the search "(support AND access) /5 child" will first look for all documents that contain the words *support* and *access*. It will then find all documents that contain the word *child* within five words of that result.

Each computerized source has its own connector priority. You must determine this priority before developing your Boolean search.

SEARCH SYNTAX

All the sources you will use for computerized legal research rely on the same Boolean logic, and all require you to have the same skills in determining and combining the appropriate keywords. But different sources may vary in their "search syntaxes" —in their proximity connectors, truncation symbols, substitution symbols, and rules for setting up the search. You will find that Boolean logic is used in one of three ways, depending on the source:

- *Full Boolean logic with the use of connectors.* You must use Boolean or proximity connectors (OR, AND, NOT, /*n*, /p, or /s) between your search terms and quotation marks surrounding an exact phrase.
- *Implied Boolean logic.* You enter search terms, but you don't use Boolean or proximity connectors. The space between keywords defaults to either OR or AND, depending on the source. Also, the use of quotation marks may default to a search for variations of the enclosed keywords, rather than searching for the exact phrase. For example, if you run a plain language search on WestlawNext Canada and use the phrase "dog owners" (in quotation marks), you will find documents in which the phrase "owners of a dog" and "dog owners" appear.
- *Predetermined language.* Some sources offer a search template that sets out a selection of connectors for you to choose, which you access from a drop-down menu.

Each computerized source has its own default implied Boolean logic that you must learn before you use the source. You must find out whether the words you enter

- are searched as an exact phrase,
- are searched as though there were an OR between them,
- are searched as though there were an AND between them, or
- require all of the Boolean connectors to be keyed in.

When using a computerized source, you must also learn what, if any, proximity connectors and truncation symbols are used by that source. For example, the substitution symbol for one source is a question mark ("?"), while for other sources it is an asterisk ("*"). Most sources use the proximity connectors /*n*, /p, and /s. Each computerized source will explain the search syntax it uses. Most computerized sources also contain a help feature that explains how to develop a Boolean search using that source.

Developing a Boolean Search

Now we offer some general guidelines for developing an effective Boolean search.

Begin by familiarizing yourself with the search syntax of the source you are using. Make sure you know the proximity connectors, substitution and truncation symbols, and connector priority employed by the source.

Next, identify your research topic. Then, using a piece of paper or a computer to record your work, go through the following steps:

1. Identify your research topic.
2. Choose appropriate keywords for the topic.
3. Consider whether any of your keywords should be joined as a phrase, and use the appropriate "phrase" syntax (for most sources, you must surround the words with quotation marks).
4. Consider whether there are any synonyms for any of your keywords, and add them to your search using the OR connector.
5. Identify keywords that may have alternative spellings or variant letters, and replace variant letters with the appropriate substitution symbol.
6. Identify keywords that have alternative endings and truncate these words using the appropriate truncation symbol.
7. Combine your keywords logically, using the appropriate Boolean and proximity connectors. When in doubt, use parentheses to force the order of processing.

Example

The following example takes you through the steps of developing a Boolean search:

The client is a tenant who is being evicted. She wants to oppose the eviction proceedings and is also thinking about bringing a human rights complaint against her landlord. Her question for you is how much of her legal costs she will recover if she wins.

1. Identify your research topic.
   - You are looking for information about costs in eviction proceedings and in human rights applications.
2. Choose appropriate keywords for the topic.
   - costs eviction human rights applications
3. Consider whether any of your keywords should be joined as a phrase, and use the appropriate "phrase" syntax (for most sources, you must surround the words with quotation marks).
   - costs eviction "human rights" applications
4. Consider whether there are any synonyms for any of your keywords, and add them to your search using the OR connector.
   - costs eviction "human rights" applications OR proceedings OR cases
5. Identify keywords that may have alternative spellings or variant letters, and replace variant letters with the appropriate substitution symbol.
   - Not applicable here
6. Identify keywords that have alternative endings and truncate these words using the appropriate truncation symbol.
   - costs evict! "human rights" applications OR proceedings OR cases

7. Combine your keywords logically, using the appropriate Boolean and proximity connectors. When in doubt, use parentheses to force the order of processing.

   – costs /25 evict! OR "human rights" /10 applications OR proceedings OR cases

This search will find documents where *evict* (or its variants) or *human rights* (or both) appears within 10 words of *applications*, *proceedings*, or *cases*, and where that result is within 25 words of *costs*.

A Final Note on Boolean Searching

There is no one perfect Boolean search for any given topic; there are only better searches or worse searches. Two people could run a search on the same topic at the same time and come up with different answers.

When searching, you are always guessing at how keywords will show up in a document, and so you will often have to refine your search based on your results. If, for example, you use a very small proximity connector between two words, such as "/5," and get zero results, try a larger connector. Your keywords may be close together in a document you are looking for, but they may be six words apart, and not four. If you're not getting any results with "/5," try using "/10." Alternatively, if you get too many results, consider adding more keywords to your search to narrow down your results. Boolean searching is challenging, especially for a beginner, but with practice, it gets easier.

How to Use an Unfamiliar Computerized Source

In Chapter 8, one of the warnings we gave you about working with computerized sources was that they can change their appearance and function without warning. Because this happens, we also warned you to take our information about particular websites and sources not as eternal truth but as illustrations of how computerized sources may look and work.

Have you ever heard the saying "Give a man a fish and you feed him for a day; teach a man to fish and you feed him for a lifetime"? Think of detailed instructions about how to use a particular computerized source as a fish. In this section, we're going to teach you a little bit about fishing—in the seas of computerized information.

The first thing we have to tell you is a comforting one. Changes in computerized sources, even if they seem disruptive, are usually intended to make research easier. They are mostly designed to make the source more user-friendly—more accessible to researchers who do not have the Boolean skills that you have now acquired!

What should you do when you are confronted with a computerized source that you have not used before, whether because it is completely new to you or because it has been remodelled since you last used it?

- Look over the homepage of the source to begin the process of familiarizing yourself with it. If it is a source you have used before, the changes may only be cosmetic, and the search features you know and love may still be intact. When a source makes significant changes, it usually alerts users to them and offers prominent explanations of them, at least for a time.
- Look for link buttons or navigational bars. The homepage typically has link buttons or bars to allow a user to navigate. The links may be so clear and obvious, or contain such good instructions, that you'll be able to start using the source immediately.
- Look for plus symbols beside topics. When you choose a topic link, you will often find that it contains levels of information. The plus (+) symbol beside a topic tells you there is more information available (a minus symbol (–) tells you that the topic is already fully expanded). Click on + signs to see more detail about a topic.
- Look for hyperlinks to take you to relevant pages. (As a rule of thumb, any text that is not black is a hyperlink.)
- Look for a Help link. Subscription services provide extensive help in the form of user's guides or manuals for the entire source, as well as quick reference guides for specific features. They also have phone numbers for a help desk. Some sites provide online video tutorials demonstrating how to use the site's features.
- Find out whether free training is available. Subscription services may offer free training at a central location.
- If the source uses Boolean searching, find the link that explains what syntax it uses (what rules apply about proximity connectors and which symbols indicate syntactic elements such as truncation and substitution).
- Practise, or even play, with the source before you start your research. If you have already gained some feeling for computer sources in general, you will probably not find it too difficult to figure out how this new source works.

KEY TERMS

Boolean search, 118
keywords, 116
plain or natural language search, 118
substitution symbol, 124
truncation symbol, 124

EXERCISES

1. Draft a Boolean search for the following research topics:

   a. Variation of child or spousal support in Ontario

   b. Demerit points for careless or dangerous driving

   c. Damages for negligence, pain and suffering, and loss of income

   d. Adopting an infant child from foster care in Ontario

   e. Estate planning using trusts, but not charitable trusts

2. You are looking for cases about liability in tort dealing with a loss resulting from reasonable reliance on a false statement negligently made. Draft an appropriate Boolean search.

3. You are researching case law to confirm whether security personnel employed to guard against theft of merchandise have greater arrest powers than citizens do. Draft an appropriate Boolean search.

PART V

Using a Legal Encyclopedia to Find a General Statement of Law

When you perform legal research, the most efficient strategy is to start by locating a general statement of the law as it applies to the legal problem you need to solve. The most efficient tool for that purpose is a legal encyclopedia. A legal encyclopedia will not only provide you with a summary of the law in the relevant area but will also refer you to the relevant statutes, regulations, and cases from which the principles of law are derived.

The two Canadian legal encyclopedias are the *Canadian Encyclopedic Digest* and *Halsbury's Laws of Canada*. Each is available in both a print and a computerized version.

Legal Encyclopedias —Paper

10

LEARNING OUTCOMES

After reading this chapter, you will understand:

- Which legal encyclopedias are available in print—the *Canadian Encyclopedic Digest* (CED) and *Halsbury's Laws of Canada* (Halsbury's)

- How the CED is organized

- How to use the CED for legal research

- How Halsbury's is organized

- How to use Halsbury's for legal research

Introduction

This chapter deals with the paper versions of the two Canadian legal encyclopedias—the *Canadian Encyclopedic Digest*, or CED, and *Halsbury's Laws of Canada*, or Halsbury's, with primary emphasis on the CED. The computerized versions of both sources are discussed in Chapter 11.

The Canadian Encyclopedic Digest

The CED is one of the most comprehensive secondary sources for legal research. It is a loose-leaf multi-volume legal encyclopedia that provides a very general overview of most areas of Canadian law, and it is an excellent place to begin when you know very little about the area of law that you are researching. The print version comprises two editions. The Ontario edition focuses on Ontario and federal laws. The Western edition focuses on the law in the four Western provinces—Manitoba, Saskatchewan, Alberta, and British Columbia.

The CED Volumes

The current (4th) edition of the CED is made up of over 200 subject titles, contained in approximately 56 loose-leaf volumes. The subject titles are broad topics of information or general areas of law, such as animals, contracts, evidence, or income tax. The volumes are organized alphabetically, by subject title. The spine of each CED volume sets out the volume number and the alphabetical range of subject titles contained in that volume.

Each subject title contains parts, sections, subsections, and sub-subsections, with the subject title broken down into increasingly specific topics. By narrowing down your research problem within the relevant subject title, you can find the general statement of law dealing with your particular topic.

At the beginning of each subject title is a detailed table of contents, called the Table of Classification. This can help you find, within that subject title, the specific topic you would like to research. Each subject title also includes an indexed Table of Cases, which identifies the cases cited within the subject title, and both a Table of Statutes and a Table of Regulations, which together identify the legislation cited within the subject title. There is also a subject index at the end of each title that refers you to relevant paragraph numbers within the subject title.

Each subject title has both a name and a title number, and each is divided into parts that are given both a number (in uppercase Roman numerals) and a name. Each part is divided into sections that are given both a number (Arabic numerals) and a name. Each section may be further divided into subsections (subtopics) that are given a letter and a name. Each subsection may be further divided into sub-subsections that are given a number (lowercase Roman numerals) and a name. Each section is divided into numbered paragraphs (preceded by the "§" symbol but without a name) that provide a summary of the law, together with references to the relevant statutes, regulations, and/or cases providing authority for the summary.

Specific topics cross-reference the topic's relevant subject classification in the *Canadian Abridgment*'s *Case Digests*. The *Canadian Abridgment* is discussed in Chapter 13.

The CED is updated regularly. Supplemental pages, found at the beginning of each subject title, update case and statute references, as well as other significant developments that have occurred since the publication date of the subject title. The paragraph numbers noted in the supplemental pages correspond to the paragraph numbers in the main body of the text.

Finding Tools

There are two separate finding tools to help you look for information in the CED:

1. the Research Guide and Key, and
2. the Index.

Research Guide and Key

The Research Guide and Key helps you find information in all the subject titles. It is found in a separate binder and contains the following:

- the Research Guide,
- the Table of Statutes,
- the Table of Rules, and
- the Table of Regulations.

RESEARCH GUIDE

The Research Guide explains how to find information using the CED.

TABLE OF STATUTES

The **Table of Statutes** provides a list, in alphabetical order, of all current federal and provincial statutes referred to in the various subject titles of the CED. It also provides the volume number, title number, and paragraph numbers for discussions of or references to specific provisions of the statute.

Table of Statutes
alphabetical list of all current federal and provincial statutes referred to in the various subject titles in the CED

TABLE OF RULES

The **Table of Rules** provides a list, in alphabetical order, of the rules of court (rules of civil procedure) referred to in the CED's subject titles. It also provides a reference to the volume and paragraph numbers where the rules are referred to.

Table of Rules
alphabetical list of the rules of court referred to in the subject titles in the CED

TABLE OF REGULATIONS

The **Table of Regulations** provides a list, in alphabetical order, of the regulations referred to in the CED's subject titles. It also provides a reference to the volume and paragraph numbers where the regulations are referred to.

Table of Regulations
alphabetical list of the regulations referred to in the subject titles in the CED

Index

CED Index
separate volume of the CED that contains the List of Titles in the CED and the Index Key

The **CED Index** is a separate binder that contains

- the List of Titles in the CED, and
- the Index Key.

The List of Titles sets out, in alphabetical order, all the subject titles in the CED. It gives both the title number of the subject title and the volume number in which the subject title can be found.

Index Key
combines the individual indexes from all the titles and contains an alphabetical list of keywords, together with extensive cross-references within and among subject titles in the CED

The **Index Key** provides an alphabetical list of keywords, together with extensive cross-references within and among subject titles. It combines the individual indexes from all the titles.

As we mentioned above, there is also a table of contents at the beginning of each subject title, and a subject index at the end. Both provide yet another way to find increasingly specific information on your research topic.

How to Use the CED

What approach you take with the CED will depend on whether you know the area of law that deals with the problem you are trying to solve.

If you know the area of law, take the following steps:

1. Choose the volume that contains the appropriate subject title. Check the Scope of Title section (if available) of the subject title to make sure that your topic is included in the subject title you have chosen. You may be directed to another subject title instead. For example, the tort of false imprisonment is not discussed under the subject title "Torts"; it is discussed under a separate subject title, "Malicious Prosecution and False Imprisonment." However, the Scope of Title section within the "Torts" subject title does direct you to see the "Malicious Prosecution and False Imprisonment" title, among others.

2. Look at the table of contents at the beginning of the title, or look at the index at the end of the title. Either will refer you to relevant paragraph numbers.

3. Find the useful paragraphs and read about your topic. It's usually a good idea to at least skim the entire section.

4. Update each relevant paragraph by looking at the supplemental pages at the beginning of the subject title.

When you don't know the area of law very well and are unsure what subject title your research topic falls under, the Index Key is the best place to start. By looking up keywords dealing with your research problem, you can easily find the relevant subject title. By looking under specific topics within the relevant subject title, you will be referred to the volume number, title number, and paragraph number that provides a general statement of law on your specific topic. Then go to the appropriate volume and follow steps 1 through 4, above.

Below, we go into more detail about how to use the CED when you do know the area of law, and how to use it when you don't. The best way to learn how to use the CED is to work through an example.

Example

A client in Toronto, Ontario, has a cocker spaniel that barks constantly. One day last month, the client's neighbour went to her apartment to complain. When the client opened the door, the dog rushed out to attack the neighbour, who fell backward and broke his leg. The neighbour is now suing the client for compensation for the injuries caused by the dog. Can the client be held legally responsible for her canine companion's dastardly act?

To advise the client, you will need to find a general statement of the law concerning whether a dog owner in Ontario is responsible for the injuries caused by his or her dog.

FINDING YOUR TOPIC WHEN YOU DON'T KNOW THE AREA OF LAW

If you don't know which area of law to look in, go to the Index and refer to the Index Key. Find the relevant subject title by looking up keywords for your problem. For example, if you search for the keyword *dogs*, you will find an entry titled "DOGS." Within it you will find the relevant subject title: "Animals." See Figure 10.1.

Figure 10.1   CED Index Key Entry

DOGS

See Agriculture; Animals; Municipal Corporations; Negligence

Next, look in the Index Key under "ANIMALS" for the relevant part: "X. Dogs." See Figure 10.2, which reproduces the relevant pages of the Index Key. Under this part, you will find the relevant section: "Liability for Injuries Inflicted by Dogs." Next, locate the relevant subsection: "(h) Ontario." Finally, locate the relevant subsubsection: "(i) Dog Owners' Liability." Note that "3-7§431" appears beneath this entry. These numbers tell you that the summary or general statement of the law on your research topic can be found in volume 3 of the CED, under subject title number 7, in paragraph number 431.

Figure 10.2 Pages of CED Index Key for Subject

ANIMALS VII.6

26

Figure 10.3   Page from the CED List of Titles

LIST OF TITLES

The following is a list of the subject titles in CED (Ont. 4th), showing the volumes in which they appear and their respective title numbers.

Title No.	Subject Title	Volume No.
1.	Aboriginal Law	1
2.	Absentees	1
3.	Actions	1
4.	Administrative Law	1
5.	Agency	2
6.	Agriculture	2
6.1	Alternative Dispute Resolution	2
7.	Animals	3
8.	Annuities	3
10.	Associations and Not-for-Profit Corporations	3
11.	Auctions	3
12.	Aviation	3
13.	Bailment	4
14.	Banking	4
15.	Bankruptcy and Insolvency	5
16.	Barristers and Solicitors	6
17.	Bills of Exchange	6
18.	Boundaries and Surveys	6
19.	Building Contracts	6
20.	Bulk Sales	7
21.	Burial and Cremation	7
22.	Business Corporations	7
23.	Carriers	8
24.	Charities	8
25.	Children	8A
26.	Citizenship	9
27.	Companies' Creditors Arrangement Act	9
29.	Condominiums	10
30.	Conflict of Laws	10

1

April 2016

FINDING YOUR TOPIC WHEN YOU KNOW THE AREA OF LAW

If you already know something about the area of law you're researching, including the relevant subject title, you can start by looking at the List of Titles (in the CED Index) to find the relevant volume number and subject title for your specific topic. A page from the List of Titles is reproduced in Figure 10.3 on the previous page. Looking at Figure 10.3, you see that "Animals" is subject title number 7 and can be found in volume 3 of the CED.

Alternatively, you can simply refer to the spine of the CED volumes to find the volume that contains your subject title. The spine of each volume provides the volume number and the alphabetical range of subject titles contained in that volume. Once you find the right volume, you can simply refer to the tab that has your subject title name on it. To find more specific information within the title, use the Table of Classification found at the beginning of the subject title or the subject index found at the end of the title.

Figure 10.4 reproduces a portion of the Table of Classification for the subject title "Animals"—the part dealing with dogs.

The following table illustrates how the research topic in this problem is progressively broken down within the subject title "Animals."

	Number	Name
Subject title	7	Animals
Part	X	Dogs
Section	6	Liability for Injuries Inflicted by Dogs
Subsection	(h)	Ontario
Sub-subsection	(i)	Dog Owners' Liability
Paragraph	431	

The subject index at the end of the subject title breaks down general topics into more specific topics using keywords and phrases, and it refers you to the relevant paragraph numbers within the subject title that contain the general statement of law on your research topic. Figure 10.5 reproduces a portion of the subject index for the subject title "Animals"—the portion that deals with injuries by dogs. It directs you to paragraphs 431 and 432 for general information on injuries by dogs in Ontario.

FINDING AND READING THE TEXT

Once you have identified your specific topic using one of the finding tools discussed above, read the relevant paragraph(s). In our example, we have been directed to paragraphs 431 and 432 of subject title 7 ("Animals") in volume 3 of the CED. Those paragraphs are reproduced in Figure 10.6.

Note that the paragraphs are preceded by a cross-reference to the classification number of the specific topic in the *Canadian Abridgment*. (The *Canadian Abridgment* is discussed in more detail in Chapter 13.) Note also that the paragraphs contain

- a statement of the law;
- footnotes citing relevant legislation; and
- in the case of paragraph 431, footnotes citing relevant case law.

Figure 10.4 Portion of the CED Table of Classification

ANIMALS

5. Seizure, Forfeiture and Disposal .... §245
    - (a) Federal .... §245
    - (b) Alberta .... §257
    - (c) British Columbia .... §258
    - (d) Manitoba .... §260
    - (e) Ontario .... §265
    - (f) Saskatchewan .... §269
6. Compensation .... §271
    - (a) Federal .... §271
    - (b) Alberta .... §280
    - (c) British Columbia .... §281
    - (d) Manitoba .... §282
    - (e) Ontario .... §284
    - (f) Saskatchewan .... §288
7. Offences and Penalties .... §290
    - (a) Federal .... §290
    - (b) Alberta .... §294
    - (c) British Columbia .... §296
    - (d) Manitoba .... §302
    - (e) Ontario .... §304
    - (f) Saskatchewan .... §309
8. Liability .... §310

VIII. Wild Birds .... §318

IX. Polar Bears .... §321

X. Dogs .... §324

1. Regulation of Dogs .... §324
2. Kennels .... §329
3. Security Patrol Dogs .... §344
4. Police and Tracking Dogs .... §350
5. Guide and Service Dogs .... §366
    - (a) Federal .... §366
    - (b) Alberta .... §367

CED (4th) 6

(Figure 10.4 is concluded on the next page.)

Figure 10.4   Concluded

TABLE OF CLASSIFICATION

7   January 2017

Figure 10.5   Portion of the CED Subject Index

ANIMALS

injuries by dogs (British Columbia) *(cont'd)*
- "dangerous dogs", 419–423
- negligence, 414
- police dogs, 416
- scienter, 414
- wildlife/endangered species/game, 418

injuries by dogs (Manitoba)
- big game animals, 430
- cattle-trespass, abolition of, 424
- damages, measure of, 427
- destruction order, effect of, 429
- general, 425
- joint liability, 428
- liability, exceptions to, 425
- "owner", 426
- scienter, abolition of, 424

injuries by dogs (negligence)
- Alberta, 411
- British Columbia, 414, 415
- causation, 400
- collisions with persons, 415
- general, 400–405, 407
- highways/streets, dogs on, 407–409
- Manitoba, 406
- municipal by-law, effect of breach of, 401
- occupiers' liability (Alberta), 411, 412
- police dogs, 403
- running at large, 401
- scienter, relationship to, 405
- trespassing cattle, driving off, 404

injuries by dogs (Ontario)
- big game hunting, 441, 442
- damages, measure of, 432
- destruction orders, 437, 439

- general, 431, 432
- "harbouring", 433
- livestock/poultry, 460–462
- occupiers' liability, 434
- offences, 440
- "owner", 433
- owner, prohibition against, 438
- pit bulls, 450–459
- proceedings, respecting, 435, 436
- search/seizure, 443–449

injuries by dogs (parties liable), 391

injuries by dogs (Saskatchewan)
- big game hunting, 467
- fine not barring action, 464
- general, 463, 466
- offences, 465
- police dogs, 468
- "protected animal", 463

injuries by dogs (scienter)
- Alberta, 411
- British Columbia, 414
- barking at horses, 396
- elements of scienter, 391, 393
- ferocious/savage nature, evidence of, 392
- Manitoba, 398, 424
- negligence, effect of, 399
- Ontario, 398
- precautions, sufficiency of, 395
- running at large, 397
- vicious, 394
- volenti non fit injuria, 395
- warning to strangers, sufficiency of, 394

injuries by dogs (statutory remedies)
- Alberta, 411–413

CED (4th)   328

Figure 10.6   CED Paragraphs on Topic

§429   ANIMALS

action by the owner or possessor of livestock for the recovery of damages for the injury done to or the killing of the livestock by the dog.[3]

    1   *Animal Liability Act*, S.M. 1998, c. 8, C.C.S.M., c. A95, s. 7(1); **see also** §481.
    2   *Animal Liability Act*, S.M. 1998, c. 8, C.C.S.M., c. A95, s. 7(5).
    3   *Animal Liability Act*, S.M. 1998, c. 8, C.C.S.M., c. A95, s. 7(7).

§430 Except as may be permitted by the regulations, no person shall: use a dog for, or be accompanied by a dog while, hunting big game animals or wild turkeys; or allow a dog to run after, pursue or molest a big game animal, a fur bearing animal or a wild turkey.[1]

    1   *Wildlife Act*, R.S.M. 1987, c. W130, C.C.S.M., c. W130, s. 35.

(h) — Ontario

(i) — Dog Owners' Liability

See Canadian Abridgment: TOR.XVI.10.a.iii Torts — Negligence — Liability of owner or possessor of animals — Injury by domestic animals — Injury by dog

§431 A dog owner must exercise reasonable precautions to prevent it from biting or attacking a person or domestic animal, or behaving in a manner that poses a menace to the safety of persons or domestic animals.[1] Failure to do so is an offence[2] and also exposes the owner to civil liability.[3]

    1   *Dog Owners' Liability Act*, R.S.O. 1990, c. D.16, s. 5.1 [en. 2005, c. 2, s. 1(15)]; *R. v. Vantroba* (2015), 2015 CarswellOnt 4982 (Ont. S.C.J.) (accused training dogs inside boards of hockey rink area; dog biting child who jumped over boards and ran across rink; *actus reus* of offence not established, namely, that accused's conduct representing marked and substantial departure from standard of care of reasonably prudent person).
    2   *Dog Owners' Liability Act*, R.S.O. 1990, c. D.16, s. 18 [en. 2005, c. 2, s. 1(16)]; **see also** §440.
    3   *Dog Owners' Liability Act*, R.S.O. 1990, c. D.16, s. 2.

§432 A dog's owner is liable for damages resulting from a bite or attack by the dog on another person or domestic animal.[1] Liability does not depend on knowledge of the propensity of the dog or fault or negligence on the part of the owner.[2] However, the court must reduce the damages awarded in proportion to the degree, if any, to which the plaintiff's fault or negligence caused or contributed to the damages.[3] An owner who is liable

CED (4th)   212

UPDATING YOUR RESEARCH

After reading the relevant paragraphs on your research topic, update your research by checking the relevant paragraph numbers in the supplemental pages found at the beginning of the subject title. If a paragraph number is not mentioned, it means that there has been no change in the law as set out in that paragraph.

Halsbury's Laws of Canada

Halsbury's Laws of Canada is another comprehensive legal encyclopedia of Canadian law, comprising 77 hardbound volumes. It is an offshoot of the English edition, *Halsbury's Laws of England*, which was first published at the beginning of the 20th century. The current (and first) edition of Halsbury's was started in 2006 and finished in 2013. The print version of Halsbury's, found only in major law libraries, is much less widely available than the print CED. When you use Halsbury's, it will almost certainly be the online version. So we'll provide you with only a short overview of the print version here.

Organization of Halsbury's

Like the CED, Halsbury's provides a summary of the law together with footnotes referring to the relevant legislation and leading case law from which the summary of law is derived. Information is arranged by subject titles, each of which covers a distinct area of Canadian law and contains a complete statement of the law. Each subject title contains a Table of Cases, a Table of Statutes, a Table of Contents, a keyword index, and a glossary of defined terms.

Subject titles are organized alphabetically into volumes. The volumes are not numbered, but each volume is labelled with the names of the titles that appear in the volume. The volumes are updated using annual supplements.

Each title is divided into increasingly specific content using the following numbering scheme:

  I Chapter
  1. Section
    (1) Subsection
    (a) Paragraph
      (i) Subparagraph
      A. Clause

Major paragraphs within a subject title represent a significant topic within the title. Each major paragraph is assigned a title identifier made up of the letter "H" (for Halsbury's) followed by an abbreviation of the subject title name, a short dash, a paragraph number, and a descriptive heading. For example, "Torts" is a subject title (abbreviation "TO"), and paragraph 1 is the first paragraph of the "Torts" title; it discusses the nature of this area of law. The title is identified as follows: "HTO-1 Nature of tort law." The title identifier is surrounded by inverted triangles ("∇HTO-1∇").

Minor paragraphs are subtopics within a major paragraph—they elaborate on the legal principles discussed in the major paragraph. Minor paragraphs contain a descriptive heading only. For example, paragraph HTO-1 includes a minor paragraph or subtopic dealing with the definition of a tort. It contains the descriptive heading "Definition." See Figure 10.7.

Figure 10.7   Paragraph from Halsbury's

I. INTRODUCTION

HTO-1 Nature of tort law.

HTO-1 Nature of tort law. The law of torts hovers over virtually every activity of modern society. The driver of every automobile on our highways, the pilot of every aeroplane in the sky, and the captain of every ship plying our waters must abide by the standards of tort law. The producers, distributors and repairers of every product, from food to machinery, must conform to tort law's counsel of caution. No profession is beyond its reach: a doctor cannot raise a scalpel, a lawyer cannot advise a client, nor can an architect design a building without being subject to potential tort liability. In the same way, teachers, government officials, police, and even jailers may be required to pay damages if someone is hurt as a result of their conduct. A blogger booting up a computer must take care. Those who engage in sports, such as golfers, hockey-players, and snowmobilers, may end up as parties to a tort action. The territory of tort law encompasses losses resulting from fires, floods, explosions, electricity, gas, terrorism, and many other catastrophes that may occur in this increasingly complex world. A person who punches another person on the nose may have to answer for it not only in a criminal case but also in the civil courts. A person who says nasty things about another may be sued for defamation. Hence, any one of us may become a plaintiff or a defendant in a tort action at any moment. Tort law, therefore, is a subject of abiding concern not only to the judges and lawyers who must administer it but also to the public at large, whose every move is regulated by it.

Definition. Although it is relatively easy to point to the activities within the compass of tort law, it is not so simple to offer a satisfactory definition of a tort. The term itself is a derivation of the Latin word, *tortus*, which means twisted or crooked. The expression found its way into the early English language as a synonym for the word "wrong". It is no longer used in everyday language, but it has survived as a technical legal term to this day.[1] Many authors have striven to define tort law and to mark it off from criminal law, contract law and quasi-contract law, but none of them has been entirely successful. Perhaps the best working definition so far produced is a civil wrong, other than a breach of contract, which the law will redress by an award of damages.[2] But even this formulation does not tell us very much. It merely asserts that a tort consists of conduct for which the courts will order compensation, which is almost as circular as saying that a tort is a tort. A tort is a legal construct which only exists where the law says it exists.[3]

Footnote(s)

1 *Lawson v. Wellesley Hospital*, [1975] O.J. No. 2443, 9 O.R. (2d) 677 at 681, *per* Dubin J.A. (Ont. C.A.), affd on another point [1977] S.C.J. No. 83, [1978] 1 S.C.R. 893 (S.C.C.).

2 Fleming, *The Law of Torts*, 10th ed. (North Ryde, N.S.W.: LBC Information Services, 2011), at 1; *Prosser and Keeton on the Law of Torts*, 5th ed. (St. Paul, Minn.: West Pub Co., 1984), at 1-2, reproduces several definitions; Williams and Hepple, *Foundations of the Law of Torts* (London: Butterworths, 1976); for an excellent treatise on the Québec law, see Baudouin, *La Responsabilité Civile*, 6th ed. (Cowansville, Qué.: Yvon Blais, 2003); see Dobbs, *The Law of Torts* (St.

Using Halsbury's

Start your research with the Companion Guide and Consolidated Index volume. Use keywords to find the relevant subject. Once you find your specific topic, the Companion Guide and Consolidated Index will provide the title identifier and paragraph numbers of the major paragraph about your topic. Find the commentary volume that contains the title identifier and then locate the specific paragraph number. Refer to the Cumulative Supplement to update your research.

KEY TERMS

CED Index, 136
Index Key, 136
Table of Regulations, 135
Table of Rules, 135
Table of Statutes, 135

EXERCISES

1. Using the print version of the CED, find a general statement of British Columbia law concerning whether the parents of a child are each equally entitled to be appointed the child's guardian. Cite the applicable legislation.

2. Using the print version of the CED, find a general statement of Ontario law concerning whether an individual's driver's licence can be suspended under the demerit point system. Cite the applicable legislation.

3. Using the print version of the CED, find a general statement of Ontario law concerning the limitation period for commencing a tort action for damages. Cite the applicable legislation.

4. Using the print version of the CED, find a general statement of the law concerning how a residential landlord can terminate a tenant's tenancy early for cause, for non-payment of rent. Cite the applicable legislation.

Legal Encyclopedias —Computerized

11

LEARNING OUTCOMES

After reading this chapter, you will understand:

- How to gain access to the *Canadian Encyclopedic Digest* (CED) online

- How to find information in the CED online by browsing the table of contents for specific content

- How to conduct a plain language search of the CED online

- How to conduct a Boolean terms and connectors search of the CED online

- How to conduct a template search of the CED online

- How to gain access to *Halsbury's Laws of Canada* (Halsbury's) online

- How to find information in Halsbury's online by browsing the table of contents for specific content

- How to conduct a Boolean terms and connectors search of Halsbury's online

Introduction

This chapter deals with the computerized versions of the two Canadian legal encyclopedias whose paper versions we discussed in Chapter 10—the *Canadian Encyclopedic Digest* (CED) and *Halsbury's Laws of Canada* (Halsbury's).

Canadian Encyclopedic Digest (CED) Online

The computerized version of the CED is available online through a subscription service offered by WestlawNext Canada (Westlaw). The online version combines the content of both the Western and the Ontario editions of the paper CED, and it uses the same classification numbering system as the paper version.

Using the Computerized Version of the CED

After signing on to Westlaw, select "Canadian Encyclopedic Digest" under the Commentary category in the Browse (All Content) section of Westlaw's homepage.

With the online version of the CED, there are two main ways to look for information. You can either browse the table of contents for specific content or search the CED using one of three available search options:

1. a plain language search,
2. a Boolean terms and connectors search, or
3. a template search.

In what follows, we are going to illustrate each of these methods, using the same example that we used to illustrate the paper version of the CED in Chapter 10.

Example

A client in Toronto, Ontario, has a cocker spaniel that barks constantly. One day last month, the client's neighbour went to her apartment to complain. When the client opened the door, the dog rushed out to attack the neighbour, who fell backward and broke his leg. The neighbour is now suing the client for compensation for the injuries caused by the dog. Can the client be held legally responsible for her canine companion's dastardly act?

To advise the client, you will need to find a general statement of the law about whether a dog owner in Ontario is responsible for injuries caused by his or her dog.

Browsing the Table of Contents

When you go to the CED homepage, a table of contents is displayed. It lists all the subject titles in the CED in alphabetical order, allowing you to browse specific content within any title easily. Each subject title in this listing acts as a hyperlink to the subject's full content. As your search advances, you will find successive links to increasingly specific information within the subject area. Figure 11.1 shows a portion of the table of contents you will find at the CED homepage.

Figure 11.1   Sample of the Online CED's Table of Contents

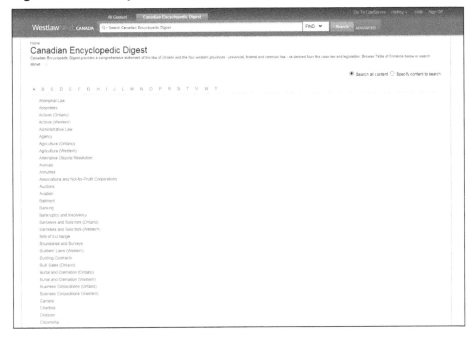

Figure 11.2 shows the topics and subtopics into which the subject title "Animals" breaks down once you select it in the table of contents.

Figure 11.2   Topics and Subtopics in the Online CED Table of Contents

As you can see, the subject title is broken down into main topic headings (identified by Roman numeral and name) and subtopic headings (identified by Arabic number and name). Browse through these two levels of numbered headings to find the ones that correspond most closely to your research topic. Under the main topic heading "X—Dogs," select the subtopic heading "6—Liability for Injuries Inflicted by Dogs." This will lead you to a new list of headings (or topics) under the main topic of "Liability for Injuries Inflicted by Dogs."

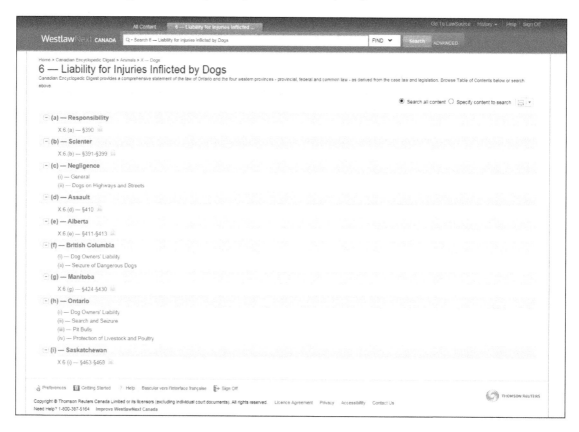

This table of contents lists further topic-specific subheadings. Next, under the entry "(h)—Ontario," choose the sub-entry "(i)—Dog Owners' Liability." This causes the classification number of the research topic ("X.6.(h).(i)") to be displayed as a link beside a reference to the relevant paragraph numbers ("§431-§442"). To the right is a document icon.

Choose either the classification number and paragraph reference, which constitute a single link, or the document icon (also a link). Either link will take you to the text of the paragraph(s) that contain the general statement of the law concerning dog owners' liability in Ontario. Figure 11.3 shows an excerpt from this text.

Figure 11.3   Excerpt from Paragraphs 431–442 (Classification X.6.(h).(i))

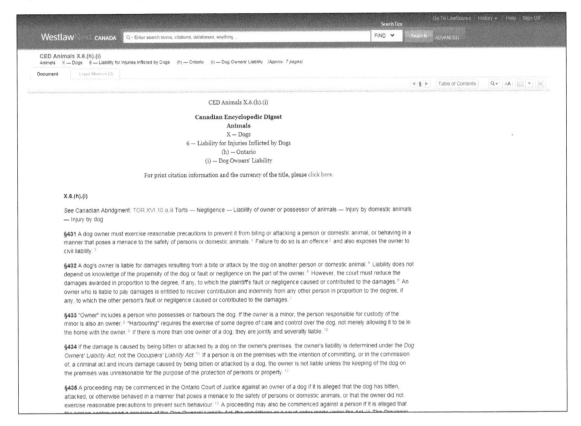

As you can see, the classification of your specific topic ("X.6.(h).(i)") is displayed at the top of the page, together with the name and title of each heading and subheading within the subject title. A cross-reference to the topic's classification number (TOR.XVI.10.a.iii) in the *Canadian Abridgment Case Digests* is provided below. (See Chapter 13 for a complete discussion of the *Canadian Abridgment Case Digests*.) Below that is the text of the relevant paragraph(s).

You can look at paragraphs of adjoining classifications by selecting the green arrows on either side of the paragraph symbol (§), at the top of the screen.

Conducting a Plain Language Search of the CED Online

At the top of the online CED's homepage (see Figure 11.1) is a search box. To conduct a **plain language search**, enter descriptive terms or keywords about your research topic into the search box and select Search. You do not need to use any operators or connectors. You do not have to draft a complete sentence or question; if

plain language search
method of searching a computerized source by means of a question, a sentence, or descriptive words, without using special syntax such as connectors and truncation symbols

you do, the CED will search only for matches of the keywords in your question. Plurals and variations of entered terms are automatically searched.

The following are examples of a plain language search into the issue of dog owners' liability:

- liability injuries dog Ontario
- are dog owners in Ontario liable for injuries caused by their dog?

Plain language searching is not precise. Searches are interpreted quite broadly by the CED online and may produce documents that include some but not all the terms you enter. You will likely receive a large number of results that you will then need to narrow down, using the filters provided. (See below, under the heading "Working with Your Search Results.") Figure 11.4 shows the results of a plain language search related to our dog example.

Figure 11.4   Plain Language Search

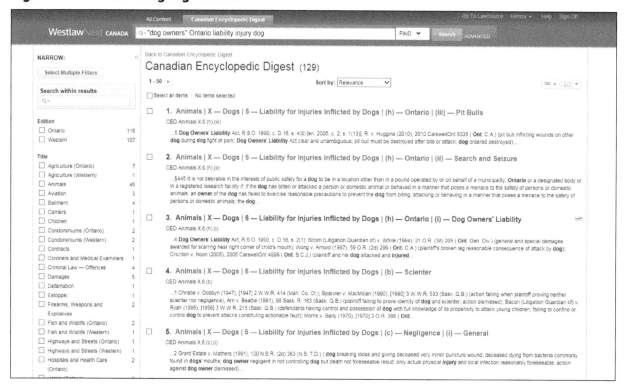

Conducting a Boolean Terms and Connectors Search of the CED Online

Boolean terms and connectors search
Boolean search—method of searching that is based on principles of logic and that requires the use of keywords together with specific syntax

To conduct a **Boolean terms and connectors search**, enter keywords together with Boolean connectors and expanders in the Search box at the top of the homepage, then select Search. A terms and connectors search is more precise than a plain language search. The latter is broad, because your search entry is interpreted loosely and some of the words you entered may be ignored. A terms and connectors search retrieves documents that contain precisely what you ask for. It offers the most control when searching, and it produces focused results.

There are two ways to trigger a terms and connectors search:

1. Preface your Boolean search with the advanced command: "advanced:" or "adv:".

2. Include a proximity or NOT connector; a truncation symbol or root expander; or a substitution symbol. (If you need to refresh your memory of Boolean searching, go back to Chapter 9.) For example, the following entry will automatically trigger a Boolean search because it contains the /*n* connector and a truncation symbol within the search:

> dog /5 owners /10 liability /10 injur! and Ontario

Keep in mind that each computerized source has its own search syntax and will provide you with an explanation of that syntax. To find the CED's explanation of its search syntax, choose the word "Advanced" beside the search box on the homepage.

Figure 11.5 illustrates a Boolean terms and connectors search.

Figure 11.5   A Boolean Terms and Connectors Search

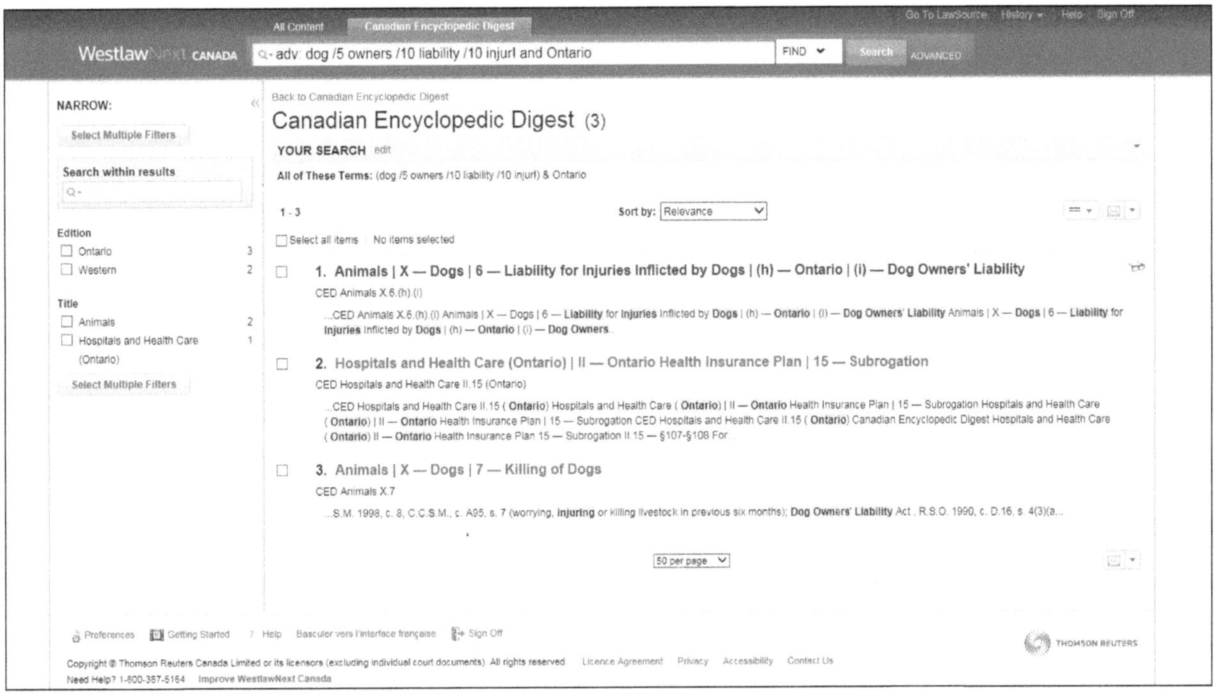

Sometimes it may be helpful to use a combination of browsing and searching when looking for information. Using our dog example, start by browsing the subject titles and select the relevant title—Animals. To search the entire subject title, enter your plain language or Boolean terms and connectors search in the search box. To further narrow your search to a specific main topic or subtopic heading, select "Specify content to search" and then select the box beside the name of the heading(s) you want to search within.

Figure 11.6 illustrates how to search the main topic heading Dogs, within the subject title Animals. As you can see, the tab above the search box confirms that your search is limited to the subject title Animals. The checked boxes confirm that your search is limited to Dogs.

Figure 11.6

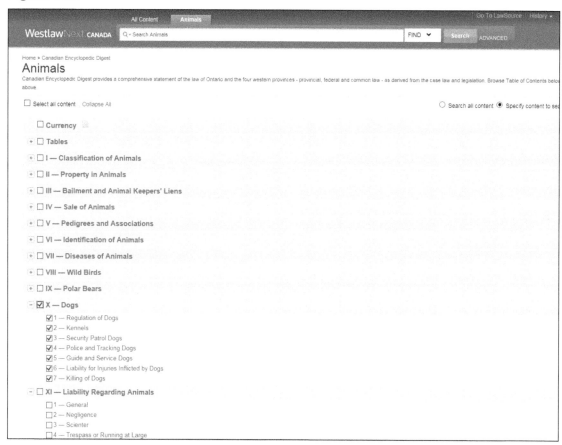

Conducting a Template Search

advanced search template
template containing pre-defined fields that help to develop a Boolean search

The **advanced search template** provides pre-defined fields that help you develop a Boolean search. (Note that using the advanced search template limits you more than an ordinary Boolean search does because it's not possible to use proximity connectors or to express multiple concepts in one search.) To access this template, choose the word "Advanced" beside the search box on the CED homepage. You can search for documents that contain

- all the terms you entered,
- any of the terms you entered, or
- the exact phrase you entered.

You can also exclude documents by specifying certain terms in the appropriate field. As you enter terms in these fields, your search will appear in the Search box at the top of the page.

The advanced search template allows you to search the entire CED (Ontario and/ or Western edition) or to limit your search to a specified subject title and/or classification. Figure 11.7 illustrates the advanced search template being used to search for information about our scenario's main legal issue—Ontario dog owners' liability for injuries caused by their dog.

Figure 11.7   Advanced Search Template

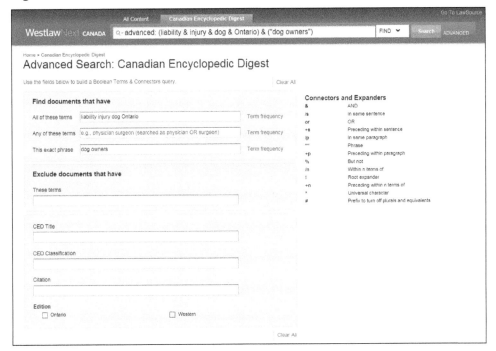

Working with Your Search Results

Using any of the search methods described above will lead you to a Results page containing links to paragraphs in the CED that provide an overview or a summary of the relevant law. Results are displayed on the right-hand side of the screen. Each result provides an excerpt from the relevant classification within a subject title, with the search keywords highlighted. Results are numbered and provide the subject title, as well as the names and classification numbers of the headings and subheadings within that title.

The left side of the screen (see Figure 11.4) shows where your results appear in both the Ontario and Western editions of the CED, across all subject titles. Use the filters to narrow your search results to a specific edition and to a specified subject title(s). You can further narrow your results by entering terms in the "Search within results" field; this will yield paragraphs that contain the additional specified terms. Once you have selected the desired filters, choose Apply Filters.

For example, in Figure 11.4 above, which illustrates the results of a plain language search, there are 129 results, across many different subject titles. (This is often the case with a plain language search, unfortunately.) By narrowing your results to Ontario (Edition) and Animals (Title), you reduce the number of results to 46, as illustrated in Figure 11.8.

When you are ready to view the text of the paragraphs that summarize the relevant law, simply choose the result in the numbered results list that corresponds most closely to your research topic.

Figure 11.9 shows the text of the paragraphs that summarize the law about liability for injuries inflicted by dogs in Ontario. As you can see, each paragraph includes one or more superscript footnote numbers; these numbers correspond to footnotes that cite the relevant legislation and leading cases. To see the information cited in the footnote, hover over the footnote number or select the footnote number to link to the text in the footnote list. There is a hyperlink to every case that is footnoted—simply select the link to see the full text of the case. There are no hyperlinks to statutes and regulations.

Figure 11.8   Search Result with Filters Applied

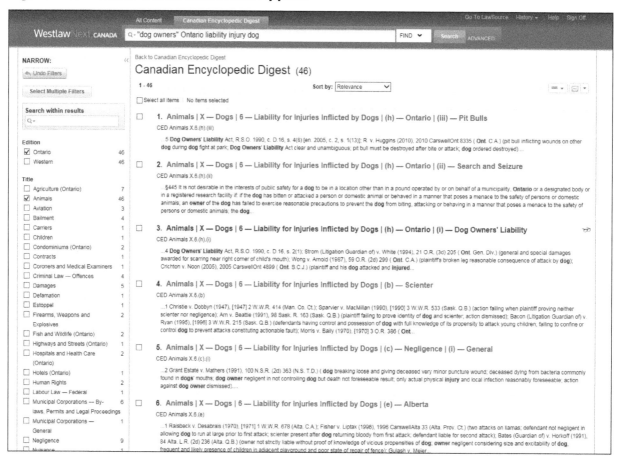

Figure 11.9   End Result of Search with Filters Applied

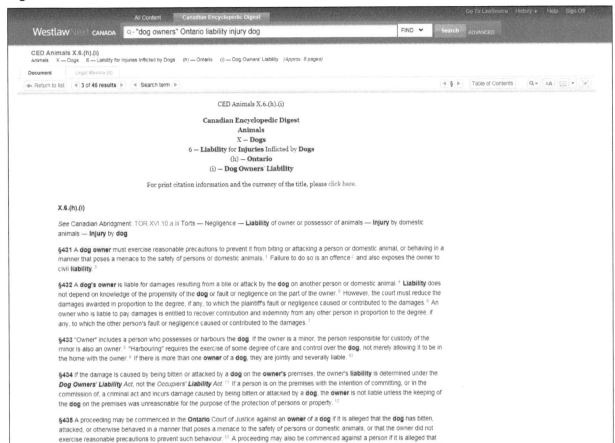

Halsbury's Laws of Canada

Halsbury's is available online as part of Lexis Advance Quicklaw (Quicklaw). As with the CED, you can look for information in the online version of Halsbury's by either searching or browsing.

Again, let's assume you are looking for a statement of the law concerning an Ontario dog owner's liability for injuries caused by her dog. If you don't know the subject title name, you can do a Boolean search.

Start by limiting your search in Quicklaw to the *Halsbury's Laws of Canada* content only. To do this, select the Browse tab at the top of Quicklaw's home page. Then, select Sources—By Category—Secondary Materials. From there, select Legal Encyclopedias (under Content Type). (Select the letter "H" to display only the Halsbury's volumes). Click on "Add All These as Search Filters" to narrow your search to *Halsbury's Laws of Canada* only. (Make sure to do this for all pages included in your results.) Figure 11.10 illustrates the addition of Halsbury's as a pre-search filter.

Figure 11.10   Searching Halsbury's on Quicklaw

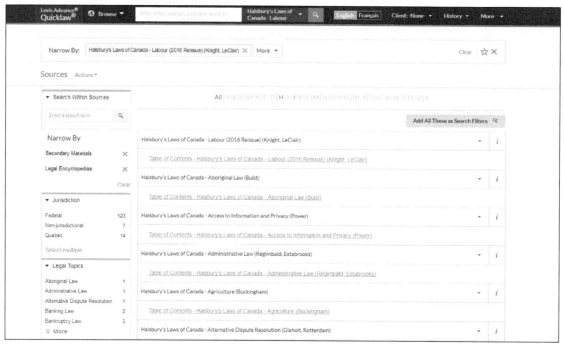

Now, you can enter your search in the search box at the top of the page. For our scenario, the following is a Boolean search phrase you may use:

dog /5 owner and liable or liability /10 injury or damage and Ontario

Figure 11.11 illustrates the results of this search.

Figure 11.11

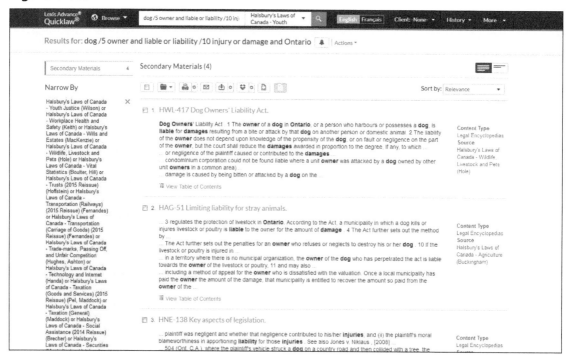

The first item in the results list ("HWL-417 Dog Owners' Liability Act") will lead you to Halsbury's summary of the law concerning this topic.

As you can see, the relevant subject title is Wildlife, Livestock and Pets, which is abbreviated as HWL. (This could be coincidental, or it might be Halsbury's little howl of a joke.) Paragraph 417 is the major paragraph in Halsbury's concerning a dog owner's liability in Ontario. The descriptive heading is *Dog Owners' Liability Act*, and the page includes footnotes that cite the relevant Ontario legislation. Figure 11.12, below, illustrates these elements.

If you know the relevant subject title (Wildlife, Livestock and Pets) to begin with, you can add that title as a search filter. After narrowing your source to Halsbury's as described above, enter the subject title name (Wildlife, Livestock and Pets) in the Search Within Sources box, or locate it in the alphabetical list of titles. Then, enter your Boolean search. Alternatively, you can continue to browse specific content within the title by clicking the Table of Contents link. Expand relevant topics by selecting the arrow beside the topic's name, as illustrated in Figure 11.13.

Here you see the text of the relevant major paragraph, as well as its location within the subject title's levels of information. The title, centred on the page, is broken down into four parts:

- Chapter VI—Torts Involving Animals
- Section 1.—Scienter and Negligence
- Subsection (3)—Legislative Modifications
- Paragraph (e)—Ontario

Paragraph (e) contains the statement of law and is the major paragraph.

Figure 11.12

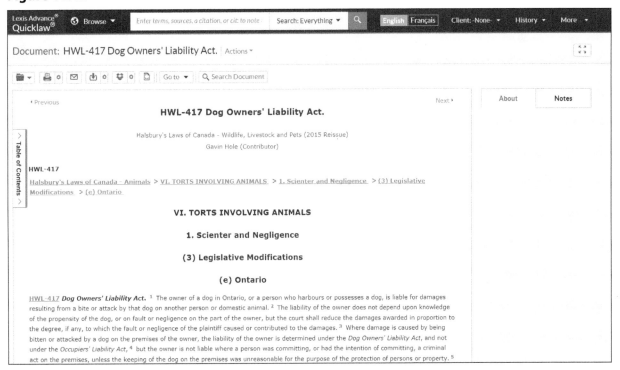

‹ Previous   Next ›

HWL-417 Dog Owners' Liability Act.

Halsbury's Laws of Canada - Wildlife, Livestock and Pets (2015 Reissue)

Gavin Hole (Contributor)

HWL-417

Halsbury's Laws of Canada - Animals > VI. TORTS INVOLVING ANIMALS > 1. Scienter and Negligence > (3) Legislative Modifications > (e) Ontario

VI. TORTS INVOLVING ANIMALS

1. Scienter and Negligence

(3) Legislative Modifications

(e) Ontario

HWL-417 **Dog Owners' Liability Act.** [1] The owner of a dog in Ontario, or a person who harbours or possesses a dog, is liable for damages resulting from a bite or attack by that dog on another person or domestic animal. [2] The liability of the owner does not depend upon knowledge of the propensity of the dog, or on fault or negligence on the part of the owner, but the court shall reduce the damages awarded in proportion to the degree, if any, to which the fault or negligence of the plaintiff caused or contributed to the damages. [3] Where damage is caused by being bitten or attacked by a dog on the premises of the owner, the liability of the owner is determined under the *Dog Owners' Liability Act*, and not under the *Occupiers' Liability*

KEY TERMS

advanced search template, 156
Boolean terms and connectors search, 154
plain language search, 153

EXERCISES

1. Using the online versions of both the CED and Halsbury's, find a general statement of Ontario law about whether both parents of a child are equally entitled to be appointed the child's guardian. Cite the applicable legislation.

2. Using the online versions of both the CED and Halsbury's, find a general statement of Ontario law concerning whether an individual's driver's licence can be suspended under the demerit point system. Cite the applicable legislation.

3. Using the online versions of both the CED and Halsbury's, find a general statement of Ontario law concerning the limitation period for commencing an action for sexual assault. Cite the applicable legislation.

4. Using the online versions of both the CED and Halsbury's, find a general statement of Ontario law about how a residential landlord can terminate a tenant's tenancy early for cause, for non-payment of rent. Cite the applicable legislation.

PART VI

Finding and Updating Statutes, Regulations, and Cases

When you research a legal issue, you have to determine whether any statutes, regulations, and cases are relevant to it. A legal encyclopedia—the best place to start your research—should refer you to any such statutes, regulations, and cases, but there are additional tools, both print and computerized, for finding these sources. We discuss these finding tools in this part.

If your initial research shows you that there *are* relevant statutes, regulations, and cases, you must have the necessary skills to locate the text of those sources and then to update the sources. This part teaches such skills, with reference to both print and computerized resources.

Finding and Updating Statutes and Regulations

LEARNING OUTCOMES

After reading this chapter, you will understand:

- How to find statutes by using computerized sources

- How to find the most current official text of a statute by using computerized sources

- How to find regulations by using computerized sources

- How to find the most current official text of a regulation by using computerized sources

- How to find and update statutes by using paper sources

Introduction

When you research a legal issue, one of your many tasks is to determine whether there is a statute relevant to it. After you determine that there is, you have to establish whether there are any regulations, made under the authority of that statute, that are relevant to your issue. Then you must locate the text of these relevant statutes and regulations. If you are using the statute or regulations as evidence in court, you will need official versions. (Note that an official version or copy of a statute or regulation is deemed to be an accurate statement of the law when adduced in a legal proceeding, subject to proof to the contrary.)

In Chapter 6, we told you that, if you know little or nothing about the issue you're researching, you should start your research with a general statement or overview of the law. You will find this in a secondary source, such as a legal encyclopedia, a legal text, or an article. These sources should refer you to statutes and regulations that are relevant to your issue. Another way to find such relevant legislation is to use finding tools, which we'll talk about in this chapter.

Although we emphasize computerized sources of statutes and regulations in our discussion, we also touch on paper sources. You will almost certainly conduct all your statutes research using computerized sources. However, we are going to mention paper sources for the obvious reason—the ever-present possibility of an apocalypse and the ensuing planet-wide Internet and computer failure, from which the Canadian justice system and all law libraries will emerge entirely intact. Another reason to mention paper sources is that, if you need to see the text of a statute as it originally read any time before approximately 2000, you will have to find it in a paper source. (A third, less compelling reason is that, as of the time of this book's publication, the Law Society of Upper Canada's* competency requirements for paralegals still include an understanding of paper statute and regulation sources.)

Is There a Statute Relevant to Your Issue?

For a researcher, the challenge of dealing with statute law lies not so much in locating the text of the statute as in finding out whether there is a statute that you need to take into account in the first place. This is one of those situations where finding the answer is relatively easy—once you've figured out what the question is.

Whether you are using paper or computerized sources, the easiest and most reliable way to find out whether a statute relevant to your subject exists is to look for general information on the subject in a secondary source, such as the following:

- a legal encyclopedia,
- a legal text, or
- an article.

If a statute figures prominently in the topic, any secondary source will almost certainly mention it. Sometimes, a table of statutes is all you need. Tables are usually found at the front of a text or an encyclopedia entry.

---

*   In September of 2017 the benchers of the Law Society of Upper Canada voted in favour of dropping "of Upper Canada" from their name. At the time this book went to press the new name had not been announced.

The *Canadian Encyclopedic Digest* (CED) and *Halsbury's Laws of Canada* (Halsbury's) are excellent secondary source tools for finding relevant statutes. Find the general statement of the law on the topic, and you will be referred to the governing statute, if there is one. The CED and Halsbury's are available in both paper and computerized versions. (Paper legal encyclopedias are discussed in Chapter 10, and computerized legal encyclopedias are discussed in Chapter 11.)

Working with Statutes: Computerized Sources

The federal government and all provincial/territorial governments now publish and consolidate (that is, incorporate updates to) their statutes electronically on their official websites. Statutes on official websites are kept current to within a few days of any change (the currency date is noted on each statute). No source will be more up to date than the official website.

We have warned in previous chapters that computerized sources are constantly changing. So keep in mind that the examples we use in this chapter reflect only the state of each source as it was at the date of this book's publication. These examples provide general principles—not iron-clad rules—about these sources and how to use them.

Government Website Search Templates: Finding Tools for Statutes

We recommended above that you use a secondary source to determine whether a statute relevant to your research issue exists. If you are feeling bold, however, you can go directly to the official government website and use its search templates to get that information.

Both the federal Justice Laws and the Ontario e-Laws websites include search templates that allow you to search for statutes by using keywords from either the statute's title or its text. Unfortunately, this method is not always swift or dependable; you may find more than one statute containing the keywords you enter. If that happens, you have to scan each statute carefully to determine whether it has anything to do with the issue you are researching.

As of the date of this book's publication, the federal Justice Laws site provides two search templates for finding current consolidated statutes:

1. The Basic Search template provides three search fields: (1) "Keyword(s)," (2) "Title," and (3) "Search in." For example, to determine what statute(s) deals with possession of a gun or firearm, you can enter those terms in the "Keyword(s)" field and choose "Acts" from the "Search in" drop-down menu. The names of all the acts that contain those keywords will be displayed (see Figure 12.1).

2. The Advanced Search template provides more search options, including the ability to search the text of statutes at a specific point in time (from January 2003 onward). (See Figure 12.2.)

Figure 12.1   Basic Search Template: Justice Laws Website

Figure 12.2   Advanced Search Template: Justice Laws Website

The Ontario e-Laws site contains a search template that allows you to search for keywords within all the statutes. You may search titles and contents, or you may restrict your search to titles alone.

Select the Search tab and enter your keyword in the search field. The e-Laws site uses a "fuzzy" search. This means that in addition to finding statutes that contain your keyword search, it will find statutes that contain words similar to your search terms. For example, a search for "legally responsible" will also find "legal responsibility." Select "Use exact search" to search exclusively for the keyword(s) you entered.

To determine the search syntax for e-Laws, select the "Advanced search help" hyperlink. As Figure 12.3 illustrates, the Ontario e-Laws site gives you the option of searching for consolidated law (current or repealed/revoked/spent statutes), source law (statutes as they read when enacted), and period in time law (statutes at a specific point in time—from January 2000 onward).

Figure 12.3   Advanced Search Template: Ontario e-Laws Website

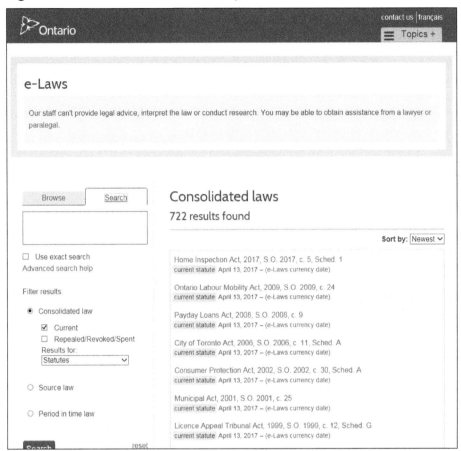

Finding the Text of a Federal Statute

Once you know the name of a federal statute, it is easy to find the text. Use any of the following online sources:

- the Justice Laws website (<http://laws-lois.justice.gc.ca/eng>),
- WestlawNext Canada (Westlaw),
- Lexis Advance Quicklaw (Quicklaw), or
- the Canadian Legal Information Institute (CanLII) website (<http://www.canlii.org>).

Justice Laws Website

The Justice Laws website is the only one of the sources listed above that provides the official version of a federal statute.

There are two ways to find the text of the consolidated version of a federal statute on this website. The first and quickest way is to enter all or part of the name of the statute in the "Find a title" search field on the homepage. A list will appear, showing the titles of all federal statutes containing the word(s) you entered. Select the relevant statute and then select "Go to table of contents." For example, to find the text of the consolidated version of the *Canada Health Act*, enter the complete name of the statute, or enter "Canada" only, or enter "Health" only. If you enter "Health" only, an alphabetical list of all statutes with the word "health" in their title appears. This method is helpful if you can't remember the entire name of the statute you are looking for. Of course, if several statutes show up and you *still* don't remember the name of the one you want, you're not much further ahead.

When you are using the Justice Laws website, the second way to find a statute whose name you know is to browse by title. Select the link "Consolidated Acts" (under the heading Laws). On the resulting page, select the first letter of the name of the statute you are looking for. All statutes that begin with that letter are displayed. Scroll down the list and choose the name of your statute. Figure 12.4 shows the listing that results from browsing by title for the letter "A."

Figure 12.4   Browsing Acts by Title: Justice Laws Website

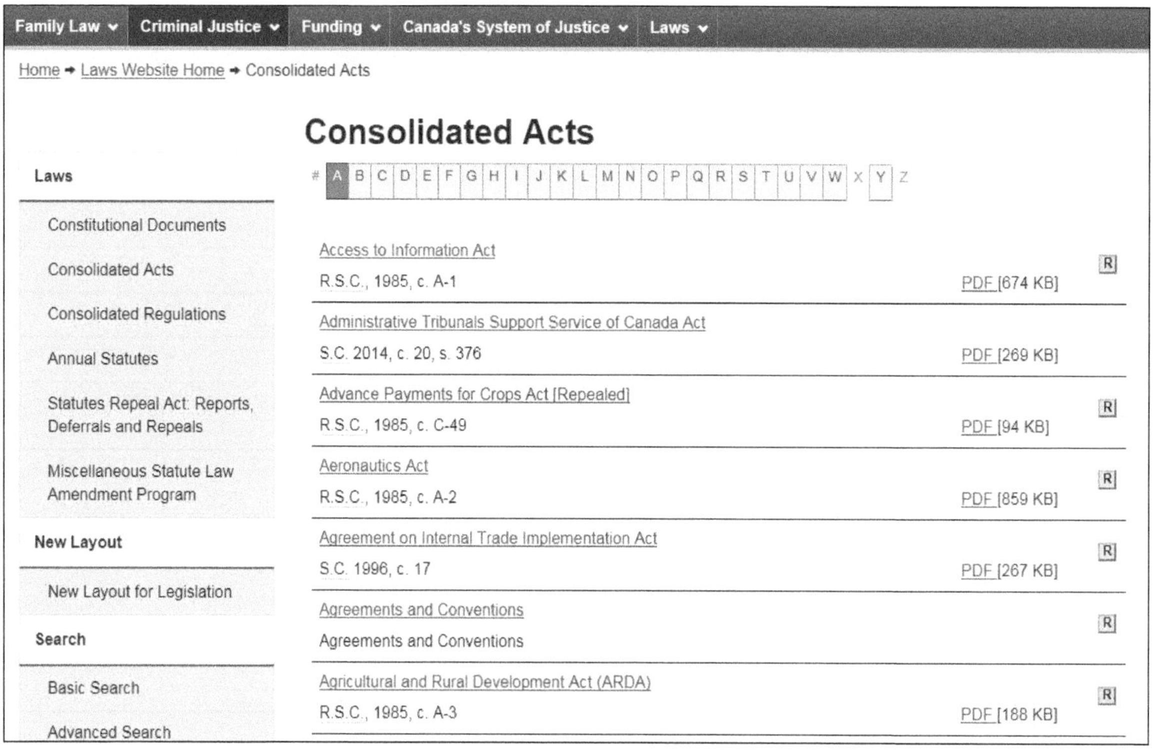

For example, if you want to use this method to find the text of the consolidated version of the *Canada Health Act*, select the letter "C," then scroll down until you find the *Canada Health Act*. Choose the name of the statute; this will take you to the statute's table of contents. (See Figure 12.5.) From the table of contents, you can link to the text of the entire Act by choosing a document format (HTML, XML, or PDF) at the top of the page.

Figure 12.5   Table of Contents for the Canada Health Act: Justice Laws Website

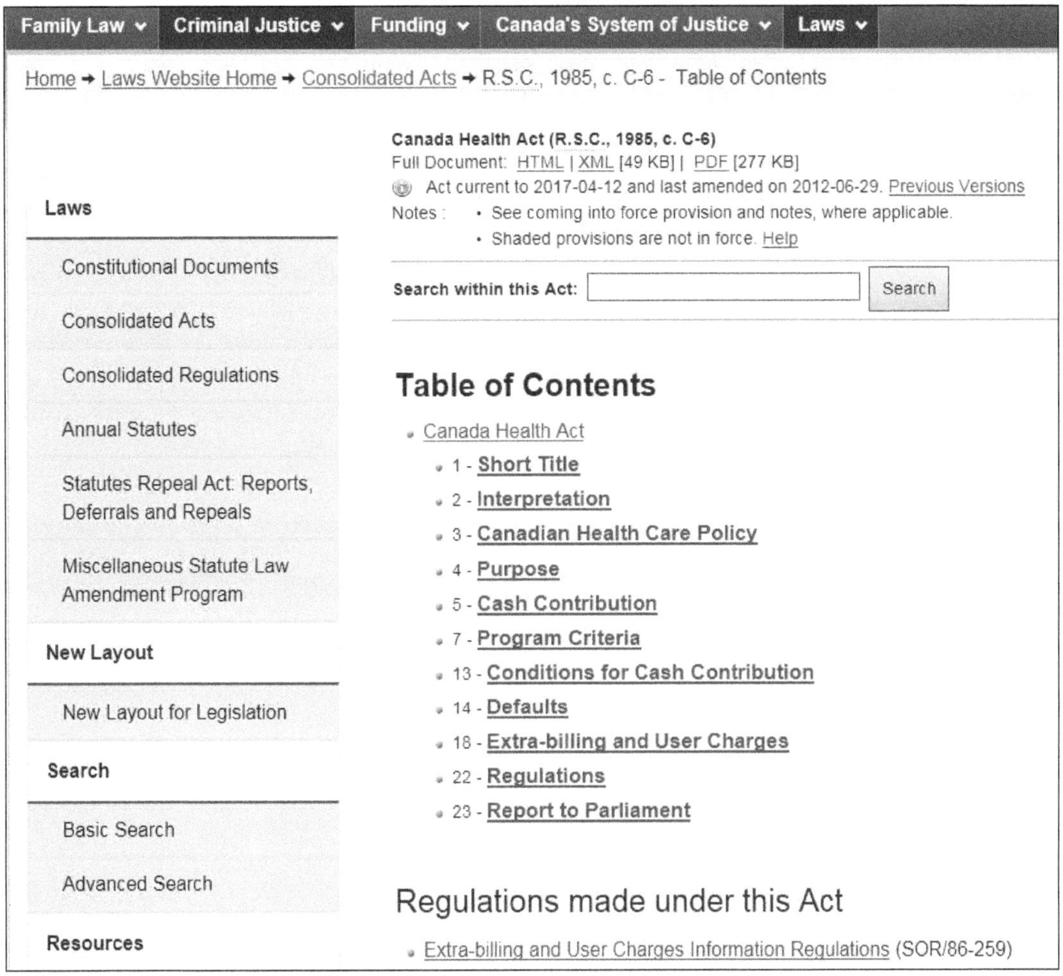

You can link to the text of a specific section of the Act by selecting the appropriate entry in the table of contents. You can move to adjoining sections of the statute by using the Previous Page and Next Page buttons at the top and bottom of each section. You can also select a specific section from the "Go to page" drop-down menu.

The page where the statute's table of contents is shown will also show whether there are regulations made under the Act, and it will provide a link to them.

If you want to see the text of a statute as it read when the statute was enacted, choose "Annual Statutes" (under the heading Laws). When you select the year that the statute was enacted, all statutes enacted in that year are listed, sorted by chapter number. The long title of the statute is listed, together with the bill number and the date that it was given royal assent. For example, to find the text of the *Physical Activity and Sport Act*, which was enacted in 2003, select "Annual Statutes" and then choose the year 2003. Find the statute's name in the list and select it to link to the text of the statute as first enacted. Annual statutes enacted before 2001 are not available on the Justice Laws website.

Westlaw

The text of federal statutes is also available as part of the Westlaw subscription service. Once you know the name of the statute, there are several different ways to find its text.

The first way is to enter the name of the statute in the Search box at the top of the homepage. This method provides a link to the statute, and it displays cases and decisions and commentary that mention the statute.

A second method is to use the Find and KeyCite a Statute or Regulation by Name search template. The easiest way to access this template is to select it from the FIND drop-down menu beside the Search box on the homepage. Note that you can also access this template using the Find and KeyCite by Name tab in the Browse section of the Westlaw homepage, or from the Find By Name links on the right side of the Law Source home page. Enter the name of the statute and select the jurisdiction ("Federal"), as follows:

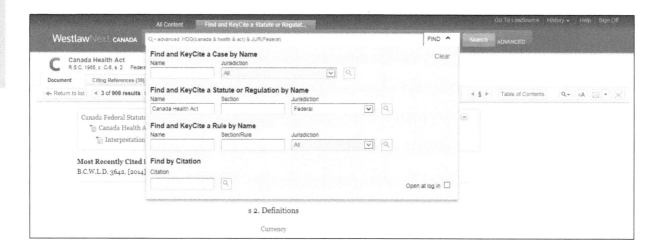

Figure 12.6 shows the results of a search for the *Canada Health Act* using this method. As you can see, the Act's contents are listed by section. Select the link to the section you want to look at. The green letter "C" to the left of each listing indicates that case law citing that section is available. Select it to link directly to the case law.

Figure 12.7 illustrates the text of s 2 of the *Canada Health Act*. From this page, you can link to the table of contents for the entire statute by selecting the name of the Act at the top of the page.

To see the text of the entire statute, start by choosing any section. Once you are viewing the text of a statute section, click on the document icon beside the name of the statute in the boxed menu at the top of the page.

A third way to find the text of federal statutes on Westlaw is by browsing Statutes and Regulations under the heading Primary Sources, available on the homepage. Select "Statutes and Regulations," then "Federal," then "Federal Statutes (English)." Browse the alphabetical list of statutes to find the name of the statute, and select it to link to the table of contents. You can then select the section(s) you want to view.

Figure 12.6   Results of Search for Canada Health Act: Westlaw

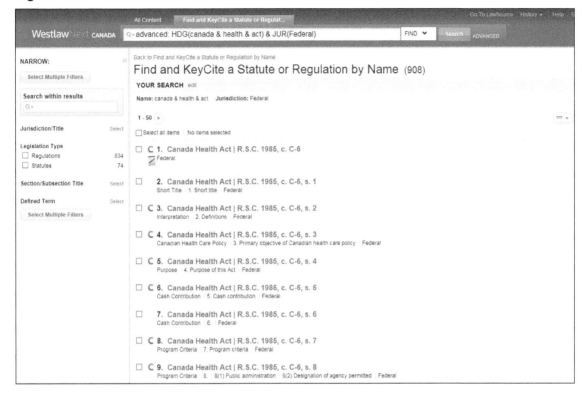

Figure 12.7   Section 2 of the Canada Health Act: Westlaw

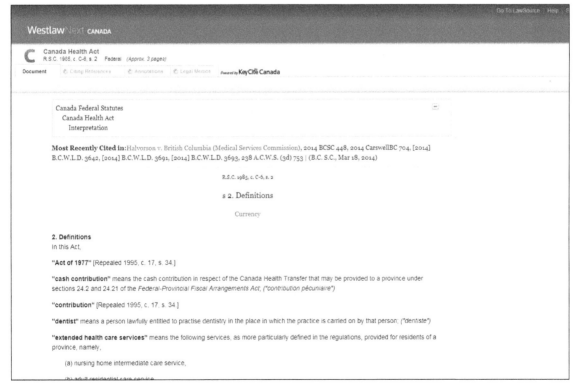

Figure 12.8 shows the *Canada Health Act*'s table of contents as shown on Westlaw.

Quicklaw

The easiest way to find the text of the current consolidation of a federal statute on Quicklaw is to enter the name of the statute in the red search box on the home page.

As you type in the name of the statute, a list of suggested documents appears in a drop-down menu as illustrated in Figure 12.9 (for a search of the *Canada Health Act*). Select the relevant document from this drop-down menu—in this case, RSC 1985, c C-6 (or type in the full name of the statute), and then click the magnifying glass (or press Enter) to run your search. If you want to find the text of a specific section of the statute, include the section number preceded by the word "section" (not s). For example, to find s 13 of the *Canada Health Act*, enter "Canada Health Act section 13" in the red search box.

From the Results list that appears, select "Legislation." Narrow the choices by "Content Type (Acts)" and "Jurisdiction (Federal)," and then choose the relevant document.

Figure 12.10 illustrates the results of a search for s 13 of the *Canada Health Act*.

Note that the results include past versions (point in time) if available, as well as the prior consolidation of the statute section.

Figure 12.8   Canada Health Act's Table of Contents: Westlaw

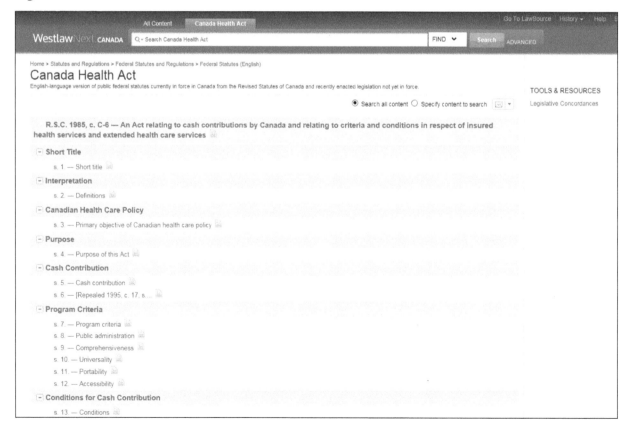

Figure 12.9   Searching for Legislation: Quicklaw

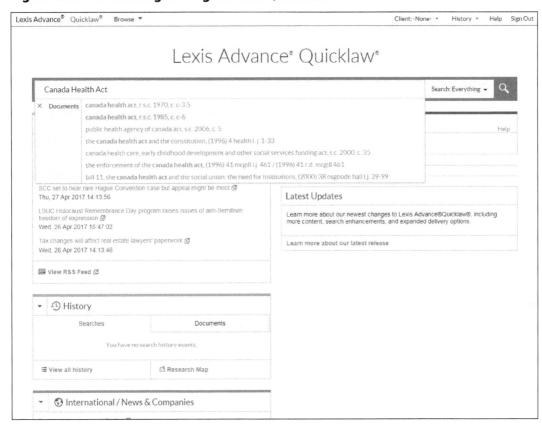

Figure 12.10   Section 13 of the Canada Health Act: Quicklaw

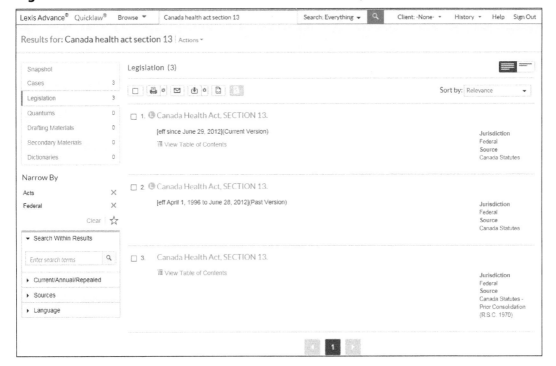

Once you select the relevant result, the text of the current version of the statute section is displayed as illustrated in Figure 12.11. As you can see, Quicklaw notes both the currency date and the effective date of the current version.

Point in time versions, if available, are displayed in the Point in Time list in the About this document box on the right side. The blue text is a hyperlink to the text of the point in time version. In our example, there is a point in time version available for s 13 of the *Canada Health Act*. To see the text of s 13 as it read in 1999, for example, click the blue text. Note that this list will not appear if no point in time versions are available.

To see surrounding sections of the statute, use the Next and Previous links at the top of the page. To see all sections of the statute, open the Table of Contents by clicking on the Table of Contents tab. You can then select any section you want to view.

You can also browse by title for federal statutes. Select the Browse drop-down on the homepage and choose "Sources" and then choose "By Category." Select "Legislation" and then "Narrow By Content Type (Acts)" and "Jurisdiction (Federal)." To see current consolidated law, select "Table of Contents—Canada Statutes." You can then browse alphabetically for the statute you want to view. Using the arrow icon, expand the statute to view the headings in the table of contents. Again, using the arrow icon, expand the section you want to view the text of. Figure 12.12 shows the results of browsing for s 2 of the *Canada Health Act* by using this method. Click Section 2 (in blue text) to view the section.

Figure 12.11   Section 1 of the Canada Health Act: Quicklaw

Figure 12.12   Section 2 of the Canada Health Act: Quicklaw

▸ Canada Employment Insurance Financing Board Act [REPEALED]	☆ Q°
▸ Canada Evidence Act	☆ Q°
▸ Canada Foundation for Sustainable Development Technology Act	☆ Q°
▸ Canada Fund for Africa Act	☆ Q°
▸ Canada Grain Act	☆ Q°
▾ Canada Health Act	☆ Q°
☐ Long Title	
☐ Preamble	
☐ Enactment Clause	
▸ SHORT TITLE	☆ Q°
▾ INTERPRETATION	☆ Q°
☐ SECTION 2	
▾ CANADIAN HEALTH CARE POLICY	☆ Q°
☐ SECTION 3	
▸ PURPOSE	☆ Q°
▸ CASH CONTRIBUTION	☆ Q°
▸ PROGRAM CRITERIA	☆ Q°
▸ CONDITIONS FOR CASH CONTRIBUTION	☆ Q°
▸ DEFAULTS	☆ Q°
▸ EXTRA-BILLING AND USER CHARGES	☆ Q°
▸ REGULATIONS	☆ Q°
▸ REPORT TO PARLIAMENT	☆ Q°
▸ Canada Health Care, Early Childhood Development and Other Social Services Funding Act	☆ Q°
▸ Canada Labour Code	☆ Q°
▸ Canada Lands Surveyors Act	☆ Q°
▸ Canada Lands Surveys Act	☆ Q°

Canadian Legal Information Institute (CanLII)

If you are using CanLII (<http://www.canlii.org>), the simplest way to find the text of a federal statute is to enter the statute's name in the search box at the top of the homepage.

You can also find the text by browsing. On the homepage, under the heading Browse, choose "Canada (Federal)." On the resulting page, under the heading Legislation, select "Statutes and Regulations." This will take you to another page. Here, under the heading Consolidated Statutes of Canada, select the letter that corresponds to the first letter of the statute's name. This will result in an alphabetical list of all federal statutes starting with the letter you've chosen. Scroll down to find the name of the statute you're looking for. The name of the statute is a link to its text.

For example, to find the text of the *Divorce Act*, select the letter "D," scroll down, and select "Divorce Act." Figure 12.13 shows the first page of the text of the *Divorce Act* as it appears on CanLII.

As you can see from Figure 12.13, the text of a statute on CanLII provides four additional options: Versions, Noteup, Regulations, and Amendments. They appear at the top of the page, under the statute's title. These options enable you to do the following, respectively: compare different versions of the statute (if different versions are available); note up the statute; link directly to any regulations associated with the statute; and view any amendments to the statute (since 2000).

Figure 12.13 First Page of the Divorce Act: CanLII

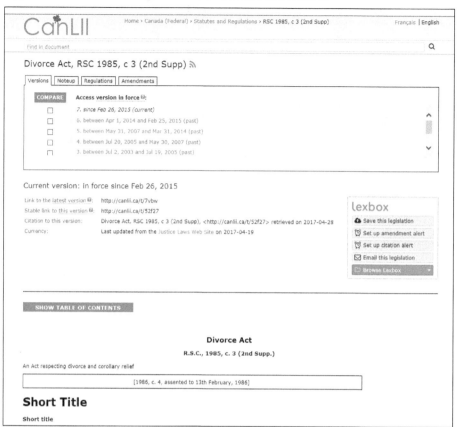

Finding the Text of an Ontario Statute

Once you know the name of an Ontario statute, you will have no difficulty finding the text online. Use any of the following sources:

- the Ontario e-Laws website (<http://www.ontario.ca/laws>),
- WestlawNext Canada (Westlaw),
- LexisAdvance Quicklaw (Quicklaw), or
- the Canadian Legal Information Institute (CanLII) website (<http://www.canlii.org>).

Ontario e-Laws Website

Note that the Ontario e-Laws website is the only one that provides the official version of an Ontario statute.

On e-Laws, there are two ways to search by name for the text of an Ontario statute whose name you know:

1. The first way is to browse by title, using the statute's name. Under the Browse tab select "Consolidated law" (to see the text of the current version)

or "Source law" (to see the text of the statute as originally enacted). With e-Laws, source law is available only as far back as the year 2000.

Select the first letter of the name of the statute to see a list of statutes starting with that letter. To link to the text of the statute, select its name. For example, to find the text of the consolidated version of the *Dog Owners' Liability Act*, select the letter "D" (under the Browse tab) and select "Current consolidated law." Next, choose "Statutes" from the "Results for" drop-down menu. When you select the green Browse button, a list of consolidated statutes starting with the letter "D" will appear. Scroll down the list of statutes until you find the *Dog Owners' Liability Act*. Select the statute's name to view the text of the entire statute. Figure 12.14 illustrates how the text of the statute is displayed. The entire statute appears after the contents.

As you can see, the consolidation period appears at the top of the page, together with links to earlier consolidations. You can link directly to regulations made under the *Dog Owners' Liability Act* by selecting the "Regulations under this Act" tab. To print the statute or download a Word version of its text, select the Print or Download buttons, as applicable.

Figure 12.14   Results of a "Browse by Title" Search for the Dog Owners' Liability Act: Ontario e-Laws Website

2. The second way to find a statute whose name you know is to use the Search tab. Select that tab and then choose "Consolidated law" (to see the text of the current version), "Source law" (to see the text of the statute as originally enacted), or "Period in time law" (to see the text of the statute as it read on a specific date).

   Enter the name of the statute, enclosed in quotation marks, in the Search field and select "Use Exact Search." Choose "Statutes" from the "Results for" drop-down menu and then select "Search."

   To find the text of the *Dog Owners' Liability Act* as it read at the end of 2004, for example, do the following. Select the Search tab and enter "dog owners' liability act" in the Search field, then select "Use Exact Search." Select "Period in time law," enter 2004-12-31 in the "On date" field, choose "Statutes" from the "Result for" drop-down menu, and select the Search button. This will provide a link to the historical version of the statute for the consolidation period December 6, 2000 to March 8, 2005.

As mentioned above, you can also search Ontario statutes on e-Laws by using the Search tab and entering keywords that appear in the title or text. However, it is not efficient to find relevant statutes in this way because you may find more than one statute containing the keywords you entered. You will then have to scan each statute carefully to determine whether it is, in fact, relevant to your research topic. The most reliable finding tool is the CED.

Westlaw

You can search or browse Westlaw to find the text of an Ontario statute online. To do this, follow the same steps you would take to find the text of a federal statute (as set out above). In other words, either (1) enter the name of the Ontario statute in the Search box on the homepage or (2) use the Find and KeyCite a Statute or Regulation by Name search template. If using the second option, simply change the jurisdiction to Ontario.

Quicklaw

You can search or browse Quicklaw to find the text of an Ontario statute. Here, as with Westlaw, simply follow the same steps you would use to find the text of a federal statute. Change the jurisdiction to Ontario and proceed.

Canadian Legal Information Institute (CanLII)

To find the text of an Ontario statute on CanLII (<http://www.canlii.org>), take the following steps. On the homepage, under the heading Browse, choose "Ontario." Then, either enter the name of the statute in the search box at the top of the page or select "Statutes and Regulations" under the heading Legislation and browse by title. On the resulting page (see Figure 12.15), under the heading Consolidated Statutes of Ontario, select the letter that corresponds to the first letter of the statute name you are looking for. This will give you an alphabetical list of statutes. Scroll down and choose the name of the statute you are seeking; this is a link to its text.

Figure 12.15   Statutes and Regulations of Ontario Page: CanLII

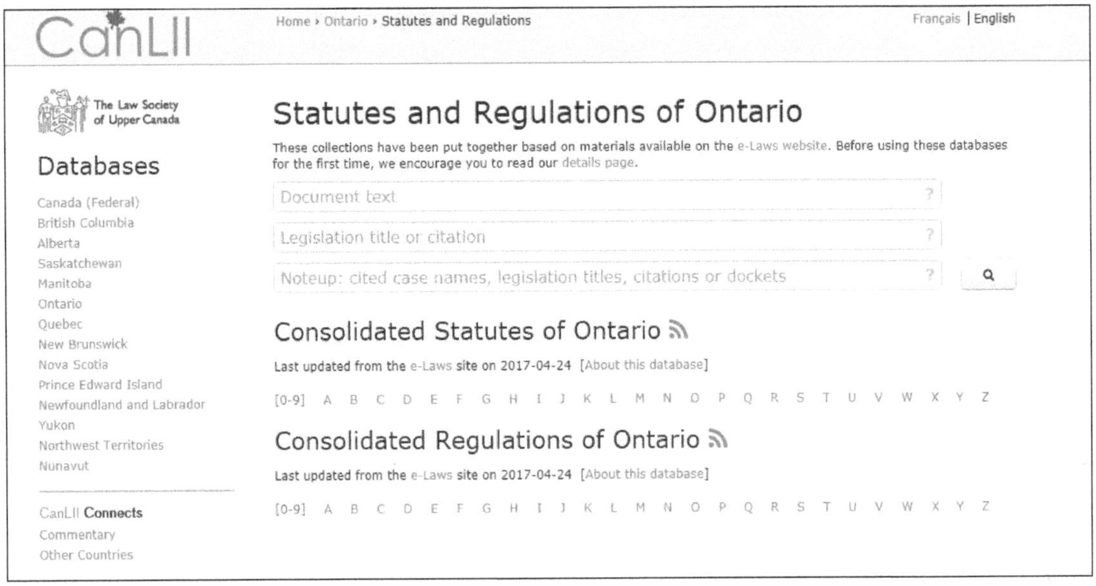

With the text of Ontario statutes on CanLII, as with the text of federal statutes, you are given four additional options: Versions, Noteup, Regulations, and Amendments. They appear at the top of the page, under the Ontario statute's title. These options enable you to do the following, respectively: compare different versions of the statute (if different versions are available); note up the statute; link directly to any regulations associated with the statute; and view any amendments to the statute (since 2000).

Finding the Text of Statutes of Territories or Provinces Other than Ontario

If you need to look at statutes of territories or provinces other than Ontario, consider the following:

- Westlaw and CanLII both provide links to the statutes of each province and territory. When using Quicklaw, use the method described above for finding Ontario statutes, but choose the relevant jurisdiction.

- All provinces and territories have a government website that provides access to their legislation. To find these websites, do a Google search for *province/ territory name* and *legislation*.

Updating Statutes: Computerized Sources

Because the versions of statutes on official government websites are consolidated on an almost daily basis, they are current. (The other electronic sources (WestlawNext Canada, Lexis Advance Quicklaw, and CanLII) are also current but not as current as the government sources.) However, you may sometimes need to update a statute almost to the minute, and that means checking the status of any bills that pertain to that statute. A **bill** is a statute that has not yet been passed by Parliament or (in the case of provincial/territorial statutes) by a provincial/territorial legislature.

bills
proposed statutes that are before Parliament or a provincial/territorial legislature but have not yet been passed

Federal Statutes

Each statute on the Justice Laws website includes a statement, in the header area, identifying both the date on which the statute was last updated and (in most cases) the date on which it was last amended. Federal statutes are generally updated every two weeks.

To find out whether any pending bills might affect a statute you're interested in, check the LEGISinfo page of the Library of Parliament website (at < http://www.parl.gc.ca/LegisInfo/Home.aspx?Language=e&Mode=1&ParliamentSession=42-1>). The status of bills is updated daily.

Ontario Statutes

Looking at the text of a statute on e-Laws, be sure to check the notice of currency, which is located at the beginning of the statute. It states whether there are outstanding amendments to be consolidated into the statute or whether the consolidation is current. The notice also gives information about proclamations (naming a day on which provisions of the statute come into force), if that information is not already reflected in the consolidated statute. Notices of currency are usually up to date to within two business days.

To find out whether any pending bills might affect a particular statute, check the Legislative Assembly of Ontario website (<http://www.ontla.on.ca/web/home.do>). The Status of Bills section is updated daily. To see the updates, go to <http://www.ontla.on.ca/lao/en/bills>. Then click on "Bills from the Current Session of Parliament" or "Bills from Previous and Current Parliaments," and select the desired bill. This provides links to the text of the bill, the bill's status, and debates about the bill.

Working with Regulations: Computerized Sources

Regulations are made under the authority of an act, which is known as the enabling act. They are not made directly by Parliament or by a legislature, but by a body or an individual empowered to make regulations under the enabling act. Typically, that power is delegated to a government minister. Regulations are sometimes referred to as "subordinate legislation." Because they do not have to go through the lengthy legislative process by which statutes are created, they can be made, revised, and repealed by a government quite quickly.

Both the federal and the provincial/territorial governments now publish and update their regulations electronically on their official websites.

Finding Federal Regulations

Use any of the following online sources to find out whether regulations have been made under a federal statute, and, in the event such regulations have been made, to find their texts:

- the Justice Laws website (<http://laws-lois.justice.gc.ca/eng>),
- WestlawNext Canada (Westlaw),
- Lexis AdvanceQuicklaw (Quicklaw), or
- the Canadian Legal Information Institute (CanLII) website (<http://www.canlii.org>).

Generally speaking, you will find the regulation in these sources by using the same general process you used to find the statute itself.

Justice Laws Website

When you use the Justice Laws website to find a statute, you do not have to conduct a separate search for regulations. Once you find the act you are looking for, you will also find a link to the regulations made under it. Beside the name of the statute, to the far right, you will see a small yellow box with the letter "R" inside it. If you select it, you will see a list of the regulations made under the act.

Another way to find regulations on the Justice Laws website is to select the name of the statute. When you retrieve the statute, the resulting table-of-contents page lists all related regulations. Figure 12.5, above, showing the table-of-contents page for the *Canada Health Act*, indicates that there is one related regulation.

Select the name of the regulation to link to its table of contents (see Figure 12.16).

There is also a Basic Search template on the Justice Laws website that lets you search directly for consolidated regulations in the same way that you search for federal statutes (as described above).

Most people know the names of statutes better than they know the names of regulations, so it is easier to find a regulation by first finding the statute. However, if you do happen to know the name of the regulation you are looking for, you can find it by choosing the "Consolidated Regulations" link (under the heading Laws) and then selecting the first letter of the name of the regulation under the heading Regulations by Title.

Westlaw

The text of federal regulations is also available on Westlaw. To browse federal regulations, select the "Statutes and Regulations" link under the Primary Sources heading of either the homepage or LawSource. Select "Federal" and then select "Federal Regulations (English)." An alphabetical list of statute names will appear. Select the name of a statute to see a list of the regulations made under it. Select the name of the regulation to link directly to its table of contents. You can then select the section(s) you want to view.

Figure 12.16   Table of Contents for Regulation Made Under the Canada Health Act: Justice Laws Website

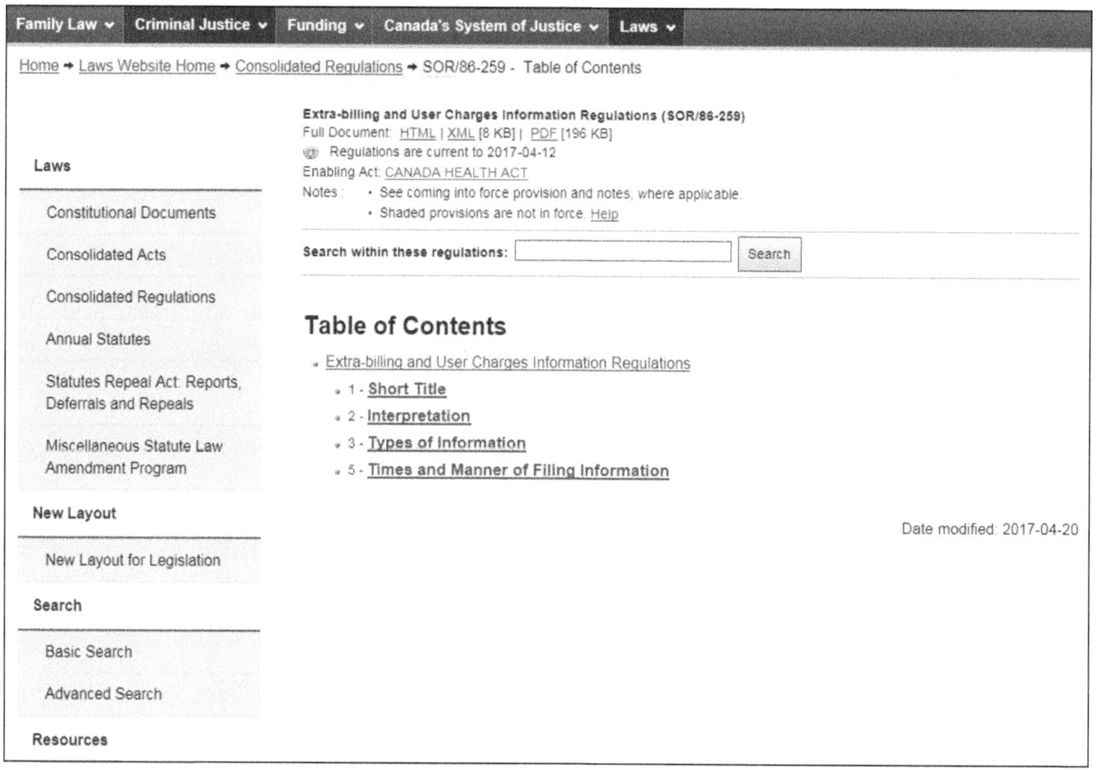

If you know the name of the regulation you are looking for, you can use the Find and KeyCite a Statute or Regulation by Name template, as discussed above for finding a statute using its name. Type in the name of the regulation and a section number, if applicable, and choose "Federal" as the jurisdiction.

Quicklaw

The texts of federal regulations are also available on Quicklaw. Start by entering the name of the enabling statute in the red search field and clicking Search. Select "Legislation" under the Results list on the top left of the page, narrow by "Content Type (Regulations)" and then choose the relevant document.

While viewing a section of a federal statute, you can link to Regulations by selecting "Regulations under this Act" from the Related Content list in the "About this document" box on the right side. It will also display the total number of regulations.

If you know the name of the regulation you are looking for, you can enter that name instead, in the red search field.

Canadian Legal Information Institute (CanLII)

On the homepage of the CanLII website, choose "Canada (Federal)" under the heading Browse. Then enter the name of the statute in the search box at the top of the page. On the resulting page, select the Regulations tab under the title of the statute, and a list of related regulations will be displayed.

Alternatively, choose "Canada (Federal)" and then select "Statutes and Regulations" under the heading Legislation. To find a regulation from this page, you may use one of two methods:

1. Under the heading Consolidated Statutes of Canada, select the letter that corresponds to the first letter of the statute's name. In the resulting list, locate the statute you are looking for. To the right of the statute's name, a link to the related regulations is provided.

2. If you know the name of the regulation you are looking for, look under the heading Consolidated Regulations of Canada and then select the letter that corresponds to the first letter of the regulation's name. This will provide you with an alphabetical list of regulations. Scroll down to find the one you're looking for.

Finding Ontario Regulations

If you are using any of the following sources to find a statute, you will also be able to find out whether regulations have been made under it, and you will be able to retrieve the text of these regulations:

- the Ontario e-Laws website (<http://www.ontario.ca/laws>),
- WestlawNext Canada (Westlaw),
- LexisAdvance Quicklaw (Quicklaw), or
- the Canadian Legal Information Institute (CanLII) website (<http://www.canlii.org>).

Ontario e-Laws Website

On the Ontario e-Laws website, you do not have to conduct separate searches for statutes and regulations. Once you find the text of the statute, regulations made pursuant to it will be listed under the "Regulations under this Act" tab (see Figure 12.14, above). By selecting this tab, you will generate a list of all regulations: select the name of the regulation to retrieve the text. Figure 12.17 shows that there is one regulation (O Reg 157/05, *Pit Bull Controls*) under the *Dog Owners' Liability Act*.

Figure 12.17   Results from Choosing Regulations Under the Dog Owners' Liability Act: Ontario e-Laws Website

If you know the name of a specific regulation, you can find its text by using the Browse or Search tabs, as discussed above with respect to statutes. Select "Regulations" from the "Results for" drop-down menu, after inputting the required information.

Westlaw

To browse Ontario regulations on Westlaw, select the "Statutes and Regulations" link under the Primary Sources heading of either the homepage or LawSource. Select "Ontario" and then select "Ontario Regulations." An alphabetical list of statutes will appear. Select the name of a statute to see a list of associated regulations. Select the name of the regulation to link directly to the regulation's table of contents. From there, you can link to the text.

If you know the name of the regulation you are looking for, you can use the Find and KeyCite a Statute or Regulation by Name template.

Quicklaw

To find the text of an Ontario regulation on Quicklaw, start by entering the name of the enabling statute in the red search field and clicking Search. Select "Legislation" under the Results list on the top left of the page, narrow by "Content Type (Regulations)" and "Jurisdiction (Ontario)," and then choose the relevant document.

While viewing a section of an Ontario statute, you can link to regulations by selecting "Regulations under this Act" from the Related Content list in the "About this document" box on the right side. It will also display the total number of regulations.

If you know the name of the regulation you are looking for, you can enter that name instead, in the red search field.

Canadian Legal Information Institute (CanLII)

To find the text of an Ontario regulation on CanLII, use one of the following methods. If you know the name of the statute but not of the regulation, choose "Ontario" under the heading Browse on the homepage, and then enter the statute's name in the search box at the top of the page. On the resulting page, under the statute's name, you will see a Regulations tab. Select it to see a list of regulations associated with the act. Locate the regulation in the list and select it to see its text.

Alternatively, choose "Ontario" under the heading Browse on the homepage, and then, under the heading Legislation, select "Statutes and Regulations." On the Statutes and Regulations of Ontario page, under the heading Consolidated Statutes of Ontario, select the letter that corresponds to the first letter of the statute's name. Scroll down the list of statutes to find the one you want; a link to associated regulations appears to the right of the statute's name, under the heading Enabled Regulations.

If you know the name of the regulation to begin with, follow the same steps to get from the homepage to the Statutes and Regulations of Ontario page. Then, under the heading Consolidated Regulations of Ontario, select the letter that corresponds to the first letter of the regulation's name. Scroll through the list of regulations until you find the one you're seeking.

Finding Regulations of Territories and Provinces Other than Ontario

All provinces and territories have a government website that provides access to their statutes and regulations. To find these websites, do a Google search for *province/ territory name* and *legislation*.

Westlaw and CanLII both provide links to the regulations of all the provinces/ territories. When using Quicklaw, use the method described above for finding Ontario regulations but choose the relevant jurisdiction.

Updating Regulations: Computerized Sources

Because the electronic versions of regulations are consolidated on an ongoing basis, most computerized sources are very current. However, to fully and obsessively update a regulation, look at the *Canada Gazette* online for federal regulations and the *Ontario Gazette* online for Ontario regulations (the other provinces and territories have their own gazettes).

Federal Regulations

Federal regulations are published in the *Canada Gazette*, Part II, available online at <http://www.gazette.gc.ca/rp-pr/p2/index-eng.html>.

Ontario Regulations

Ontario regulations are published in the *Ontario Gazette*, available online at <http://www.ontario.ca/ontario-gazette>.

Working with Statutes: Paper Sources

There was a time when computerized versions of statutes and regulations were not official; they could not be used for evidentiary purposes in a legal proceeding. You had to introduce the print version. This meant that learning how to use print sources was unavoidable. Today, however, the laws on e-Laws and Justice Laws have official status. For Ontario legislation, this has been the case since 2006. For federal legislation, it has been the case since 2009.

The federal and provincial/territorial governments still publish annual volumes of statutes in print form. However, the most recent consolidation of federal statutes was in 1985, and the most recent consolidation of Ontario statutes was in 1990. This being the case, you are not likely to look for a print statute unless you have no access to computerized sources. One of the few reasons left to learn how to use print sources is that print is currently the only way to see the text of a statute as it originally read at any time before approximately 2000.

Finding Tools: Print Sources of Statutes

Annual statute volumes do not contain a subject index. Revised statute series and consolidated statutes do have index volumes, arranged by subject matter. However, note that these indexes are no more up to date than the revisions themselves. For example, an index to an Ontario statute series will direct you only to statutes that existed, and in the form they existed, in 1990. In the case of a federal statute, the date would be 1985.

To find statutes published since the last annual volume appeared, you will need to use an "index to current bills" tool to locate bills that have been enacted recently. The available finding tools are as follows:

- For federal or provincial bills, use *Canadian Current Law—Legislation*, "Progress of Bills," or *Canadian Abridgment—Legislation Annual*;
- For federal bills only, you can check the *Canada Legislative Index* under the "Titles Index," or the *Canada Statute Citator*; and
- For Ontario bills only, look at the *Ontario Legislative Digest Service* under "Acts Affected," or the *Ontario Statute Citator*.

Finding the Paper Version of a Statute Using Its Citation

The statutory citation gives you the information you need to find the text of the statute in the provincial/territorial or federal annual or revised statute volumes. (See Chapter 2.) The volume title abbreviation will direct you to either the revised statute volumes or the annual statute volumes.

If you are directed to the revised statute volumes, all the statutes are organized in alphabetical order and divided into volumes. Look on the spine of the volumes until you find the one containing the alphanumeric chapter number of your statute.

If you are directed to an annual volume, look for the one for the year indicated in the volume title abbreviation. The statutes for each year are organized in numerical order by chapter number.

Keep in mind that the version of the statute that you find is only as current as the publication date of the revised or annual volume, and will therefore have to be updated (see more below).

Other Print Sources of Statutes

Consolidated and annotated versions of important statutes are published by commercial legal publishers, often annually. If you can find the statute edition for the current year, it will shorten the work involved in checking for amendments. These commercial editions of statutes do not provide official versions of the legislation, but they are usually reliable.

Finding the Text of Bills and Recent Statutes: Paper Sources

As we mentioned above, proposed statutes (statutes that are before Parliament or before a provincial/territorial legislature and have not yet been passed) are called bills. To look for current bills, use the *Ontario Statute Citator* or *Canada Statute Citator*, both of which are discussed more fully below.

Statutes may have come into existence through receiving royal assent, but they may not yet have been bound into an annual volume of statutes. Again, to find these statutes, use the *Ontario Statute Citator* or *Canada Statute Citator*.

Updating Statutes: Paper Sources

Once you've found the text of a statute, you have to update it to find out whether any part of it has been amended or repealed. If you're dealing with a recently enacted statute, you may also need to find out whether it has actually been "proclaimed in force"—that is, whether it has come into effect. Some statutes that have received royal assent sit on the books for a while before anyone has to obey them. Updating a statute using paper sources involves taking the original statute, finding any and all subsequent statutes that have amended the statute, and then cutting and pasting each amendment into the original statute.

Federal Statutes

For amendments to federal statutes, check one of the following sources:

- *Canada Statute Citator*, or
- *Canadian Current Law—Legislation*.

The *Canada Statute Citator* gives the full citations of all statutes in RSC 1985 (*Revised Statutes of Canada*, 1985 revision) and of all federal statutes to date, and it sets out the text of any amendments to those statutes.

Canadian Current Law—Legislation is part of Carswell's *Canadian Abridgment*. Check under "Statutes Amended, Repealed or Proclaimed in Force." Note that *Canadian Current Law—Legislation* has been published only since 1989–90, and it does not provide a cumulative overview of amendments. If you are looking for amendments earlier than the most recent, you will have to go through each annual volume of *Canadian Current Law—Legislation*, as well as through the pamphlets, which are published regularly throughout the year.

To determine the dates on which new or amending statutes were proclaimed in force, check the following:

- the date proposed in the statute itself (this information is usually found at the end of the statute);
- the actual date identified in *Canadian Current Law—Legislation*, under "Statutes Amended, Repealed or Proclaimed in Force"; and
- the date given in the *Canada Statute Citator*, under the name of the individual statute and in the "Monthly Bulletin" (the green pages at the front).

To find proclamation-in-force dates more recent than the date of whichever source you are using, look in a table of proclamations. Use either the one in the

Canada Gazette, Part III or the one in the quarterly index of the *Canada Gazette*, Part I. For the most recent information on proclamations, check individual issues of the *Canada Gazette*, Part I.

Ontario Statutes

For amendments to Ontario statutes, check one of the following sources:

- *Ontario Statute Citator*, or
- *Canadian Current Law—Legislation*.

The *Ontario Statute Citator* gives the full citations of all statutes in RSO 1990 (*Revised Statutes of Ontario*, 1990 revision) and of all subsequent statutes to date, and it sets out the text of all amendments to those statutes.

In *Canadian Current Law—Legislation*, check under "Statutes Amended, Repealed or Proclaimed in Force," under Ontario. Again, note that *Canadian Current Law—Legislation* has been published only since 1989–90 and does not provide a cumulative overview of amendments. You'll have to go through each annual volume, as well as through the pamphlets, to find amendments earlier than the most recent.

For proclamation-in-force dates of new Ontario statutes and amendments, look for the proposed dates in the statute itself and for the actual date of proclamation in any of the following sources:

- *Canadian Current Law—Legislation* under "Statutes Amended, Repealed or Proclaimed in Force (Ontario)";
- the *Ontario Legislative Digest Service*;
- the *Ontario Statute Citator*—the pink "Weekly Bulletin Service" pages at the front of the volume; or
- individual issues of the *Ontario Gazette*.

Working with Regulations: Paper Sources

Finding and updating regulations using paper sources is, and always has been, incredibly difficult and time-consuming. As a result, it is also subject to error. Before regulations were published electronically, there was no choice but to slog through this awful task. Fortunately, though regulations are still published in paper format (see Chapter 2, if you've forgotten the gory details), they are also now published electronically, in up-to-date, reliable versions. This being the case, we cannot bring ourselves to encourage you to try to find and update regulations using paper sources. It would just be too cruel.

KEY TERM

bills, 184

EXERCISES

1. Go to the government website for Manitoba legislation and search the Continuing Consolidation of the Statutes of Manitoba for the *Condominium Act*. What is the full citation of this statute?

2. On e-Laws, browse by title for an Ontario consolidated statute called the *Justices of the Peace Act*.

3. On e-Laws, browse source law for an Ontario public statute enacted in 2001 called the *Good Samaritan Act, 2001*. Find the text of this statute as enacted. What is the purpose of this statute?

4. On e-Laws, browse source law for a regulation(s) filed in 2005 under the Ontario *Tenant Protection Act*. Provide the citation of the regulation(s).

5. On e-Laws, browse period in time law for the Ontario *Medicine Act, 1991* and find the text of the earliest version available on this site. What is the date of this version?

6. Using the Government of Canada (Justice Laws) website, search "Consolidated Acts" for a federal statute called the *Judges Act*.

7. Is there an Ontario statute that governs the transplanting of human organs after death? Include three elements in your response: (a) the kind of information you're being asked for (statute, regulation, update, or something else); (b) what paper research tools and computerized sources you should use; and (c) an answer to the question, with a correct citation of any statute or regulation you are asked to find.

8. What federal statute deals with the sentencing of young offenders? Include three elements in your response: (a) the kind of information you're being asked for (statute, regulation, update, or something else); (b) what paper research tools and computerized sources you should use; and (c) an answer to the question, with a correct citation of any statute or regulation you are asked to find.

9. What Ontario statute provides information about who may adopt infants and children? Are there any regulations made under it? Include three elements in your response: (a) the kind of information you're being asked for (statute, regulation, update, or something else); (b) what paper research tools and computerized sources you should use; and (c) an answer to the question, with a correct citation of any statute or regulation you are asked to find.

10. Your firm's client resides in British Columbia. She recently defaulted on her mortgage payments and the mortgagee is suing for a final order for foreclosure. Which BC statute provides information about the effect of a final order for foreclosure? How do you find the text of this statute? Include three elements in your response: (a) the kind of information you're being asked for (statute, regulation, update, or something else); (b) what paper research tools and computerized sources you should use; and (c) an answer to the question, with a correct citation of any statute or regulation you are asked to find.

Finding and Updating Cases

13

LEARNING OUTCOMES

After reading this chapter, you will understand:

- Why case law is an important part of legal research
- How to find cases using print sources
- How to update cases using print sources
- How to find cases using computerized sources
- How to update cases using computerized sources

Introduction

After determining whether any statutes or regulations are relevant to the issue you are researching (see Chapter 12), you must find out whether there is any case law relevant to it. Case law may interpret or comment on the statutory or regulatory provisions that govern the issue. It may also be a source of binding law. In the case of a common law (judge-made) issue, the case law will be decisive. Therefore, even if your search for a relevant statute produces nothing, you must not assume there is no binding law concerning your issue. You must check the case law. If there is relevant case law, you first have to find the text of the case(s), and then you must update the case(s) to see whether the law is still relevant.

The online coverage of statutes and regulations, as we have seen, is very thorough and generally free. The online coverage of cases is less thorough by comparison, and it tends to be more expensive (though CanLII now offers free access to case law). A further complication, where case law is concerned, is that you may have to turn to print sources when you are looking for the text of a court or tribunal decision, because not all older cases have been computerized.

This chapter discusses how to find and update case law using both print and computer sources.

Getting the Big Picture

With case law, as with statutes and regulations, your first task is to determine whether there is in fact any law relevant to the topic you are researching. And, as with statutes and regulations, we encourage you to start your research by looking in a secondary source, such as

- a legal encyclopedia,
- a textbook,
- an article, or
- a case digest.

The legal encyclopedias (*Canadian Encyclopedic Digest* [CED] and *Halsbury's Laws of Canada* [Halsbury's]) will provide a general statement of the law on the topic and cite relevant case law. However, you may find in these sources only references to the leading cases and not to those that wander into the finer points and minor byways of your issue. The CED and Halsbury's are available in both paper and computerized versions. (Paper legal encyclopedias are discussed in Chapter 10, and computerized legal encyclopedias are discussed in Chapter 11.)

To find a textbook on your topic, check in a law library catalogue under the topic name. (Library catalogues are usually computerized, so you should not have to deal with a print catalogue.)

To find an article on a subject, consult the *Index to Canadian Legal Literature*, which is part of Carswell's *Canadian Abridgment*. The *Canadian Abridgment* is available in print and through the subscription service WestlawNext Canada (Westlaw).

If you want to look beyond the leading cases, look at Carswell's *Canadian Abridgment Case Digests*, discussed in detail below.

Finding and Updating Cases: Print Sources

This part of the chapter covers print sources only and discusses the following topics:

- how to look for cases about a particular subject;
- how to look for cases that interpret a statute;
- how to look for cases that consider a word or a phrase;
- how to look for a case when you have a partial or an incorrect citation (also known as *treasure hunting*);
- how to look for unreported cases;
- how to look for the text of a case by using its citation; and
- how to update cases.

There are a number of different secondary sources that you can use to find case law on the issue you are researching. Which source you use will depend on the reason you are looking for case law. The following questions will help you determine which source you should use:

1. Are you looking for case law dealing with a specific subject or legal issue?

   If so, you should use the *Canadian Abridgment Case Digests*.

2. Are you looking for cases that have interpreted a statute or a section of a statute?

   If so, you should use *Canadian Statute Citations* (part of the *Canadian Abridgment*) or a Canadian or provincial/territorial statute citator.

3. Are you looking for case law that considers a word or a phrase?

   If so, you should use *Words & Phrases Judicially Defined in Canadian Courts and Tribunals* (also part of the *Canadian Abridgment*).

4. Are you treasure hunting—that is, trying to find a case using a partial or an incorrect citation?

   If so, you should use the *Consolidated Table of Cases* or the *Canadian Case Citations* volumes of the *Canadian Abridgment*.

5. Are you looking for an unreported case?

   If so, you should use a digest service such as the *All-Canada Weekly Summaries*.

Looking for Cases About a Particular Subject: Canadian Abridgment Case Digests

If you want to look beyond the leading cases on a subject, the most comprehensive research tool is Carswell's *Canadian Abridgment Case Digests*. This is a multi-volume publication that collects **case digests**, or summaries of cases, from Canadian courts and administrative tribunals, and organizes them by subject area. Each digest pro-

case digests
summaries of how legal issues were decided in particular cases

vides a brief summary of how a legal issue was decided in a particular case, together with a summary of all necessary background facts and the reasons for the decision. Each digest covers only a single legal issue. If a case deals with several legal issues, there is a separate digest for each issue.

Organization of the Canadian Abridgment Case Digests

The current (third) edition of the *Canadian Abridgment Case Digests* contains 55 subject titles. These subject titles fill over 150 hardcover volumes, organized alphabetically by broad subject area. Each of these volumes is numbered, and each is updated by a softcover supplement volume. The supplement volumes are issued annually. Each new annual supplement is cumulative—that is, it incorporates the contents of each previous supplement—and replaces the previous supplement. As a result, there is only one supplement volume for each hardcover volume. The supplements are further updated by monthly softcover editions of *Canadian Current Law—Case Digests*.

Within the hardcover and supplement volumes, the digests are organized by subject and arranged according to a multi-level classification system, called the **key classification system**. Each digest is classified under one of the *Case Digests'* subject titles. Each subject title is given a name and broken down into increasingly specific levels. Main topics within the subject title are identified by a Roman numeral, sub-topics by numbers, and sub-subtopics by letters. All digests that deal with the same topic have the same classification number.

Take, for example, the following classification: CIVIL PRACTICE AND PROCEDURE III.2.d. This represents the following:

> CIVIL PRACTICE AND PROCEDURE
> >   III. Institution of Proceedings
> > >   2. Writ of Summons
> > > >   d. Issuance

In other words, "Civil Practice and Procedure" is a subject title, "Institution of Proceedings" is a main topic (represented by "III"), "Writ of Summons" is a subtopic (represented by "2"), and "Issuance" is a sub-subtopic (represented by "d"). All digests that deal with issuing a writ of summons when instituting civil proceedings have the key classification number III.2.d. Each digest also has its own individual case digest number.

Finding Tools

There are two main tools to help you locate all the digested cases on a particular issue in the *Case Digests*: (1) the Key and Research Guide, and (2) the General Index. Both will direct you to the relevant case digests dealing with your legal issue or topic. Only the Key and Research Guide, however, uses the key classification system.

The **Key and Research Guide** is really an elaborate table of contents. It groups subjects together according to the key classification system. You start by looking up

key classification system
multi-level classification system used in the hardcover and supplement volumes of the *Canadian Abridgment Case Digests*

Key and Research Guide
one of two finding tools used to locate digested cases in the *Canadian Abridgment Case Digests*; uses the key classification system

a term that describes your issue. You will be referred to relevant subject titles and their subtopics according to the key classification system. From there you will be referred to the digests that fall under those titles and subtopics in the relevant permanent volume and supplement. The Key and Research Guide thus allows you to locate your issue within the classification scheme and then look through all the digests that fall under the appropriate title and subtopic. It also provides you with the classification number you will need to use in searching for your issue in any part of the *Canadian Abridgment*. In the current edition of the *Case Digests*, some subject titles are so large that it takes more than one volume to cover them. When that happens, the classification table indicates the volume number in which each main topic of the subject title appears.

The **General Index** arranges terms and keywords alphabetically. Each entry locates the relevant case digests by volume number(s) and case digest numbers. The General Index does not give you the classification number.

General Index
one of two finding tools used to locate digested cases in the *Canadian Abridgment Case Digests*; locates the relevant case digests by volume number(s) and case digest numbers

How to Use the Case Digests

Follow these steps when using the *Case Digests*:

1. Look in the General Index or the Key and Research Guide to find where the relevant case digests are located.
   - The General Index will give you the relevant case digest volume number and the digest numbers.
   - The Key and Research Guide will give you the relevant volume number and the key classification number.
2. Find the hardcover volume that contains your subject title. Look at the digest numbers from the General Index or the classification number from the Key and Research Guide.
   - Scan the digests under the appropriate subject title and classification number, and make a note of the names and citations of important cases.
   - Within each classification number, the digests are set out in reverse chronological order. In other words, the most recent cases come first. Each digest is identified by the key classification number, which is found in the upper right-hand corner of the digest entry, and each is given a digest number, which is found in the upper left-hand corner of the digest entry. The digest entries are numbered consecutively within each volume.
3. Look in the softcover supplement volume to find cases reported after the cut-off date for inclusion in the hardcover volume. Find the subject title in the supplement volume, and then look at the digests under the key classification number.
4. To find cases reported after the cut-off date for inclusion in the supplement volume, consult the monthly softcover issues of *Canadian Current Law— Case Digests*.
   - To find the digests in the monthly issues, look up your topic in the index at the back. The subject titles are set out in alphabetical order.

- The March, June, September, and December issues contain a cumulative index of all digests that have appeared to that date during the year, so begin your search with the most current volume that contains a cumulative index. Then check each subsequent monthly issue.

- You can also use the case law update section provided in the General Index to direct you. The "scope note" at the start of the case law update section sets out the *Canadian Current Law—Case Digests* issues covered in the update section. Look for the subject title and classification number.

An Example

The best way to learn how to use the *Case Digests* is to work through an example. Assume that you are continuing to work on the research problem discussed in Chapters 10 and 11—the one with the cocker spaniel. It reads as follows:

> A client in Toronto, Ontario, has a cocker spaniel that barks constantly. One day last month, the client's neighbour went to her apartment to complain. When the client opened the door, the dog rushed out to attack the neighbour, who fell backward and broke his leg. The neighbour is now suing the client for compensation for the injuries caused by the dog. Can the client be held legally responsible for her canine companion's dastardly act?

In Chapter 10, we used the *Canadian Encyclopedic Digest* to find a general statement of the law relating to injuries caused by dogs, and we found both case law and statute law there. Now we want to use the *Case Digests* to find case law in this area.

USING THE GENERAL INDEX TO FIND THE RELEVANT CASE DIGESTS

Start by looking up the word "Dog" in the General Index. You will be referred to the main topic "Animals." This part of the index is set out in Figure 13.1.

Next, look up the word "Animals" in the General Index. You will be referred to all the topics and subtopics under this main topic. The topic "Injury by animals" tells you to refer to the main topic "Negligence" and the subtopic "Liability of owner or possessor of animals," as illustrated in Figure 13.2. Note that the main topic ("Animals") is in boldface type. Bullets are used to identify the level of each subtopic under the main topic "Animals." Main subtopics have one bullet, subtopics under this main subtopic have two bullets, and sub-subtopics under this subtopic have three bullets.

Next, look up the word "Negligence." This part of the index is set out in Figure 13.3. Note that "Negligence" is the main topic. "Liability of owner or possessor of animals" is a main subtopic under this main topic. "Injury by domestic animals" is a more specific subtopic and "Injury by dog" is an even more specific subtopic.

As you can see, the General Index gives you the relevant volume numbers and case digest numbers in those volumes that deal with your specific topic. For cases dealing with the liability of an owner for injuries caused by his or her dog, you are referred to **TOR 114.**2476-2605 and **TOR 114 Supp.**444-469.

Figure 13.1   Case Digests General Index Showing "Dog"

General Index   Domestic contracts and settlements

Doctrine of cy-près
- General principles, **EST 35Reis.**723-731
- Miscellaneous, **EST 35Reis.**859-862; **EST 35Supp.**27
- Schemes, **EST 35Reis.**850-858
- When cy-près doctrine applicable
- •• Beneficiary ceasing to exist, **EST 35Reis.**757-780; **EST 35Supp.**23-26
- •• Change in purpose of beneficiary, **EST 35Reis.**781-785
- •• Impracticability of carrying out purpose
- ••• General principles, **EST 35Reis.**793-806
- ••• Insufficient funds, **EST 35Reis.**807-813
- •• Miscellaneous, **EST 35Reis.**821-826
- •• Non-existent beneficiary, **EST 35Reis.**732-756
- •• Obsolescence of purpose, **EST 35Reis.**786-792
- •• Sale of devised property, **EST 35Reis.**814
- •• Surplus funds, **EST 35Reis.**815-820
- When doctrine not applicable
- •• Absence of general charitable intent, **EST 35Reis.**827-842
- •• Continuing possibility of original application, **EST 35Reis.**843-849

Documentary evidence, *see* Children in need of protection; Evidence; Motor vehicles, Evidence

Dog, *see* Animals

Domestic animals, *see* Agricultural products, Property in domestic animals

Domestic contracts
- Effect of contract
- •• On spousal support
- ••• Effect on application under dependants' relief legislation, *see* Dependants' relief legislation
- Marriage settlements, *see* Domestic contracts and settlements
- Variation of terms
- •• By inconsistent disposition in will, *see* Estates

Domestic contracts and settlements
- Effect of contract
- •• Miscellaneous, **FAM 47Reis.**3606-3674; **FAM 47Supp.**790-805
- •• On child support, **FAM 47Reis.**3046-3472; **FAM 47Supp.**708-760

- •• On custody and access, **FAM 47Reis.**3473-3605; **FAM 47Supp.**761-789
- •• On division of family property
- ••• General principles, **FAM 47Reis.**1830-2099; **FAM 47Supp.**559-601
- ••• Matrimonial home, **FAM 47Reis.**2100-2220; **FAM 47Supp.**602-618
- ••• Pensions, **FAM 47Reis.**2221-2273; **FAM 47Supp.**619-632
- •• On spousal support
- ••• Terms regarding cost of living adjustments, **FAM 47Reis.**3042-3045; **FAM 47Supp.**706-707
- ••• Under Divorce Act, **FAM 47Reis.**2274-2927; **FAM 47Supp.**633-691
- ••• Under provincial legislation, **FAM 47Reis.**2928-3041; **FAM 47Supp.**692-705
- Enforcement
- •• Effect of death, **FAM 47AReis.**610-630; **FAM 47ASupp.**115-119
- •• Effect of divorce, **FAM 47AReis.**590-609; **FAM 47ASupp.**114
- •• Effect of electing alternate remedy, **FAM 47AReis.**678-694
- •• Effect of reconciliation, **FAM 47AReis.**631-672; **FAM 47ASupp.**120-121
- •• Effect of release against estates, **FAM 47AReis.**673-677; **FAM 47ASupp.**122
- •• General principles, **FAM 47AReis.**322-456; **FAM 47ASupp.**71-93
- •• Jurisdiction of courts, **FAM 47AReis.**457-504; **FAM 47ASupp.**94-103
- •• Practice and procedure, **FAM 47AReis.**505-589; **FAM 47ASupp.**104-113
- General principles, **FAM 47Reis.**950-985; **FAM 47Supp.**381-384
- Incorporation into divorce decree or court order, **FAM 47AReis.**695-748; **FAM 47ASupp.**123-135
- Interpretation, **FAM 47Reis.**3675-3805; **FAM 47Supp.**806-837
- Marriage settlements, **FAM 47AReis.**749-797; **FAM 47ASupp.**136-140
- Miscellaneous, **FAM 47AReis.**822-860; **FAM 47ASupp.**148-172
- Settlements between counsel, **FAM 47AReis.**798-821; **FAM 47ASupp.**141-147
- Termination, **FAM 47Reis.**3806-3834; **FAM 47Supp.**838-844

Figure 13.2 Case Digests General Index Showing "Animals"

* * Miscellaneous, **ADR 2Reis.**710-751; **ADR 2Supp.**180-194

* * Stay of court proceedings

* * * Discretion of court to grant stay, **ADR 2Reis.**443-513; **ADR 2Supp.**83-103

Amortization, *see* Mortgages

Ancillary letters probate, *see* Estates

Animals

* Diseases of animals

18

General Index   Annulment

* * Compensation, **PER 85.**369-385; **PER 85Supp.**22-26

* * Destruction of animals, **PER 85.**351-367; **PER 85Supp.**21

* * General principles, **PER 85.**348-350; **PER 85Supp.**19-20

* * Miscellaneous, **PER 85.**386-390; **PER 85Supp.**27-28

* Injury by animals, *see* Negligence, Liability of owner or possessor of animals

* Injury to animals

* * By railway, **PER 85.**100-265

* * Cattle, **PER 85.**266-276; **PER 85Supp.**8

* * General principles, **PER 85.**1-7; **PER 85Supp.**1-6

* * Malicious injury, **PER 85.**277-329

* * Miscellaneous, **PER 85.**330-347; **PER 85Supp.**9-18

* * On streets and highways

* * * Duty of motorist, **PER 85.**33-87

* * * Miscellaneous, **PER 85.**88-99; **PER 85Supp.**7

* * Stray animals, **PER 85.**8-32

* Miscellaneous, **PER 85.**405-413; **PER 85Supp.**35-73

* Stray animals, **PER 85.**391-404; **PER 85Supp.**29-34

* * General principles, **INS 57AReis.**3190-3192

* * Miscellaneous, **INS 57AReis.**3248-3250

* * Rights of residuary legate, **INS 57AReis.**3246-3247

* * Where annuity in arrears

* * * General principles, **INS 57AReis.**3235-3239

* * * Interest on arrears, **INS 57AReis.**3240-3245

* * Whether corpus chargeable

* * * Where annuity charged on income only, **INS 57AReis.**3229-3231

* * * Where corpus generally chargeable, **INS 57AReis.**3232-3234

Annulment

* Decree or judgment, **FAM 47AReis.**1163-1187

* Effect of annulment on family rights

* * Property, **FAM 47AReis.**1188

* Essential validity

* * Consanguinity and affinity, **FAM 47AReis.**1038-1049

* * Impotence

* * * Evidence, **FAM 47AReis.**1019-1037

* * * General principles, **FAM 47AReis.**962-1004

19   General Index Binder 2015-1

Figure 13.3   Case Digests General Index Showing "Negligence"

Necessity   General Index

- Failure to provide, *see* Failure to provide necessaries
- Jurisdiction of Admiralty Courts, *see* Maritime and admiralty law, Courts with admiralty jurisdiction

Necessity, *see* Criminal law, Defences

Negative easement, *see* Easements, Definitions

Neglected children, *see* Children in need of protection

Negligence
- Causation
- • Concurrent negligence, **TOR 113**.2090-2091; **TOR 113Supp.**1249-1257
- • Foreseeability and remoteness, **TOR 113**.1844-2027; **TOR 113Supp.**1121-1209
- • General principles, **TOR 113**.1837-1842; **TOR 113Supp.**969-1120
- • Intervening causes, **TOR 113**.2028-2080; **TOR 113Supp.**1210-1241
- • Mental and nervous shock, **TOR 113**.2081-2089; **TOR 113Supp.**1242-1248
- • Miscellaneous, **TOR 113**.2092-2410; **TOR 113Supp.**1258-1423
- Contributory negligence
- • Apportionment of liability
- • • Effect on damages, **TOR 113**.3441-3473; **TOR 113Supp.**1863-1878
- • • Equal apportionment, **TOR 113**.3285-3369; **TOR 113Supp.**1819-1857
- • • General principles, **TOR 113**.3275-3283; **TOR 113Supp.**1754-1818
- • • Miscellaneous, **TOR 113**.3475-3633; **TOR 113Supp.**1879-1933
- • • Variation on appeal, **TOR 113**.3370-3440; **TOR 113Supp.**1858-1862
- • At common law
- • • As absolute defence, **TOR 113**.2439-2456; **TOR 113Supp.**1475-1476
- • • Miscellaneous, **TOR 113**.2457-2463; **TOR 113Supp.**1477
- • Defence to breach of statutory duty, **TOR 113**.3072-3083; **TOR 113Supp.**1713-1715
- • General principles, **TOR 113**.2424-2438; **TOR 113Supp.**1428-1474
- • Joint and independent tortfeasors
- • • Contributory negligence of parent or child, *see* Status and capacities of children, Torts

- • • Joint and several liability, **TOR 113**.3125-3161; **TOR 113Supp.**1716-1726
- • • Miscellaneous, **TOR 113**.3270-3274; **TOR 113Supp.**1750-1753
- • • Right of indemnification and contribution, **TOR 113**.3162-3269; **TOR 113Supp.**1727-1749
- • Liability of master for injuries to servant, *see* Employment law
- • Miscellaneous, **TOR 114**.150-269; **TOR 114Supp.**9-27
- • Negligence statutes, **TOR 113**.2464-2489; **TOR 113Supp.**1478-1483
- • Proof of contributory negligence
- • • Duty of care, **TOR 113**.2512-2821; **TOR 113Supp.**1493-1615
- • • Miscellaneous, **TOR 113**.3063-3071; **TOR 113Supp.**1698-1712
- • • Onus of proof, **TOR 113**.2490-2511; **TOR 113Supp.**1484-1492
- • • Plaintiff's knowledge of danger, **TOR 113**.2822-2984; **TOR 113Supp.**1616-1687
- • • Relation to causation, **TOR 113**.2985-3062; **TOR 113Supp.**1688-1697
- • Third party identification
- • • Gratuitous passengers, **TOR 113**.3084-3108
- • • Miscellaneous, **TOR 113**.3109-3124
- • Ultimate negligence
- • • Application to particular situations, **TOR 114**.87-121; **TOR 114Supp.**2-8
- • • Avoidability of negligence, **TOR 114**.139-149
- • • Definition, **TOR 114**.1-10
- • • Knowledge of danger, **TOR 114**.66-75
- • • Loach doctrine, **TOR 114**.122-138
- • • Need for subsequent and severable conduct, **TOR 114**.33-65
- • • Relation to causation, **TOR 114**.76-86
- • • Relevance of doctrine, **TOR 114**.11-32; **TOR 114Supp.**1
- Criminal negligence causing bodily harm, *see* Criminal law, Offences
- Criminal negligence causing death, *see* Criminal law, Offences
- Defences
- • Act of God (vis major)

398

(Figure 13.3 is concluded on the next page.)

Figure 13.3   Concluded

General Index   Negligence

- • • Application of principles, **TOR 114**.3321-3334; **TOR 114Supp.**605
- • • Miscellaneous, **TOR 114**.3336-3342; **TOR 114Supp.**606
- • Common practice, **TOR 114**.3215-3224; **TOR 114Supp.**595-596
- • Exculpatory clauses, **TOR 114**.3184-3214; **TOR 114Supp.**587-594
- • Inevitable accident
- • • Application of principles, **TOR 114**.3225-3288; **TOR 114Supp.**597-600
- • • Miscellaneous, **TOR 114**.3289-3320; **TOR 114Supp.**601-604
- • Mental illness, **TOR 115**.147-149
- • Miscellaneous, **TOR 115**.164-178; **TOR 115Supp.**14-22
- • Plaintiff's carelessness as sole cause of injury, **TOR 115**.151-163; **TOR 115Supp.**8-13
- • Volenti non fit injuria
- • • Intoxicated driver, **TOR 115**.33-128; **TOR 115Supp.**3
- • • Knowledge and appreciation of risk, **TOR 114**.3343-3384; **TOR 114Supp.**607-608
- • • Miscellaneous, **TOR 115**.146
- • • Sporting events, **TOR 115**.129-145; **TOR 115Supp.**4-7
- • • Statutory breach, **TOR 114**.3488-3495
- • • Voluntary acceptance of risk, **TOR 114**.3386-3459; **TOR 114Supp.**609-614
- • • Waiving right of action, **TOR 114**.3460-3487; **TOR 114Supp.**615-618
- • • Willing passengers, **TOR 115**.1-32; **TOR 115Supp.**1-2
- • Duty and standard of care
- • • After accidents, **TOR 113**.1679-1688; **TOR 113Supp.**840-841
- • • Duty of care, **TOR 113**.1033-1362; **TOR 113Supp.**343-600
- • • Emergencies, **TOR 113**.1597-1651; **TOR 113Supp.**834-837
- • • Exercise of statutory powers, **TOR 113**.1707-1731; **TOR 113Supp.**845-859
- • • Fiduciary duty, **TOR 113**.1756-1781; **TOR 113Supp.**878-938
- • • Gratuitous undertakings, **TOR 113**.1689-1706; **TOR 113Supp.**842-844
- • • Gross negligence, **TOR 113**.1732-1743; **TOR 113Supp.**860-872

- • • Intoxication, **TOR 113**.1744-1755; **TOR 113Supp.**873-877
- • • Miscellaneous, **TOR 113**.1782-1836; **TOR 113Supp.**939-968
- • • Rescue, **TOR 113**.1652-1678; **TOR 113Supp.**838-839
- • • Standard of care, **TOR 113**.1363-1596; **TOR 113Supp.**601-833
- • Effect of wrongful conduct, **TOR 113**.2411-2423; **TOR 113Supp.**1424-1427
- • Fatal Accidents Acts, *see* Fatal accidents acts
- • General principles, **TOR 113**.998-1032; **TOR 113Supp.**310-342
- • Liability for environmental damage, *see* Environmental law
- • Liability of owner or possessor of animals ⬅
- • • Criminal liability, **TOR 114**.2814-2830; **TOR 114Supp.**477-479
- • • Distress damage feasant, **TOR 114**.2765-2813
- • • Injury by domestic animals ⬅
- • • • At common law, **TOR 114**.2436-2469
- • • • Injury by dog, **TOR 114**.2476-2605; ⬅ **TOR 114Supp.**444-469
- • • • On highway, **TOR 114**.2606-2698; **TOR 114Supp.**470-473
- • • • Under by-law or statute, **TOR 114**.2470-2475; **TOR 114Supp.**440-443
- • • Injury by wild animals, **TOR 114**.2699-2706; **TOR 114Supp.**474-475
- • • Liability for nuisance, **TOR 114**.2831-2845; **TOR 114Supp.**480
- • • Miscellaneous, **TOR 114**.2874-2881; **TOR 114Supp.**494-498
- • • Regulation of dangerous animals, **TOR 114**.2846-2873; **TOR 114Supp.**481-493
- • • Trespass by animals, **TOR 114**.2707-2764; **TOR 114Supp.**476
- • Miscellaneous, **TOR 115**.1764-1844; **TOR 115Supp.**429-458
- • Motor vehicles, *see* Motor vehicles
- • Occupiers' liability
- • • Definitions
- • • • Contractual entrant, **TOR 114**.964-966; **TOR 114Supp.**165
- • • • Invitee, **TOR 114**.967-999
- • • • Licensee, **TOR 114**.1000-1017
- • • • Occupier, **TOR 114**.905-963; **TOR 114Supp.**146-164

399   General Index Binder 2015-1

TOR refers to the subject title abbreviation for the relevant subject title: "Torts." The number 114 refers to the volume number of the *Case Digests* that contains the subject title "Torts." 114 Supp refers to the corresponding supplement volume. The numbers 2476-2605 refer to the case digest numbers of the case digests in the hard-cover volume that deal with the specific topic. The numbers 444-469 refer to the case digest numbers of case digests in the corresponding supplement volume.

USING THE KEY AND RESEARCH GUIDE TO FIND THE RELEVANT CASE DIGESTS

The *Case Digests* divides the law into main subject titles, and every topic falls under one of these subject titles. If you look up a word or topic that is not an actual subject title, you will be referred to the subject title under which the word or topic falls.

A subject titles table, found at the beginning of the Key and Research Guide, lists all the subject titles in the *Case Digests* and refers you directly to the pages in the key that contain information about each title. If you already know that "Torts" is the subject title relevant to your issue, you can look at the subject titles table; it refers you to page 2-741 of the key (see Figure 13.4).

If you don't know the subject title, use the index portion of the key to look up "Dogs." It refers you to the subject titles that contain information about dogs and provides the relevant main topic and subtopic of each subject title. In our example, the relevant subject title is "Torts." The relevant main topic is topic XVI, and the relevant subtopic is section 10 (see Figure 13.5). Figure 13.6 shows the contents of the subject title "Torts." It tells you that topic XVI (Negligence) is dealt with in volumes 113-115. Next, look at section 10 of topic XVI in the Table of Classification for the subject title "Torts," set out in Figure 13.7. The Table of Classification breaks down, or "classifies," the subject title into increasingly specific subtopics.

As Figure 13.7 shows, section 10 of topic XVI (XVI.10) is broken down into subtopics and sub-subtopics, as follows:

> **10. Liability of owner or possessor of animals**
> a. Injury by domestic animals
>   i. At common law
>   ii. Under by-law or statute
>   iii. Injury by dog
>   A. At common law
>   B. Under by-law or statute
>   C. Injury to other animals

Using this information, you can "classify" your topic. In our example, you are looking for cases dealing with a dog owner's liability under the relevant Ontario statute. The classification number for this specific topic is XVI.10.a.iii.B. All the case digests dealing with this specific topic will have the same classification number. Find the volumes that contain the subject title "Torts" and then find the volume that contains this classification number. Note that when a subject title is contained in more than one volume of the *Case Digests*, the Table of Classification for the subject title will indicate which classifications appear in each volume.

Figure 13.4   Case Digests Subject Titles Table Showing "Torts"

SUBJECT TITLES TABLE

> **EDITOR'S NOTE:** The list of subject titles below is supplemented in the Key by an extensive system of cross-references. The cross-references appear in bold-face and may be of assistance in locating specific topics or related issues. In addition, each subject title includes a Scope Note describing its contents and the location of related issues in other subject titles.

i   Key & Research Guide 2014–1

(Figure 13.4 is concluded on the next page.)

Figure 13.4   Concluded

Figure 13.5   Case Digests Key and Research Guide Showing "Dogs"

DISSOLUTION — *see Business associations IV.3.d, IV.5, VI.4; Financial institutions III; Municipal law II.2; Remedies II.4.i*

DISTINCTIVENESS — *see Intellectual property III.4.g*

DISTRESS — *see Commercial law III.7, IV.7 ; Criminal law V.8; Municipal law XXI.7.f; Public law I; Real property V.18*

DISTRIBUTION — *see Bankruptcy and insolvency XIII.2; Estates and trusts I.6.l*

DISTURBANCE DAMAGES — *see Real property VI.9*

DITCHES — *see Natural resources V; Real property IX*

DIVIDED SUCCESS *effect on costs* — *see Civil practice and procedure XXIII.6.c*

DIVIDENDS — *see Bankruptcy and insolvency XIII; Business associations III.2.b*

DIVISION OF PROPERTY — *see Family law III*

DIVORCE — *see Conflict of laws III.4, III.5.b.ii.C; Constitutional law; Family law VIII*

DNA TESTING — *see Criminal law V.8.j, VII.1.d.i, VIII.2.d; Evidence II.8.j.v, XVI.5.b.iv; Family law XIV.2.d.vi*

DOCKS — *see Maritime and admiralty law VII; Natural resources V.3.d*

DOCTORS — *see Health law III.2.o*

DOCUMENTARY EVIDENCE — *see Criminal law VI.21.c.iv.C; Evidence VII; Motor vehicles XI.1.a.i*

DOCUMENTS — *see Civil practice and procedure X.2; Contracts; Criminal law VI.49, VI.55.d.i.A, VI.55.g.i.A; Evidence VII*

DOGS — *see Personal property I; Torts XVI.10*

DOMAIN NAME — *see Information technology II*

DOMESTIC CONTRACTS — *see Family law V*

DOMESTIC TRIBUNALS — *see Administrative law*

DOMICILE — *see Business associations III.5.a; Conflict of laws*

DOMINANT TENEMENT — *see Real property VIII*

DONATIO MORTIS CAUSA — *see Estates and trusts I.15.d.iii, IV.1.b*

DOUBLE ASPECT — *see Constitutional law VII.5.d; Public law I*

DOUBLE JEOPARDY RULE — *see Criminal law IV.23*

DOUBLE POSSIBILITIES — *see Estates and trusts IX.2*

DOWER — *see Civil practice and procedure XXII.3.b.iii; Family law II.8.a; Real property VII*

DRIVING WHILE DISQUALIFIED — *see Criminal law VI.113*

DRUGGISTS — *see Health law III.2.n*

DRUGS — *see Criminal law XVIII*

DRUNKENNESS — *see Criminal law V.12, VI.98.c.iii, VI.125.b.iv.A; Equity IV.1.c*

**Figure 13.6   Case Digests Key and Research Guide Showing the
Contents of the Subject Title "Torts"**

TORTS
• THIRD EDITION •

CONTENTS

RELATED TITLES

- Tort of passing off — see INTELLECTUAL PROPERTY III.10
- Injunctions to restrain tortuous conduct generally — see REMEDIES II
- Injunctions as remedy for nuisance — see REMEDIES II.2.a.ix.A, II.2.f.i
- Limitation of actions in tort — see CIVIL PRACTICE AND PROCEDURE XXII.5
- Damages for assault and battery — see REMEDIES I.5.a.ii.C
- Exemplary, punitive and aggravated damages for assault and battery — see REMEDIES I.7.c.i
- Damages as remedy for nuisance — see REMEDIES I.5.d.i.C
- Damages for trespass to land — see REMEDIES I.5.d.i.D
- Grounds for awarding exemplary, punitive or aggravated damages for trespass to land — see REMEDIES I.7.c.iv.B

1

Figure 13.7   Table of Classification for Topic XVI.10 of "Torts"

TABLE OF CLASSIFICATION

FINDING AND READING THE TEXT

After you have identified your specific topic by using one of the finding tools discussed above, locate the appropriate volume—in this case, 114—and refer to the digest numbers (2476-2605 in the main volume and 444-469 in the supplement volume) obtained from the General Index, or to the key classification number (XVI.10.a.iii.B) obtained from the Key and Research Guide.

Scan the appropriate digests, and write down the names and citations of the relevant cases.

If you used the General Index, look for appropriate case digest numbers in the upper left-hand corner of each digest. From your research of our sample issue in the *Canadian Encyclopedic Digest* (see Chapter 10), you know that there is statute law—the *Dog Owners' Liability Act*—governing it. As a result, you can go directly to the digest entries dealing with liability under statute law. The first digest under this heading is number 2526.

If you used the Key and Research Guide, look for the key classification number, which appears in the upper right-hand corner of each digest. All the case digests dealing with the research topic will be under classification number XVI.10.a.iii.B. The relevant digests for our example, beginning with digest number 2526, *Crichton v Noon*, are shown in Figure 13.8.

UPDATING YOUR RESEARCH

Look in the supplement volume of the *Case Digests* for digests of any cases that may have been reported after the cut-off date of the permanent volume. If you used the General Index as your finding tool, it will provide the digest numbers in the supplement volume—in this case, 444-469. If you used the Key and Research Guide, find your subject title—in this case, "Torts"—and then look under the relevant classification number, in this case, XVI.10.a.iii.B.

To update beyond the supplement's cut-off date (the end of the previous calendar year), check each monthly softcover issue of *Canadian Current Law—Case Digests*.

Looking for Cases That Interpret a Statute

You can consult a number of different sources to find cases that have interpreted or applied a statute, including

- the *Canadian Abridgment*'s *Canadian Statute Citations*,
- statute citators, and
- annotated statutes.

Canadian Statute Citations

Canadian Statute Citations is part of the *Canadian Abridgment* and contains citations of cases that interpret both federal and provincial/territorial statutes. Federal and provincial/territorial statutes are located in separate volumes. First, locate the hardcover volumes for Canada or for the province in which you are interested; then

Figure 13.8   Case Digests for Classification Number XVI.10.a.iii.B

XVI.10.a.iii.A   TORTS   [2524–2529]

jury by dog — At common law —— Vicious propensities of dog — Owner's knowledge — Scienter — Damages.

Action was brought for damages for injuries inflicted by a dog owned or harboured by defendant. It was shown that the dog was formerly owned by a man in defendant's employ, who lived at defendant's house. The man went away and left the dog with defendant's son to be kept until sent for. The dog went every day with defendant or defendant's son to defendant's place of business. On two occasions, the dog's savage disposition was shown in evidence to have been exhibited, once in the presence of defendant and once in the presence of defendant's son. **Held:** There was ample evidence for the jury that defendant harboured the dog with knowledge of its vicious propensities.

Vaughan v. Wood (1890), 18 S.C.R. 703, 1890 CarswellNB 70 (S.C.C.); affirming (1889), 28 N.B.R. 472, 1889 CarswellNB 36 (C.A.).

2525.   (XVI.10.a.iii.A)

Negligence — Liability of owner or possessor of animals — Injury by domestic animals — Injury by dog — At common law —— Dog biting person — Evidence of previous and subsequent attacks by dog — Admissibility thereof — Owner's knowledge of dog's vicious propensity — Negligence.

In an action brought for an injury inflicted by a dog, it is necessary to allege and prove that defendant had knowledge of the animal's vicious propensity. As soon as that knowledge is shown, the same responsibility attaches to the owner to keep him from doing mischief, as the keeper of an animal, naturally ferocious, would be subject to, and there is no necessity for proving negligence. Plaintiff was bitten by defendant's dog. In an action for damages, 1 witness testified that he had been bitten by the dog one year previously and that he informed defendant of it and another witness testified that he had been bitten by the same dog subsequently to the action having been brought. **Held:** The evidence with reference to the dog's biting on the occasion subsequent to the action having been started, was improperly received, but since the trial Judge expressly withdrew it from the consideration of the jury, the verdict should not be interfered with.

Wilmot v. Vanwart (1877), 17 N.B.R. 456, 1877 CarswellNB 58 (C.A.).

B. *Under by-law or statute*

2526.   (XVI.10.a.iii.B)

Negligence — Liability of owner or possessor of animals — Injury by domestic animals — Injury by dog — Under by-law or statute.

Crichton v. Noon (2005), 2005 CarswellOnt 4899, Searle D.J. (Ont. S.C.J.).

2527.   (XVI.10.a.iii.B)

Negligence — Liability of owner or possessor of animals — Injury by domestic animals — Injury by dog — Under by-law or statute.

Graham (Litigation Guardian of) v. 640847 Ontario Ltd. (2005), 2005 CarswellOnt 3866, Belleghem J. (Ont. S.C.J.).

2528.   (XVI.10.a.iii.B)

Negligence — Liability of owner or possessor of animals — Injury by domestic animals — Injury by dog — Under by-law or statute.

R. v. Callero (2005), 2005 CarswellOnt 3943, 2005 ONCJ 381, De Morais J.P. (Ont. C.J.).

2529.   (XVI.10.a.iii.B)

Negligence — Liability of owner or possessor of animals — Injury by domestic animals — Injury by dog — Under by-law or statute —— Dog jumped onto fence and lunged at victim, injuring her lip — Accused owner of dog was charged under s. 8(4) of Dangerous Dog By-law for owning dog that, "without provocation, attacked, assaulted, wounded, bit, injured or killed person or domestic animal" — Crown provided specific particulars, namely that dog "bit lady on right side upper lip" — Justice of peace acquitted owner, finding reasonable doubt existed as to whether victim's injury was consequence of bite per se, and not accident — Crown appealed — Appeal dismissed — Contrary to Crown's contention that justice of peace erred in finding there was provocation, justice of peace in fact made no finding of provocation, nor did he address legal test for provocation, as no evidence existed on issue — In choosing to charge accused as being owner of dog that "without provocation . . . bit . . . person", Crown had to prove dog bit victim, not merely injured or wounded victim as was open to Crown in drawing information — Justice of peace correctly focused upon offence of dog bite — Sufficient evidence existed to support justice of peace's conclusion.

R. v. Florness (2005), 273 Sask. R. 173, 2005 SKQB 517, 2005 CarswellSask 856, Sandomirsky J. (Sask. Q.B.).

564

find the name of the statute. Look up the statutory provision by statute name and then by section number. Cases that consider statutes as a whole appear at the beginning of the entry for that statute, under the heading "generally." The statutes are listed alphabetically and then, within that order, chronologically by statute revision. Make sure that you look under the correct revision of the statute (for example, 1990, 1980, or 1970).

After looking in the hardcover volume of *Canadian Statute Citations*, check the corresponding supplement volume to find cases that were decided after the cut-off date of the hardcover volume. You should check the corresponding supplement volume even if you don't see the name of the statute or the section of the statute you are looking for in the hardcover volume, because cases may have been decided after the cut-off date of the hardcover volume. Complete your search by consulting the monthly issues of *Canadian Statute Citations*.

Each case citation is preceded by a code inside a small circle that indicates the court's treatment of the statute. (See Figure 13.9.)

Figure 13.9   Canadian Statute Citations' Treatment Symbols for Statutes

Symbol	Meaning
U	**Unconstitutional:** The case decided that a section of the statute was unconstitutional or invalid.
C	**Considered:** The case analyzed or interpreted a section of the statute.
P	**Pursuant to:** The case was brought pursuant to a section of the statute.
R	**Referred to:** The case mentions a section of the statute in passing, but does not consider it directly.

Statute Citators

Statute citators provide another way of looking for cases that interpret a statute or a specific provision of a statute. The citator will refer you to important cases that have dealt with a statute. For cases involving federal statutes, consult the *Canada Statute Citator*. For cases involving Ontario statutes, for example, consult the *Ontario Statute Citator*. Cases are listed under the statutory provision to which they are related. The citator is not comprehensive and should be used only with another source.

Annotated Statutes

There is a third way to find cases that interpret a statute. A commercially published annotated version of the statute will list relevant cases under the section of the statute that the cases considered.

Looking for Cases That Consider a Word or Phrase

The *Canadian Abridgment* has a set of volumes called *Words & Phrases Judicially Defined in Canadian Courts and Tribunals*. Use this source to find cases that have considered particular legal terms or phrases. Words and phrases are arranged alphabetically in the volumes. Each entry includes an extract from the judgment in which the word or phrase was considered. It also gives you the name, citation, and jurisdiction for each case. First check the hardcover volumes of *Words & Phrases Judicially Defined in Canadian Courts and Tribunals*; next, look in the supplement volumes to update your search for cases reported after the cut-off date of the hardcover volume.

Treasure Hunting

When using print sources, you cannot find a case report with only the name of the case—you need the entire correct citation. Sometimes, you won't be able to find a case that you're looking for because you have been given a wrong or partial citation.

If you know the complete name of the case you are looking for but have an incomplete or incorrect citation, you can find the correct citation by looking in either the *Consolidated Table of Cases* volumes or the *Canadian Case Citations* volumes of the *Canadian Abridgment*. Cases are arranged alphabetically by name and are cross-referenced by alternative case names and by the defendant's name.

If you cannot find the name of a case in the hardcover volumes, check the supplement volumes. It may be that the case you are looking for was decided or reported after the cut-off date of the main volume.

Note: Before you do the above, you may wish to check (1) the table of cases in the case report volume you pulled that was *supposed* to contain the case but didn't, and/or (2) the index volume of that case report series. Incorrect citations are often a matter of a wrong page number or volume number.

If the above steps do not work, recheck the source of the citation, because you may have the wrong name.

If you know only part of the name of the case you are looking for, you can try to find the full name in the permanent volumes, as well as in all the supplements, of the *Consolidated Table of Cases* or *Canadian Case Citations*.

If you still cannot find the correct name, you have probably been given a completely wrong name reference. In this situation, find out what precisely is the subject of the case, then proceed to research the matter as you would research a subject. By this method, you may eventually come across the case under a variation of its originally suggested name.

reported case
judge's decision and reasons about a case published in a law report series or a legal database

unreported case
case not published in a law report series

Looking for Unreported Cases

With a **reported case**, the judge's decision and reasons concerning a case are published in a law report series. Many more cases are decided than are reported. Lawyers used to think that an **unreported case** was not worth showing to the court. That has now changed, partly because so many decisions are handed down that not all the important ones can be reported, and partly because computer databases have made it possible to find more and more unreported decisions.

One print source of unreported cases is digest services. Digest services are published weekly or monthly and contain summaries of recent cases of interest. An unreported decision is usually available on request from the publisher of the service. There are various digests available:

- general digests—*Canadian Current Law—Case Digests*;
- civil cases digests, from all jurisdictions—*All-Canada Weekly Summaries* (ACWS); and
- topical digests, with cases from all jurisdictions—for example, the *Weekly Digest of Family Law* and the *Weekly Criminal Bulletin* (WCB).

Finding the Text of the Case Using the Case Citation

After you have found the name and citation of relevant cases, you still need to find the text of the cases. The citation of a case contains all the information you need to find the actual case report; it provides the name and volume numbers of the report series in which the case has been published. (See Chapter 4 for a refresher on case citations.)

Start your search for a cited case by finding the law report series, including the correct series number. Then look for the appropriate volume number. Finally, turn to the page number set out in the citation. The case starts on that page.

Updating Cases

After you find relevant case law, you must make sure that it is current by updating each case. This means finding out the following:

- *The case's **appeal history** or case history*. Has it been confirmed or overturned on appeal? What was the highest court that reviewed the decision?
- *How the case has been treated by other judges*. Has it been followed or not? Has it been distinguished?

Why do you need to know these details about the case? First, a case in your favour is useless if it has been reversed on appeal. Second, a case that has not been followed by other judges has less persuasive value than one that has been followed consistently.

If a case has been appealed to higher courts, the citation you have may include a complete appeal history or case history of the case's journey through the court system. (Again, see Chapter 4 for a refresher on case citations.)

If you don't have a full citation showing the case history, or if you think the citation may not be complete because the case is still in play, use either the *Consolidated Table of Cases* or *Canadian Case Citations* (both series are part of the *Canadian Abridgment*) to find the history of the case. *Canadian Case Citations* may be slightly more thorough in listing cases. For either series, look in both the hardcover main volumes and the softcover supplementary volumes.

appeal history
history of a case—for example, whether the case has been confirmed or overturned on appeal and the name of the highest court that reviewed the decision

Figure 13.10   Canadian Case Citations Sample Page

(1961), 38 C.R. 19 (B.C. Co. Ct.)

Stewart v. R.
(March 11, 1902)
(1902), 32 S.C.R. 483 (S.C.C.)

Cases citing S.C.C.
ⓕ Lawson v. W.R. Carpenter
     Oversea Shipping Ltd., [1945]
     1 W.W.R. 5 (B.C. C.A.)
ⓒ Klimack Construction Ltd. v.
     Belleville (City), [1951]
     O.W.N. 705 (Ont. H.C.)

Stewart v. R.
(1901), 7 Ex. C.R. 55 (Can. Ex.
Ct.)

Cases citing Can. Ex. Ct.
ⓒ Klimack Construction Ltd. v.
     Belleville (City), [1951]
     O.W.N. 705 (Ont. H.C.)

Stewart; R. c., *see R. c. Stewart*

Stewart; R. v., *see R. v. Stewart*

Stewart v. R. (No. 2)
(1977), 35 C.C.C. (2d) 281 (Ont.
C.A.)

Cases citing Ont. C.A.
ⓕ Myers v. R. (1991), 65 C.C.C.
     (3d) 135 (Nfld. C.A.)
ⓓ R. v. Pearson (1978), 7 C.R.
     (3d) 175 (Que. S.C.)
ⓒ Desbiens v. Québec (Procureur
     général), [1986] R.J.Q. 2488
     (Que. S.C.)
ⓒ R. v. Skogman, [1984] 2
     S.C.R. 93 (S.C.C.)
ⓒ Stolar v. R. (1983), 32 C.R.
     (3d) 342 (Man. C.A.)
ⓒ Bourget v. Northwest Territo-
     ries (1982), 47 A.R. 220
     (N.W.T. S.C.)

Stewart v. Ray
(October 27, 1941)
[1941] 3 W.W.R. 881, [1941] 4
D.L.R. 718 (Sask. C.A.)

Stewart v. Reavell's Garage
[1952] 2 Q.B. 545, [1952] 1 All
E.R. 1191 (Eng. Q.B.)

Cases citing Eng. Q.B.
ⓕ Walsh Insurance & Real Estate
     Ltd. v. Trans North Holdings
     Ltd. (1978), 20 A.R. 108 (Alta.
     T.D.)
ⓕ Raiche's Steel Works Ltd. v. J.
     Clark & Son Ltd. (1977), 16
     N.B.R. (2d) 535 (N.B. Q.B.)
ⓕ Scott Maritimes Pulp Ltd. v. B.
     F. Goodrich Canada Ltd.
     (1977), 19 N.S.R. (2d) 181
     (N.S. C.A.)

Stewart v. Rempel
(November 5, 1991), Doc. Van-
couver B880462
[1991] B.C.W.L.D. 2603 (B.C.
S.C.)

Stewart v. Rennie
(1836), 5 U.C.Q.B. (O.S.) 151

Stewart v. Rhodes
[1900] 1 Ch. 386 (Eng. Ch. Div.)

Cases citing Eng. Ch. Div.
ⓒ Jacobson Brothers v. Anderson
     (1962), 48 M.P.R. 29 (N.S.
     C.A.)

Stewart v. Richard
(1885), 3 Man. R. 610 (Man.
Q.B.)

Cases citing Man. Q.B.
ⓕ Canada Settlers Loan Co. v.
     Fullerton (1893), 9 Man. R.
     327 (Man. C.A.)
ⓓ Morris (Rural Municipality) v.
     London & Canadian Loan &
     Agency Co. (1890), 7 Man. R.
     128 (Man. C.A.)

Stewart v. Richardson
(February 18, 1870)
(1870), 17 Gr. 150

**Stewart v. Richardson Securities
of Canada**
(February 12, 1982), Doc. GDC-
3210
(1982), 35 Nfld. & P.E.I.R. 325,
99 A.P.R. 325 (P.E.I. S.C.)

**Stewart v. Richardson Sons &
Co.**
(June 10, 1920)
[1920] 3 W.W.R. 134, 30 Man. R.
481, 53 D.L.R. 625 (Man. C.A.)

Stewart; Robertson v., *see
Robertson v. Stewart*

Stewart; Robichaud v., *see
Robichaud v. Stewart*

Stewart v. Rogers
(June 30, 1905)
(1905), 6 O.W.R. 195 (Ont. H.C.)

Stewart v. Roop
(1983), 58 N.S.R. (2d) 407, 123
A.P.R. 407 (N.S. T.D.)

Stewart v. Ross
Doc. Q.B. J.C.R. 4226/86
(1988), 64 Sask. R. 271 (Sask.
Q.B.)

Stewart v. Rounds
(1882), 7 O.A.R. 515

Cases citing 1st level
ⓕ Weaver v. Sawyer & Co.
     (1889), 16 O.A.R. 422 (Ont.
     C.A.)
ⓒ Bate v. Canadian Pacific Rail-
     way (1888), 15 O.A.R. 388

Stewart v. Routhier
(December 21, 1971)
(1971), 4 N.B.R. (2d) 340 (N.B.
Q.B.)
affirmed / confirmé (March 9,
1972) (1972), 4 N.B.R. (2d) 332,
26 D.L.R. (3d) 752 (N.B. C.A.)
**which was reversed / qui a été
infirmé** (1973), [1975] 1 S.C.R.
566, 7 N.B.R. (2d) 251, 45 D.L.R.
(3d) 383, 1 N.R. 183 (S.C.C.)
**which was varied / qui a été
modifiée** (April 2, 1974) (1974),
[1975] 1 S.C.R. 588, 7 N.B.R.
(2d) 558, 53 D.L.R. (3d) 77, 1
N.R. 630 (S.C.C.)

and which was reversed / et qui
a été infirmé (1973), [1975] 1
S.C.R. 566, 7 N.B.R. (2d) 251, 45
D.L.R. (3d) 383, 1 N.R. 183
(S.C.C.)
which was varied / qui a été
modifiée (April 2, 1974) (1974),
[1975] 1 S.C.R. 588, 7 N.B.R.
(2d) 558, 53 D.L.R. (3d) 77, 1
N.R. 630 (S.C.C.)

Cases citing S.C.C.
ⓕ Bate v. Kileel Enterprises Ltd.
     (1976), 14 N.B.R. (2d) 204
     (N.B. C.A.)
ⓕ Brekka v. Reid (1975), 14
     N.S.R. (2d) 677 (N.S. C.A.)
ⓕ Lessard v. Paquin, [1975] 1
     S.C.R. 665 (S.C.C.)
ⓓ Lewis Realty Ltd. v. Skalbania
     (1980), 25 B.C.L.R. 17 (B.C.
     C.A.)

Cases citing S.C.C.
ⓓ Canadian Aero Service Ltd. v.
     O'Malley (1975), 10 O.R. (2d)
     239 (Ont. H.C.)

Stewart v. Rowlands
(1864), 14 U.C.C.P. 485

Stewart v. Rowsom
(1892), 22 O.R. 533

Stewart v. Royal Bank
(1930), 1 M.P.R. 302, [1930] 2
D.L.R. 617 (N.S. C.A.)
reversed / infirmé (June 11,
1930), [1930] S.C.R. 544, [1930]
4 D.L.R. 694 (S.C.C.)

Cases citing N.S. C.A.
ⓒ Laidlaw Waste Systems Ltd. v.
     C.U.P.E., Local 1045 (1993),
     37 L.A.C. (4th) 146 (Ont. Arb.
     Bd.)
ⓒ Landymore v. Hardy (1991),
     21 R.P.R. (2d) 174 (N.S. T.D.)
ⓒ Landymore v. Hardy (Decem-
     ber 23, 1991), Doc. S.H.
     77533/91 (N.S. T.D.)
Cases citing S.C.C.
ⓕ El-Zayed v. Bank of N.S.
     (1988), 87 N.S.R. (2d) 171
     (N.S. T.D.)
ⓕ Booth Fisheries Canadian Co.
     v. Banque provinciale du Can-
     ada (1972), 7 N.B.R. (2d) 138
     (N.B. Q.B.)
ⓒ Levasseur v. Banque de Mon-
     tréal, [1978] C.S. 1157

Stewart; Royal Bank v., *see
Royal Bank v. Stewart*

Stewart; Royal Trust Co. v., *see
Royal Trust Co. v. Stewart*

Stewart v. Royds
(1904), 118 L.T. 176

Cases citing 1st level
ⓕ Richardson v. McCaffrey
     (1919), 45 O.L.R. 153 (Ont.
     C.A.)

Stewart v. Rundle
(April 13, 1940)

Figure 13.11   Treatment Symbols for Cases

Symbol	Meaning
F	**Followed:** This case followed the principle of law in the cited case.
D	**Distinguished:** This case distinguished the cited case—that is, the principle of law was not applied because of a difference in facts or law.
N	**Not Followed/Overruled:** This case ruled that the cited case was wrongly decided.
C	**Considered:** This case considered or mentioned the cited case.

To find out whether a case has been followed by other judges, use *Canadian Case Citations*.

Figure 13.10 reproduces a page from *Canadian Case Citations*. Note how the cases are listed alphabetically with parallel citations. If a case has been mentioned in other cases, those cases are listed at the end of the entry. Each case is preceded by a circled explanatory letter called a treatment symbol. The meanings of those treatment symbols are provided in Figure 13.11.

Finding and Updating Cases: Computerized Sources

When you're using computerized legal research sources, the two most comprehensive case finding sources are WestlawNext Canada (Westlaw) and LexisAdvance Quicklaw (Quicklaw). Both of these sources contain extensive databases of case decisions and can be used in all the same situations discussed above for print sources. Both sources allow you to find relevant case law by using keyword searches.

Westlaw also includes the *Canadian Abridgment Digests*, which, unlike Quicklaw, is an edited source, and allows you to browse through a table of contents related to your topic. This feature makes it easier to focus your search by looking for a specific issue within the relevant subject title.

You can also find case law using BestCase Library, which is one of the subscriber sources offered by Westlaw, and the Canadian Legal Information Institute (CanLII). Each of these sources contains a broad collection of Canadian case law.

Canadian Abridgment Digests

The *Canadian Abridgment Digests* (CAD) is available online via Westlaw. You can access the CAD below the heading Finding Tools (not in "federated search"), either directly from the Westlaw homepage or by selecting "LawSource" from the My Subscriptions section on the homepage. The online CAD acts as a finding tool, allowing you to obtain the names and citations of relevant cases. It also gives you access to the text of the cases by linking directly to Westlaw's large database of case decisions.

The online CAD uses the same key classification system as the print version.

To find relevant case law using the online version of the CAD, you can do the following:

- browse the table of contents,
- search the table of contents, or
- search using a plain language or Boolean (terms and connectors) search.

Browsing the Table of Contents

The table of contents lists all the subject titles in the CAD in alphabetical order. Select the subject title's name to see the content within the title. Figure 13.12 shows how the subject title "Torts" is broken down in the table of contents, the first page of which is shown below.

After you have identified your subject title in the table of contents, scroll through the levels until you find your specific research topic, and then select the words to display the relevant case digests. The top of the screen shows the classification of your research topic, as well as the name and title of each heading and subheading within the title. It also displays the total number of case digests in your specific topic, as well as the number of digests within each heading and subheading in the subject title. The text of the case digests dealing with the topic is displayed below, on the right-hand side of the screen, in reverse chronological order. Each case digest provides a link to the full text of the decision.

The left side of the screen provides filters that allow you to narrow your search results. You can search within the case digests to find a particular term or phrase, or filter by date, Abridgment Classification, and jurisdiction.

Figure 13.13 shows the end result of a table of contents search, under the subject title "Torts," for dog owners' liability for injuries caused by their dog (under bylaw or statute).

Searching the Table of Contents

Instead of browsing the table of contents by subject title, you can search there for a specific term or phrase. This is helpful if you don't know the relevant subject title for your research issue.

For example, you will find, when you search in the CAD for the issue of a dog owner's liability for injuries caused by his or her dog, that no subject title includes the word "animals." If you enter the term "dog" in the Search Abridgment Headings and Subheadings search box, it will show the relevant subject title—TORTS—and it will show the classification number, which includes the word "dog." You can choose to search all content in the Abridgment Digests (the default option), or you can choose to search only specific titles by choosing the "Specify content to search" option.

Figure 13.12   First Page of Table of Contents for the Subject Title "Torts": CAD Online

Figure 13.13   Result of Table of Contents Search Under the Subject Title "Torts" (Dog Owners' Liability for Injuries Caused by Their Dog Under Bylaw or Statute)

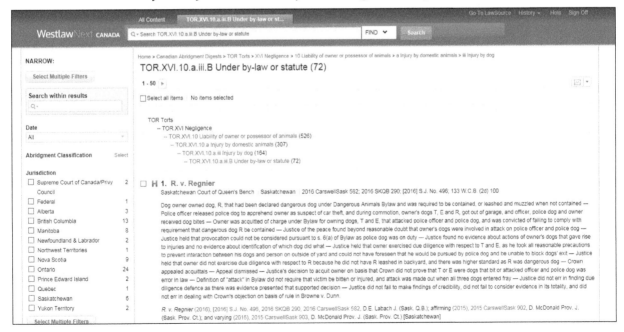

Searching for Cases Using a Plain Language Search

To undertake a plain language search for cases, enter descriptive terms or keywords (plain language) that describe your research topic into the Search box at the top of the page. You do not need to use any operators or connectors. You can even enter a complete question. You might enter one of the following, for example, for a plain language search into the cocker spaniel issue we've been discussing:

- "dog owners" liability injury dog Ontario
- Are dog owners in Ontario liable for an injury caused by their dog?

This type of search retrieves many results because your keywords are searched across the entire *Canadian Abridgment Digests* database. The results list will display each subject title in which your terms appear. Scroll through the results to find the relevant classification. Alternatively, use the Abridgment Classification. Select link in the "Narrow search" section on the left side of the screen. This allows you to easily scroll through a list of subject titles, which show the number of digests within each title. Select the title that is most relevant to your research topic.

Searching for Cases Using a Terms and Connectors (Boolean) Search

terms and connectors (Boolean) search method of searching that is based on principles of logic and that requires the use of keywords together with specific syntax

A **terms and connectors (Boolean) search** allows you to construct a search using keywords and Boolean connectors and expanders. (See Chapter 9 for a refresher on Boolean searching.) To run a Boolean terms and connectors search, preface your search with "adv:" or "advanced:". Including Boolean connectors (other than AND, OR, or a phrase) in your search will also trigger a Boolean terms and connectors search. For example, the search phrase "dog /5 owner /p liability AND injur! AND Ontario AND statute" will automatically trigger a Boolean terms and connectors search (because it contains the "/*n*" and "/p" connectors within the search). The following will trigger the same search: "adv: dog /5 owner /p liability AND injur! AND Ontario AND statute."

As we said in Chapter 8 (under the heading "Working with Computerized Sources: Pros and Cons"), each computerized source has its own search syntax, which will be explained by the source. The search syntax for the online CAD is the same as the syntax used in the online version of the CED. (For a discussion of the CED search syntax, see Chapter 11.)

It's a good idea to search both the CED and the CAD when using Westlaw. In addition to giving you a general statement of the law, the CED provides a link to the relevant *Canadian Abridgment* classification; it is located above the first paragraph of the CED's statement of the law. Select this link to see all the case digests about the particular subject.

Working with Your Search Results

Using any of the above methods to find case digests will lead you to the results page. The classification number for the topic is displayed at the top of the page, along with the total number of digests. Below that is a list of all the headings and subheadings along with the total number of digests within each. You can easily link to a heading by selecting its classification.

Each digest provides a summary of the point of law discussed in the case and includes the name, citation, and jurisdiction of the case being summarized. Both the name of the case at the top of the digest and the citation below provide a hyperlink to the text of the case. By selecting either hyperlink, you can retrieve the full text of the case.

You will likely find many case digests that are relevant to your research topic. You can reduce this number by using the filters available on the left side of the results page. You can filter by date, jurisdiction (that is, federal, provincial, or territorial—the number of digests within each jurisdiction is displayed), and search terms. You will have to scan them all to determine which cases you should read in full.

You may encounter various symbols or icons beside the name of the case. Most of the icons are KeyCite icons; these tell you something about the status of the case. Hover your cursor over the symbol for an explanation. Using KeyCite is discussed below.

Westlaw's Cases and Decisions Database

A number of search tools will give you direct access to the case decisions in Westlaw's cases and decisions database. These tools include the following:

- searching cases and decisions using keywords,
- finding a case by name or citation,
- using the Find and KeyCite a Case by Name search template, and
- using the Find and KeyCite a Statute or Regulation by Name search template.

Searching Cases and Decisions Using Keywords

Westlaw allows you to find relevant case law by using keywords to search its cases and decisions database directly. This is useful if you have a specific case in mind and have some information about it but don't know the complete citation.

From the Browse–All Content section of the Westlaw homepage (or from Law-Source), select the "Cases and Decisions" link under the heading Primary Sources.

From here you can conduct a plain language search, a terms and connectors search, or an advanced template search of the entire cases and decisions database. You can narrow your search by adding a jurisdiction or topic filter to your plain language or terms and connectors search. As you apply filters, the Search box displays the revised database. For example, if you select Ontario as your jurisdiction, the Search box will be narrowed to Ontario cases and decisions, as shown in Figure 13.14.

Select a specific topic and the screen will display the ten most recent cases from the topic and jurisdiction you selected. To find other Ontario cases and decisions, enter your plain language search or your terms and connectors search in the Search box.

Figure 13.14   Search of Westlaw's Cases and Decisions Database, Narrowed to Ontario

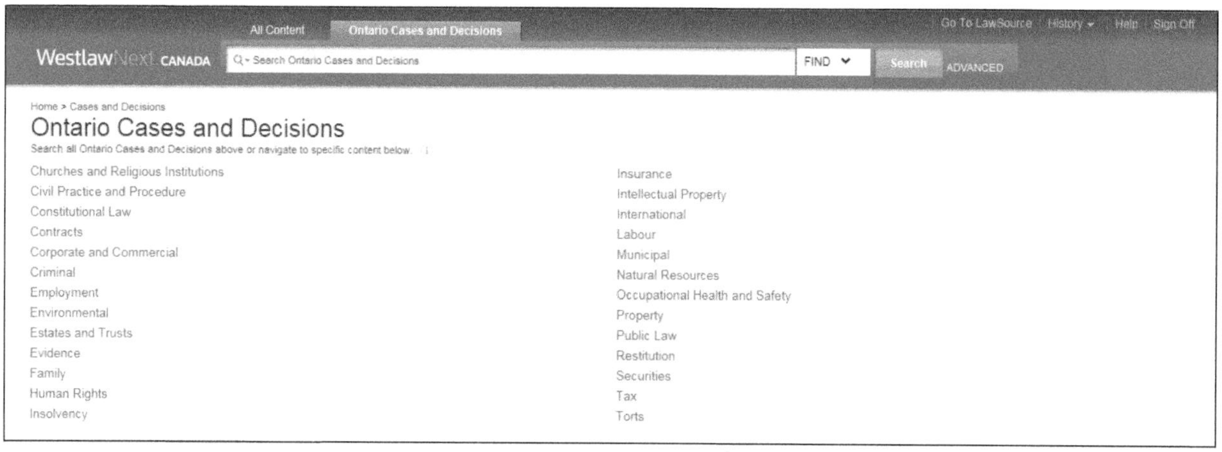

Alternatively, you can search for cases and decisions using the various fields and filters provided in the Advanced Search template (see Figure 13.15). To use this template, enter your search terms, then use the fields under the heading Document Fields (Boolean Terms & Connectors Only) to narrow your search. In these fields, enter any information you have about the name, court, jurisdiction, judge, counsel, classification number, law report, or year of the case, and Westlaw will search for your keywords in cases with the filters you have specified.

For example, assume you are looking for an Ontario case about dog owners' liability and you know that one party's name is Strom. Enter the keywords *dog*, *owner*, and *liability* in the "All of these terms" text box. Enter "Strom" in the "Case Name" field. Choose "Ontario" to limit your search to this jurisdiction only. Figure 13.15 illustrates how to do this.

The resulting page will display the full case report with the search keywords highlighted.

You can narrow your jurisdiction and topic before using the Advanced Search template. If you do this, the template will reflect those choices.

Finding a Case by Name or Citation

You can also find a case by entering its name or citation in the Search box on the Westlaw homepage. If the case you are searching for has been appealed, the search will retrieve the decision of all the levels of court that heard the case. For example, a search of *Dunmore v Ontario (Attorney General)* will find decisions from the Ontario Court of Justice, General Division, Ontario Court of Appeal, and Supreme Court of Canada, as illustrated in Figure 13.16. You must then locate the relevant decision.

If you have the citation of the case you are trying to find, use that instead. When you search for a case using its citation, the search will retrieve one decision only—the decision whose citation is the one you entered. Enter the citation in the Search box on the homepage, or in the Citation field of the Find by Citation template. You can access this template using the "Find" drop-down menu beside the Search box on the homepage.

Figure 13.15   Using Westlaw's Advanced Search Template, with Filters

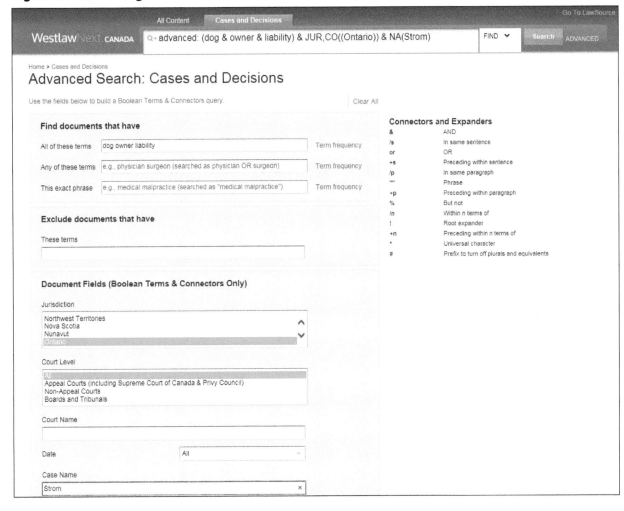

Figure 13.16   Using Westlaw's Search Box to Find a Case by Name

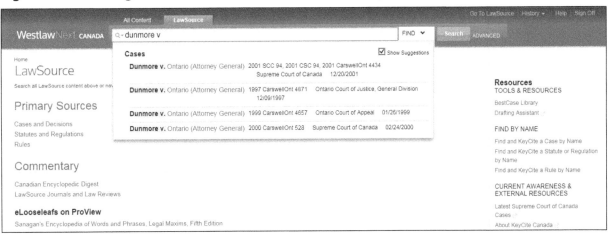

To search by citation, include the year of the case only if it is in square brackets, followed by a space. The rest of the citation can be entered without including brackets, punctuation, capitalization, or spaces. Include the abbreviation for the series number (2d, 3d, 4th). For example, to find the case whose citation is "(1996), 134 DLR (4th) 252," enter any of the following:

- 134 dlr (4th) 252,
- 134 dlr 4th 252, or
- 134dlr4th252.

To find the case whose citation is "[1996] 2 SCR 27," enter any of the following:

- [1996] 2 scr 27,
- 1996 2 scr 27, or
- 1996 2scr27.

Note: When the year is in square brackets in the citation you are searching for, you must include a space after the year in your search phrase (whether or not you are including the square brackets in that phrase).

Using the Find and KeyCite a Case by Name Template

Westlaw allows you to find and/or update a case using all or part of the case's name. The easiest way to access this template is to select it from the "Find" drop-down menu beside the Search box on the homepage. Note that you can also access this template using the Find and KeyCite by Name tab on the Westlaw homepage, or from the Find By Name links on the right side of the Law Source homepage. Enter all or part of the name of the case in the Name field and select the jurisdiction (if known) from the drop-down menu in the Jurisdiction field. Then select "Search." The results list will show cases that match your search terms.

To return to our earlier example, assume you are looking for an Ontario case dealing with dog owners' liability and you know that one of the parties is named Strom. Choose "Find and KeyCite a Case by Name" (from the "Find" drop-down menu) and enter "Strom" for the case name. Then choose "Ontario" under the "Jurisdiction" drop-down menu and select "Search." Figure 13.17 illustrates the results of that search. All Ontario cases containing Strom in their names are listed.

Use the filters on the left side of the page to help you narrow your results. The subject-area filters show the subject areas from which results may be drawn. Select "Torts" to find cases dealing with dog owners' liability. To see the text of a case, simply select its name from the results list. The screen will then display the full text of the case with your keyword(s) highlighted, as shown in Figure 13.18. Also provided are a headnote and a summary of the case, as well as links to related classifications in the *Abridgment*, which let you go directly to the *Abridgment Case Digests*.

Figure 13.17   Using Westlaw's Find and KeyCite a Case by Name Template

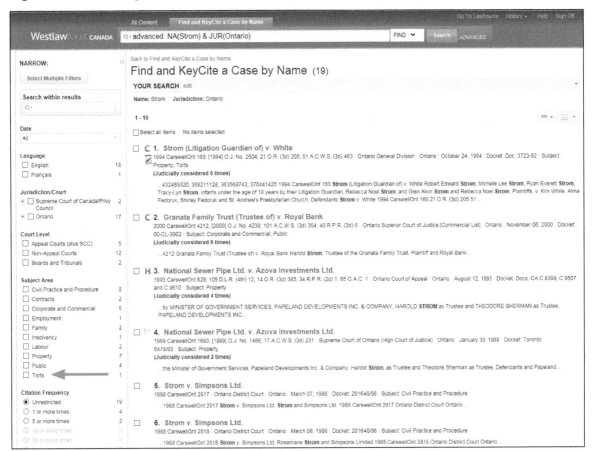

After you find a case, Westlaw provides direct access to the history of the case (if available) and to all citing references. It also provides a link to any associated legal memos. See below under the heading "Updating Cases with Online Sources" for a more detailed discussion of KeyCiting cases using Westlaw.

Using Westlaw's Find and KeyCite a Statute or Regulation by Name Template

The Find and KeyCite a Statute or Regulation by Name template on Westlaw allows you to search for case law that cites an entire statute or a specific section of one. Select this option using the "Find" drop-down menu beside the Search box on the homepage. Note that you can also access this template from the tab in the Browse section of the Westlaw homepage, or from the "Find By Name" links on the right side of the Law Source homepage. In the fields of the template provided, enter the name, section number(s), and jurisdiction of the statute you are researching.

The result displays the name and citation of the statute together with a link to citing references. Select the green "C" beside the name of the statute to see the cases that cite it.

Figure 13.18   Results of Searching Using the Find and KeyCite a Case by Name Template

Lexis Advance Quicklaw (Quicklaw)

Quicklaw, a subscription service, is also a popular case-finding tool. It provides an extensive collection of full text decisions (including case law summaries) from courts and tribunals across Canada.

To find relevant case law using Quicklaw, you can do the following:

- browse by legal topic, or
- search using a natural language or Boolean (terms and connectors) search.

Browsing Legal Topics

To browse for cases by legal topic, select the Browse tab at the top of the homepage and choose "Topics." You can then select a topic as a starting point either from the alphabetical list or by entering the topic in the "Find a topic" search box. From there, you can drill down to increasingly more specific subtopics. For example, assume you are looking for cases about whether a person can bring an action in nuisance against a neighbour who had dangerous contaminants on his land. Browse by

"Topics" and select "Tort Law and Civil Liability." Choose "Common Law Jurisdictions (Tort Law)," "Nuisance," "Factors giving rise to right of action," and "Nature of property or non-natural use of land," as illustrated in Figure 13.19.

Figure 13.19   Quicklaw's Browse Legal Topics Tab

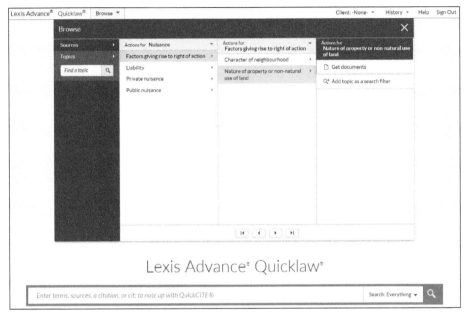

Select "Get documents" to see all cases on this specific legal topic. You can narrow your results using the filters under the Narrow By heading on the left side. For example, to see only Ontario Appeal Court decisions expand "Jurisdiction" and choose "Ontario," and then expand "Court" and choose "Court of Appeal for Ontario." Figure 13.20 illustrates the Topic Results with the applied filters. Click the name of the case to view its full text.

Figure 13.20   Quicklaw's Topic Results with Filters Applied

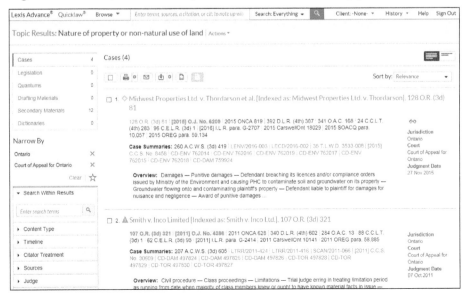

Browsing for case law this way may not be as effective as searching, especially when your legal issue doesn't fit easily (or at all!) within one of Quicklaw's predetermined topics. To have complete freedom and control when searching for case law about a specific legal topic, it is better to use a natural language or terms and connectors search.

Searching for Cases Using a Natural Language or Boolean (Terms and Connectors) Search

To find relevant cases about a legal topic, enter your search in the red search box. By default, Quicklaw searches for case law across all content and all jurisdictions. Your search will retrieve many results, which you can then refine and narrow using one or more post-search filters (discussed below).

You can also narrow your search up front (to a specific jurisdiction, court, and/ or legal topic) by adding pre-search filters before running your search. To do this, click the "Search: Everything" drop-down at the right of the search box, and select the desired filters. For example, to limit your search of case law to Ontario appeal decisions only, select "Ontario (Jurisdiction)" and "Appellate Courts (By Court)." You can also add one of the broad legal topics to your search to focus your research on that area of law.

Figure 13.21 shows pre-search filters for a search of Ontario appeal decisions limited to the area of tort law and civil liability. As you can see, your selected filters are displayed both within and below the red search box. Click the X within a filter tab to remove the filter; click "Clear" to remove all filters.

Figure 13.21   Quicklaw's Pre-Search Filters

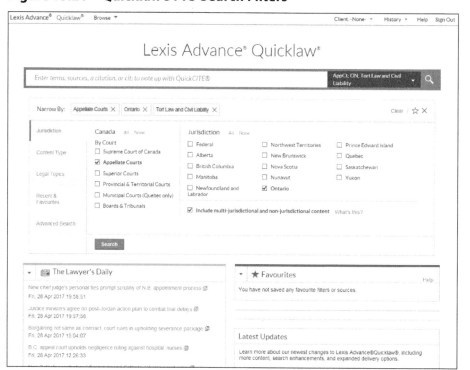

Note that although you can use pre-search filters to limit your search for case law at the outset to, for example, a specific jurisdiction and court, you don't have to. You can instead run your search broadly across all content in your subscription and then use post-search filters to refine and narrow your results. The post-search filters also allow you to narrow by jurisdiction, court, source, and legal topic but include many additional filters. (Post-search filters are discussed below under the heading "Working with Your Search Results.")

Searching for Cases Using a Natural Language Search

Enter descriptive terms or keywords (natural language) that describe your research topic into the red Search box at the top of the page. As was discussed above for plain language searches using Westlaw, you do not need to use any operators or connectors. You can even enter a complete question. You might enter one of the following, for example, for a natural language search into the cocker spaniel issue we've been discussing:

- "dog owners" liability injury dog Ontario
- Are dog owners in Ontario liable for an injury caused by their dog?

This type of search retrieves many results because your keywords are searched across the entire content in Quicklaw—all sources, content type, and jurisdictions (assuming you did not apply any pre-search filters).

Figure 13.22 illustrates the results of a natural language search (using keywords) for whether dog owners in Ontario are liable for an injury caused by their dog.

Figure 13.22   Quicklaw's Natural Language Search

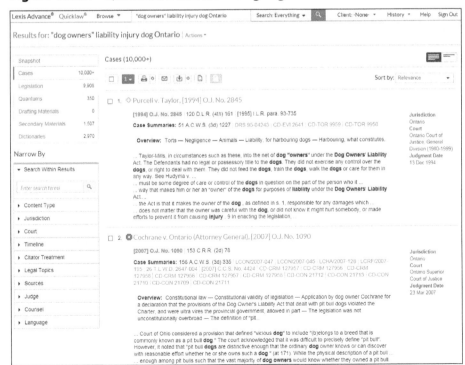

As you can see, the search retrieved more than 10,000 cases, which is typical of a natural language search. By applying the relevant post-search filters, you can easily narrow this list to an appropriate number of cases about your research topic. Post-search filters are discussed below under the heading "Working with Your Search Results".

Searching for Cases Using a Terms and Connectors (Boolean) Search

A terms and connectors (Boolean) search allows you to construct a search using keywords together with Boolean connectors and expanders. (See Chapter 9 for a refresher on Boolean searching.) Enter your Boolean search in the red search box and click the magnifying glass or hit Enter.

Remember, before entering a Boolean search, you must familiarize yourself with the search syntax used by Quicklaw. A detailed explanation of its search syntax is available on the Quicklaw site.

Quicklaw provides a template to help you develop a terms and connectors search. To access this template, choose the "Search: Everything" drop-down and select "Assisted Search." You can use this template to develop a terms and connectors search from scratch or to add terms and connectors to an existing search. When using this template, you simply enter your keywords and then select how to treat them from a predefined list of options. Figure 13.23 illustrates the Assisted Search template.

Figure 13.23   Quicklaw's Assisted Search Template

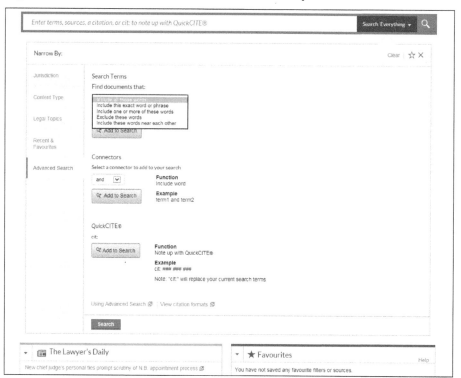

Working with Your Search Results

After running a natural language or terms and connectors search, use post-search filters to narrow to the most relevant results. The "Narrow By" pane will display all available post-search filters that change depending on which category you are viewing.

Let's review the post-search filters available for the results of a natural language search about whether dog owners are liable for injuries caused by their dog (see Figure 13.22). Since we are looking for case law, make sure "Cases" is selected as your content type. You can then narrow results by "Content Type" (court decisions, case summaries, and/or tribunal decisions), "Jurisdiction," "Court," "Timeline," "Citator Treatment," "Legal Topics," "Sources," "Judge," "Counsel," and "Language" (English or French). You can also narrow your results by adding additional search terms in the "Search Within Results" field, using a natural language or Boolean search.

Assume we want to find cases decided in the last two years that are from Ontario appeal courts and that have positive treatment. Select "Ontario" (Jurisdiction), "Court of Appeal for Ontario" (Court), "01 Jan 2015–31 Dec 2017" (Timeline), "Positive or Neutral treatment" (Citator Treatment). Note that as you select your post-search filters, Quicklaw displays the number of cases for each filter. Figure 13.24 shows the results of your search after applying your post-search filters. As you can see, the number of cases has decreased from over 10,000 to 20!

The case name and citation is a hyperlink to the text of the case. You can also link to the text of case summaries by clicking the citation hyperlink. Each result also contains an overview or summary about the case before the actual judgment.

Figure 13.24   Quicklaw's Post-Search Filters

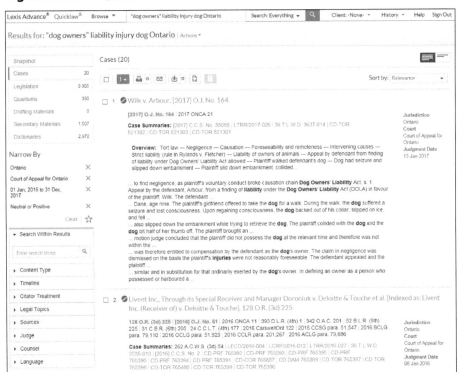

Finding a Case by Name or Citation

You can also find a case by entering its name or citation in the red search box on the Quicklaw homepage. If searching by citation, you do not need to enter any brackets, punctuation, capitalization, or spaces. As when using Westlaw, include the year of the case only if it is in square brackets, followed by a space.

Finding Cases that Cite Legislation

Quicklaw contains the QuickCITE Legislation Citator, which allows you to find cases citing a statutory provision. There are several ways to access the QuickCITE record.

The quickest way is to enter "cit:" followed by the name of the statute, in the red search box on the homepage.

You can also access the QuickCITE record while viewing the text of the statute section you want to update. (See Chapter 12 for a discussion on how to find legislation using Quicklaw.)

While viewing the text of the statutory provision, select the blue "L" beside the name of the statute or the link to the citing cases under the Related Content heading in the "About this document" box to view the QuickCITE citator record. (See Figure 12.11.)

Figure 13.25 illustrates the QuickCITE record for s 1 of the *Dog Owners' Liability Act*.

The record displays a list of cases that have cited the statute section (including any subsections) and provides a hyperlink to the text of each case.

See below under the heading "Updating Cases with Online Sources" for a more detailed discussion of the QuickCITE record.

Figure 13.25   Quicklaw's QuickCITE Legislation Citator

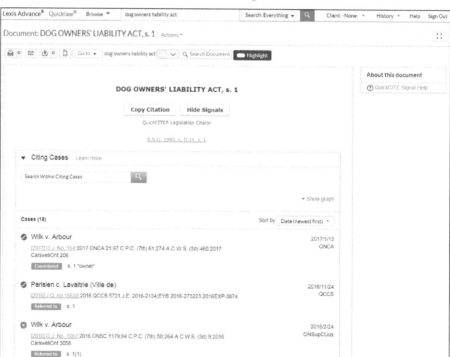

BestCase Library

BestCase, as mentioned above, is a web-based subscription case law research service available through WestlawNext Canada. It contains Canada's leading law reports and case summary services. You can access BestCase Library by selecting it from the My Subscriptions section on the Westlaw homepage. You can also select BestCase Library from the LawSource start page, under the heading Tools and Resources. The BestCase Library start page provides a list of the available law reports. Enter your plain language or Boolean (terms and connectors) search into the Search box at the top of the page to search across the entire BestCase Library database. Alternatively, select "Advanced" to use the Advanced search template. Figure 13.26 illustrates the BestCase Library start page.

Figure 13.26   BestCase Library Start Page

If you search across the entire BestCase Library database, you can then filter your results from the "View" section of the results page. For example, assume you want to find cases about Ontario dog owners' liability for injuries caused by their dog. Enter the following Boolean search in the Search box and select "Search":

dog /5 owner /p liability and injur! and Ontario

Figure 13.27 illustrates the results page for this search.

As you can see, there are many results—108 of them, at the time of writing—and the number will continue to increase as new cases are reported. They are located in four different reports. The "View" section, on the left side of the results page, illustrates which reports contain the results, including the number of results in each of those reports. The right side of the results page shows the first results from each of the reports that contain results of your search.

Select a specific report from the "View" section to see the results in that report and to narrow your results further using customized filters. For example, if you select "Dominion Law Reports (D.L.R.)," the right side of the screen displays a summary of each of the cases in that report (with your search terms highlighted), together with a link to the full text of the case and to citing references. The left side of the screen allows you to narrow your search results by selecting the desired options in the "Narrow" section (located below the "View" section), as illustrated in

Figure 13.27   Results of Boolean Search of Entire BestCase Library Database (Ontario Dog Owners' Liability for Injuries Caused by Their Dog)

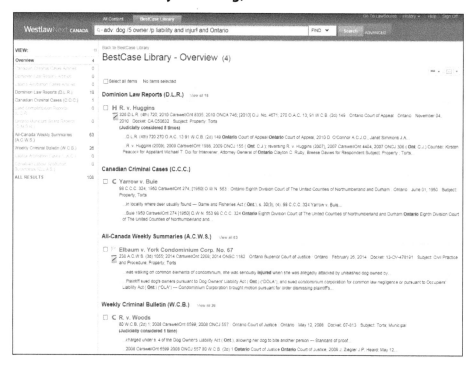

Figure 13.28   Narrowing the Results of a Boolean Search (Ontario Dog Owners' Liability for Injuries Caused by Their Dog)

Figure 13.28. As you can see, you can search for specific keywords within the results you have found.

You can also narrow your results by date, jurisdiction, court level, subject area, and citation frequency, and include the name of a party, the judge/adjudicator, or counsel, and the docket number, if you have this information. Finally, you can include any keywords that may appear in the headnote of the case you are looking for. For example, assume you want to see Ontario Court of Appeal decisions since 2000 regarding dog owners' liability in cases that involved dogs hurting children. Choose the "Select Multiple Filters" button and add your desired filters. When you are done, select "Apply Filters." You will retrieve the two results that satisfy your search requirements.

Select the case you want to view by selecting its name. The full text of the case decision will be displayed (with your search terms highlighted) on the resulting page, including links to "History" and "Citing References" (see the toolbar near the top of the page), and a link to a PDF copy of the decision (see Figure 13.29).

The "Case Views" section appears on the right side of the page. It provides different case views of the case, as well as related resources. For example, select "Source" to see Carswell's view, which includes *Abridgment* classifications and headnotes, a Table of Authorities section, and a "Statutes considered" section. A link to "Abridgment digests and classifications for all levels of this case" is provided in the "Related Resources" section, as shown in Figure 13.29.

To see a PDF of the case you are viewing, select the button with the PDF icon on the toolbar at the top of the page.

Figure 13.29   Carswell's View of Case Decision

Canadian Legal Information Institute (CanLII)

CanLII, as mentioned above, is a free Internet site containing a comprehensive collection of Canadian case law. CanLII's website is <http://www.canlii.org>.

To search for case law by topic on CanLII, enter your search terms in the appropriate fields of the default search template. The search template's scope changes depending on whether you are searching across all CanLII databases or within a specific jurisdiction only.

From the homepage, the template searches across the entire CanLII collection. To search for case law by topic across all CanLII databases, enter your search terms, using the CanLII search syntax, in the Search box at the top of the homepage. To see the search syntax, hover your cursor over the question mark ("?") that appears at the right end of the Search box. Note that, by default, words that are entered with a space between them will be searched as if there was an AND between them, not an OR.

To search for cases by topic from a specific jurisdiction, select the jurisdiction from the list under the heading Browse. The search template that appears is the same as the one on the homepage, but its scope is limited to the jurisdiction you select. You can search for case law from that jurisdiction by entering your search terms in the Search box, as on the homepage. Alternatively, you can narrow the scope further by selecting a specific court, board, or tribunal. This takes you to a search page that shows, again, the same default search template but with its scope now limited to the court, board, or tribunal you selected.

To search for cases from more than one jurisdiction, run your search across all CanLII databases and then use the available filters on the results page to define your scope. For example, assume you are looking for Canadian case law concerning the amount of damages awarded in cases of wrongful dismissal of a manager. On the homepage, enter the following in the Search box:

damages /10 award and "wrongful dismissal" /5 manager

Figure 13.30 shows the results of this search.

Next, select the Cases tab, and then use the resulting drop-down menus to select a jurisdiction, court/tribunal, and date. The drop-down menu for "All jurisdictions," displaying the number of cases relevant to each jurisdiction, is shown in Figure 13.31.

Finding the Text of a Case

When you know the name and citation of a case, it is easy to find the text of the case using any of the computerized sources discussed above.

- Using Quicklaw and Westlaw you can retrieve the text of a case simply by providing its name or its citation in the Search box. Westlaw also contains the Find and KeyCite a Case by Name template, which allows you to find the text of a case using the case's name.

Figure 13.30   Case Search Across All CanLII Databases (Damages Awarded in Cases of Wrongful Dismissal of a Manager)

Figure 13.31   Search for Cases by Jurisdiction (Damages Awarded in Cases of Wrongful Dismissal of a Manager): CanLII

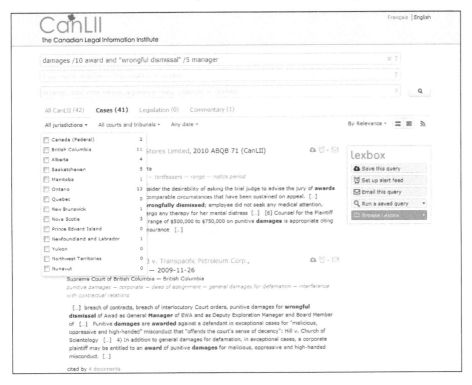

- Using CanLII, enter the name or citation of a case you want to see the text of in the "Case name, legislation title, citation or docket" field on the homepage.
- BestCase Library also provides access to the text of many Canadian cases. Enter the name of the case in the Search box to search for the case across all the reporters in the BestCase Library database. Or, if you know the citation of the case, you can select that specific reporter (if available) and then run your search for the case using its name in the Search box.

Updating Cases with Online Sources

As we mentioned earlier in this chapter (in our discussion of print sources, under the heading "Updating Cases"), it is important to update the cases you are researching. You have to update any relevant case you find to make sure that it is still "good law" that is useful to your research. By updating, in other words, you will find out the following:

- *The case history or appeal history*. Has the case been confirmed or overturned on appeal? What was the highest court that reviewed the decision?
- *The standing of the case*. How has the case been treated by other judges? Has it been followed? Has it been distinguished?

Quicklaw, Westlaw, BestCase Library, and CanLII all have comprehensive case citators that allow you to update cases easily. Each source has its own codes to indicate the judicial treatment of a case, so you will need to know the citator treatment codes for each source.

Quicklaw

As previously mentioned, Quicklaw's case citator is called QuickCITE. You can access this updating tool in the following ways:

- by entering "cit:" followed by citation of the case you want to update in the red search box on the homepage; or
- while viewing the text of a case, by selecting:
  - the treatment indicator beside the name of the case; or
  - the "Citing Cases" link (under the Related Content heading in the "About this document" box).

For example, assume you want to update the case of *Dunmore v Ontario (Attorney General)* [2001] 3 SCR 1016.

Enter "cit: 2001 3 scr 1016" in the red Search bar. (Or find the case using any of the methods described above under the heading "Finding a Case by Name or Citation" [using Quicklaw]).

Figure 13.32 illustrates the case citator record for the Dunmore case.

As you can see, the History of Case tab shows the lower courts' decisions with links to those decisions.

Figure 13.32   Quicklaw's Case Citator Record

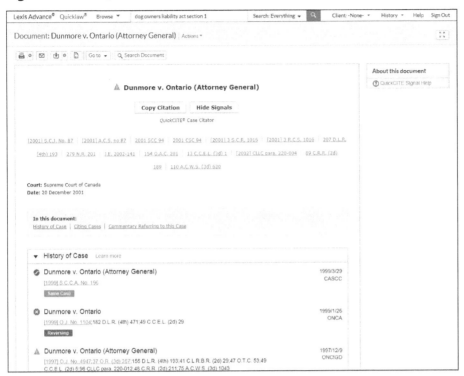

The Citing Cases tab provides a list of all cases citing the Dunmore case, including a graphical summary that easily allows you to filter your results by court, year, jurisdiction and treatment. Figure 13.33 illustrates the graphical summary of all cases citing Dunmore, across all jurisdictions, and including all treatment.

Figure 13.34 illustrates the graphical summary of only Ontario cases with positive treatment (citing the Dunmore decision).

Note that you can further refine your results to cases containing specific keywords by adding those words in the "Search Within Citing Cases" box. The list of citing cases provides the treatment indicator below the name of the case. The symbol beside the name of the case tells you whether the case has positive, cautionary, negative, or neutral treatment. Figure 13.34, for instance, shows a cautionary symbol beside the case name. Click "QuickCITE Signal Help" in the "About this Document" box for a detailed explanation of the QuickCITE signals.

The list of citing cases also provides a direct link to the text of the citing cases. Use the citation hyperlink to link directly to the entire case report. Use the Locus para number hyperlink to link directly to the first section of the case that mentions the case you noted up.

Figure 13.33   Quicklaw's Graphical Summary of All Cases

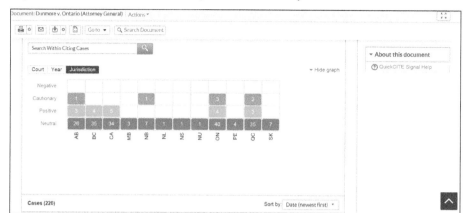

Figure 13.34   Quicklaw's Graphical Summary of Only Ontario Cases

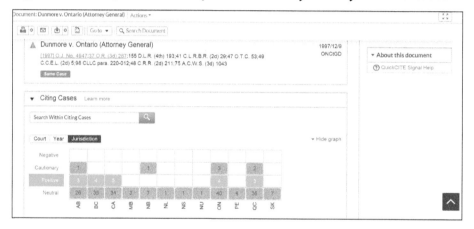

Westlaw

After you find the text of a case on Westlaw, you can quickly note up the case using KeyCite Canada by selecting the appropriate tabs.

For example, find the Ontario Court of Appeal decision of *Dunmore v Ontario (Attorney General)*. The citation for this case is 182 DLR (4th) 471. (See Figure 13.35.)

KeyCite flags and icons tell you about history and citing references. Select the icons (beside the case name), or select the History and Citing References tabs at the top of the case.

Selecting the History tab shows how the case has moved through the courts—whether it was appealed and what happened—displayed in both a list and a graphical view. In our example, the History tab shows that this decision was appealed to the Supreme Court of Canada and the decision was reversed, as illustrated in Figure 13.36.

Figure 13.35   Westlaw's KeyCite Canada Tab

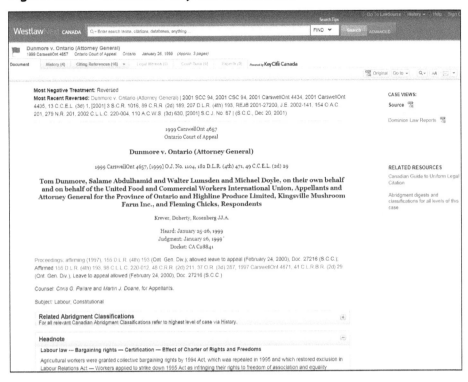

Figure 13.36   Westlaw's Case History Tab

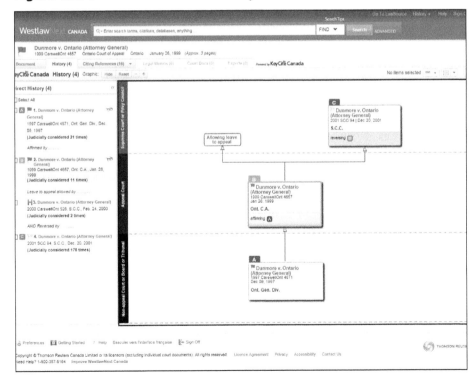

Choose the Citing References tab to see a list of all cases and secondary sources (if available) that have cited the case.

To view citing cases and decisions only, click that link under the View heading on the left side. Then, as illustrated in Figure 13.37, you can sort the results by treatment type (default), date, court level, citation frequency, or depth of treatment. You can narrow the result list by date, jurisdiction, court level, treatment type, and citation frequency by selecting the appropriate filters. You can also refine your results by entering keywords in the "Search within results" box. For an explanation of the KeyCite Canada flags and icons, hover your mouse over the flag/icon or click the "Powered by KeyCite Canada" logo at the top of the page.

Figure 13.37   Westlaw's Sorting Results Tab

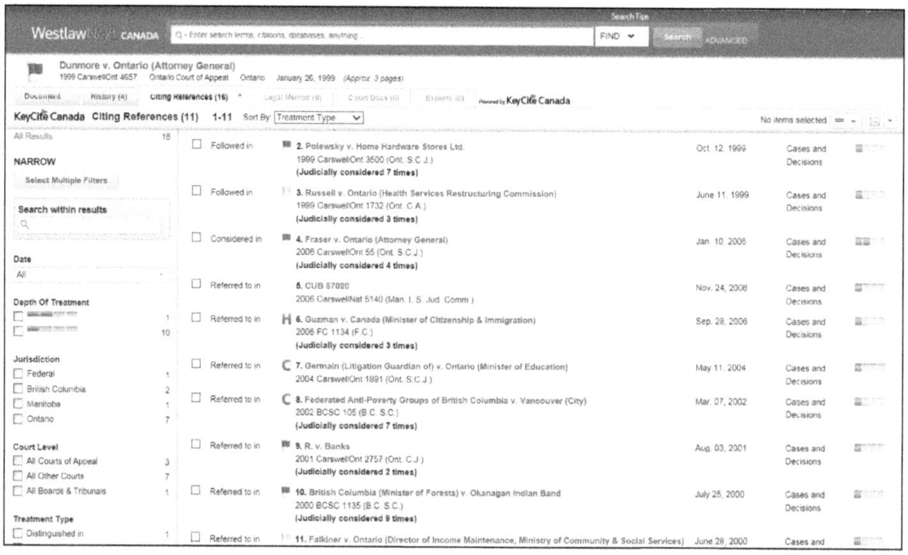

BestCase Library

To use BestCase Library to update cases, select the History and Citing References tabs that appear at the top of the screen when you are viewing the text of a case. Updates in BestCase Library are powered by KeyCite Canada (KeyCite), as discussed above for Westlaw.

CanLII

To update cases on CanLII, enter the name or citation of the case in the Noteup field on the homepage. A drop-down menu will appear showing cases with the name you've entered. Select the relevant case. You will see a link to citing references if the case has been cited in other decisions. Figure 13.38 illustrates the note up results for the Supreme Court of Canada decision of *Dunmore v Ontario (Attorney General)*, [2001] 3 SCR 1016.

Figure 13.38   CanLII's Note Up Results Tab

There are 192 cases that cited this decision, across all jurisdictions, courts and dates. You can refine this list using the drop-down tabs. For example, to see only Ontario decisions select "Ontario" from the "All jurisdictions" drop-down list. The list shows the number of results for each jurisdiction. As you can see, five Ontario cases cite the *Dunmore* case. You can further narrow your results by selecting a specific court and date from the "All courts and tribunals" and the "Any date" drop-down list,

You can also update a case while viewing its text. Next to the words "Cited by" (just above the case report) the number of documents provides a hyperlink to the same note up results page illustrated in Figure 13.38.

KEY TERMS

EXERCISES

1. Are there any cases in your province that followed the Supreme Court of Canada decision in *Crocker v Sundance Northwest Resorts Ltd*, [1988] 1 SCR 1186?

2. Was the 1992 Ontario case *Dunn v Dunn Estate* appealed? If so, what happened on appeal?

3. Are there any Manitoba Court of Appeal cases dealing with renewal of franchising contracts?

4. Are there any cases decided in 2014 that cited s 181(2) of the 1985 federal *Bankruptcy and Insolvency Act*, RSC 1985, c B-3?

5. There is a 1982 Alberta Court of Appeal case involving Holt Renfrew and another corporation. Find the name and citation of this case. Locate the case report and provide the names of all the judges.

6. Find the name and citation of two New Brunswick cases decided between 2000 and 2005 about an inmate who was assaulted with a hockey stick.

PART VII

Putting It All Together

In Part VII, we put together for you everything we've covered in this book, taking you through a research problem from beginning to end. Then we focus on two common forms of legal writing: memos of law and opinion letters. Finally, we discuss some of the key requirements of good legal writing.

A Sample Research Problem: From Start to Finish

14

LEARNING OUTCOMES

After reading this chapter, you will understand:

- How to examine a fact situation and identify the issues that arise from it

- How to find the law that applies to the fact situation and to the issues that arise from it

- Why you should preserve your research in a memo of law

- What a memo of law looks like

- What an opinion letter looks like

Introduction

In this chapter, we put it all together for you, taking you through a research problem from start to finish. We'll be using the fact situation we set out in Chapter 5, which concerned the tribulations of Elwood Blues.

Researching a Problem: A Recap of the Steps

Before we get into the specifics of our research problem, we want to remind you of the steps involved in conducting legal research. We explained them in Part III of this book.

In Chapter 5, we told you that, generally speaking, the need to research something is triggered when a client comes to you or to your firm seeking advice about a legal problem that has arisen from a particular fact situation. Therefore, the best way to start your research is by examining the fact situation with a view to identifying the issues that arise from it. The steps involved in such an examination are

1. identifying on a preliminary basis the issues arising out of the facts,
2. formulating the issues,
3. considering whether there are any issues that are not immediately obvious on hearing the fact situation, and
4. identifying the need for further information.

Then, in Chapter 6, we told you that your goal, after you have analyzed a given fact situation and identified the legal issue(s) involved, is to find the law that applies to the fact situation. The steps involved in finding this applicable law are as follows:

1. Orienting yourself in the law by using secondary sources to find a general statement or overview of the law concerning the issues you have identified.
2. Finding the primary sources of law—the statutes, the bylaws, the regulations (if any), and the case law—that govern the issue(s) you are researching. You need to find the binding and persuasive law that is in favour of the client, as well as the binding and persuasive law that goes against the client.
3. Updating any statute, regulation, or case you find to make sure it is still good law.
4. Physically locating the primary law that applies to the client's fact situation, then reading and understanding it.
5. Applying the law you have found to the client's fact situation to determine the answers to the issues you identified—and therefore the likely outcome of your client's case.

With these steps in mind, we're ready to revisit the information provided to us by the client, Elwood Blues.

The Client's Tale

Sixteen-year-old Elwood Blues went into the Kwik-e-Mart, a convenience store close to his home. He walked all around the store looking for his favourite brand of cookies. He didn't find what he was looking for and was about to leave the store when he found his way blocked by the clerk, a husky man named Steve Barnes. Barnes said, "You put something into your pocket!" Elwood replied, "No, I didn't." "We'll see about that!" Barnes said. Barnes then told Elwood that he was making a citizen's arrest, called the police, and told Elwood that he couldn't leave the store until the police got there. Barnes stayed in front of the door until the police arrived, blocking the store's only exit. When the police arrived, Barnes told the officer, "I think this boy shoplifted something from my store and put it into his pocket." The police officer asked Elwood for his side of the story. Elwood said, "I didn't take anything. See?" and emptied his pockets. There was nothing belonging to the store in his pockets, so the police officer told Elwood he was free to go. Elwood left. Elwood and his parents have now come to your firm because they want to know whether Elwood can sue the store for every nickel it's got for the way he was treated.

Analysis of the Fact Situation

- What does the client want?
  - The client wants to know whether he can sue the store for financial compensation.
- What are the relevant facts?
  - The store clerk suspected Elwood of shoplifting.
  - The store clerk prevented Elwood from leaving the store until the police arrived.
  - Elwood had not shoplifted.
- What is the area of law?
  - General area—tort law
  - Specific area—false imprisonment
- What keywords helped you identify the area of law?
  - "shoplifted"
  - "citizen's arrest"
  - "blocking the store's only exit"
- What is the objective of your research?
  - To determine whether Elwood has a cause of action in tort law, specifically for false imprisonment.
- What are the central issues?
  - Whether there was false imprisonment.
  - Whether a store clerk (a citizen, not a peace officer) can arrest a customer whom he suspects has committed a crime but who has not in fact committed a crime.

Note: In Chapter 5, we identified some hidden issues, including the following:

- Can a 16-year-old bring a lawsuit?
- Who are the defendants—the store clerk, the store, or both?
- Is there a course of action open to the clients that is more appropriate than a lawsuit?

For simplicity's sake, we are omitting consideration of these hidden issues here and concentrating on the central issues.

Finding a General Statement of the Law

After our analysis of the fact situation, we have concluded that we need to research false imprisonment—in particular, whether a citizen, as opposed to a peace officer, can arrest (and detain) an individual whom he suspects of committing a crime but who has not in fact committed a crime.

We start our research by going to a legal encyclopedia to find a summary of the law of false imprisonment and to find references to the statutes, regulations, and cases that formulate the applicable principles of law. We choose the *Canadian Encyclopedic Digest* (CED), which is available in both paper and computerized formats.

Using the Paper Version of the CED

Because you don't know the subject title in the CED, start by looking for "false imprisonment" in the Index Key of the CED Index. See Figure 14.1.

Figure 14.1 Page from CED Index Key, Showing Entry for "False Imprisonment"

FAMILY LAW - DIVORCE I.1

(a) Appeals from Committal ....26–66§92
(b) Judicial Review of the Minister's Order....26–66§98
(c) Appeals to Supreme Court of Canada....26–66§102
7. Surrender....26–66§103
8. Temporary Surrender ....26–66§105
9. Consents and Waiver ....26–66§109
10. Transit....26–66§113
III. Extradition to Canada ....26–66§115
1. Making of Request....26–66§115

FAIR REPRESENTATION

See Labour Law

FALSE ARREST

See Damages; Malicious Prosecution and False Imprisonment; Mental Incapacity; Police; Public Authorities and Public Officers

FALSE IMPRISONMENT

See Criminal Law — Offences; Damages; Hospitals and Health Care; Malicious Prosecution and False Imprisonment; Mental Incapacity; Police; Public Authorities and Public Officers; Trespass

The Index Key entry directs you to a number of subject titles, the most relevant of which is "Malicious Prosecution and False Imprisonment." The index to that title includes the listings shown in Figure 14.2.

Figure 14.2   Pages from CED Index Key for "Malicious Prosecution and False Imprisonment"

MALICIOUS PROSECUTION AND FALSE IMPRISONMENT II.8(d)

(d) Nominal Damages
...................................37–97§126

(e) Excessive or Insufficient
Award ....37–97§127

9. Vicarious Liability ......37–97§129

10. Practice and Procedure
...................................37–97§135

(a) Jurisdiction of Courts
...................................37–97§135

(b) Pleadings ....37–97§137

(c) Burden of Proof ...37–97§142

(d) Proving Record in Criminal
Case ....37–97§144

(e) Discretion as to Costs
...................................37–97§146

11. Jury Trials ....37–97§149

(a) Demand or Direction for
Jury Trial ....37–97§149

(b) Respective Functions of
Judge and Jury ....37–97§150

(i) General.............37–97§150

(ii) Reasonable and Probable
Cause ....37–97§153

(iii) Malice............37–97§159

(c) Instructions to Jury
...................................37–97§161

(i) General.............37–97§161

(ii) Reasonable and Probable
Cause ....37–97§162

(iii) Malice............37–97§166

(iv) Damages ....37–97§168

(d) Setting Aside Verdict on
Appeal......................37–97§169

(e) Ordering New Trial
...................................37–97§171

(i) Misdirection.....37–97§171

(ii) Other Grounds
..........................37–97§174

12. Limitation of Actions
...................................37–97§175

13. Related Actions.........37–97§177

(a) Malicious Arrest for Debt
...................................37–97§177

(b) Malicious Issue and Execution of Search Warrant
...................................37–97§185

(c) Malicious Abuse Of Process
...................................37–97§189

(i) General.............37–97§189

(ii) Elements of Cause of
Action.................37–97§193

A. General ....37–97§193

B. Improper Purpose
.......................37–97§197

C. Overt Conduct
.......................37–97§202

D. Damages .....37–97§203

(iii) Defences ....37–97§205

(d) Vexatious Use Of Process
...................................37–97§207

**III. False Imprisonment and False
Arrest**...................................37–97§208

1. Public Policy..............37–97§208

2. False Imprisonment ....37–97§211

(a) General ....37–97§211

(b) Deprivation of Liberty
...................................37–97§216

(c) Defendant Causing Deprivation of Liberty ....37–97§224

3. False Arrest................37–97§231

(a) General ....37–97§231

(b) Arrest by Peace Officer
...................................37–97§234

(i) With Warrant...37–97§234

(ii) Without Warrant
..........................37–97§240

(c) Arrest by Private Citizen
...................................37–97§246

(d) Obligations Upon Arrest
...................................37–97§251

(i) Charter Rights
..........................37–97§251

460

Under the main heading (Malicious Prosecution and False Imprisonment) is the relevant part, "III. False Imprisonment and False Arrest," and then the relevant sections: "1. Public Policy," "2. False Imprisonment," and "3. False Arrest." We need to read them and to pay particular attention to the subsection referred to in section 3: "(c)—Arrest by Private Citizen." The paragraph under that subsection is shown in Figure 14.3, as are the footnotes listing relevant legislation and case law.

Figure 14.3   General Statement of Law in Print CED (Arrest by Private Citizen)

(c) — Arrest by Private Citizen

See Canadian Abridgment: TOR.XIV.1.d Torts — Malicious prosecution and false imprisonment — Elements of cause of action — Miscellaneous; TOR.XIV.3.d.ii Torts — Malicious prosecution and false imprisonment — Defences — Lawful authority — Arrest by private citizen

§246 Anyone may arrest without warrant a person whom he finds committing an indictable offence.[1] A hybrid offence is deemed to be indictable until the Crown elects otherwise; hence an ordinary citizen may validly arrest someone for committing it.[2] However, this does not alter the common law that an arrest by a private citizen, including a security guard or store detective,[3] is only justified if a felony was actually committed and there were reasonable and probable grounds for believing that the detained person committed it.[4] Reasonable grounds for believing that an offence was committed are not sufficient.[5]

1   Criminal Code, R.S.C. 1985, c. C-46, s. 494(1)(a); *R. v. Cunningham* (1979), 49 C.C.C. (2d) 390 (Man. Co. Ct.) ("finds committing" not meaning that person effecting arrest must actually witness commission of offence; sufficient if offence apparently committed).

2   Interpretation Act, R.S.C. 1985, c. I-21, s. 34(1)(a); *R. v. Huff* (1979), 50 C.C.C. (2d) 324 (Alta. C.A.) (dangerous driving); *Kovacs v. Ontario Jockey Club* (1995), 126 D.L.R. (4th) 576 (Ont. Gen. Div.) (attempted fraud); *R. v. Cunningham* (1979), 49 C.C.C. (2d) 390 (Man. Co. Ct.) (mischief).

3   *Banyasz v. K-Mart Canada Ltd.* (1986), 39 C.C.L.T. 266 (Ont. Div. Ct.); *Kendall v. Gambles Canada Ltd.*, [1981] 4 W.W.R. 718 (Sask. Q.B.); *R. v. Kendall* (1980), 3 Sask. R. 417 (Sask. Dist. Ct.) (unless security guard able to prove commission of indictable offence, guard having no jurisdiction to arrest without warrant, and any disturbance caused in resisting unlawful arrest justified); *R. v. Orban*, [1972] 5 W.W.R. 222 (Sask. Q.B.).

4   *Kendall v. Gambles Canada Ltd.*, [1981] 4 W.W.R. 718 (Sask. Q.B.); *Kovacs v. Ontario Jockey Club* (1995), 126 D.L.R. (4th) 576 (Ont. Gen. Div.); *Kavanagh v. Canadian Tire Corp.* (1989), 74 Nfld. & P.E.I.R. 205 (Nfld. T.D.); *Smart v. Simpson Sears Ltd.* (1984), 51 Nfld. & P.E.I.R.

137   June 2009

Using the Computerized Version of the CED

We can either browse the CED table of contents or search the CED generally, by keyword.

Browsing the Table of Contents

The CED table of contents lists all the subject titles in alphabetical order. When we browse the table of contents, we see that there is no entry for "false imprisonment" because it is not a subject title. However, when we continue to browse the titles, we find an entry for "Malicious Prosecution and False Imprisonment." When we select it, it expands as shown in Figure 14.4.

Figure 14.4   CED Online Table of Contents for Subject Title "Malicious Prosecution and False Imprisonment"

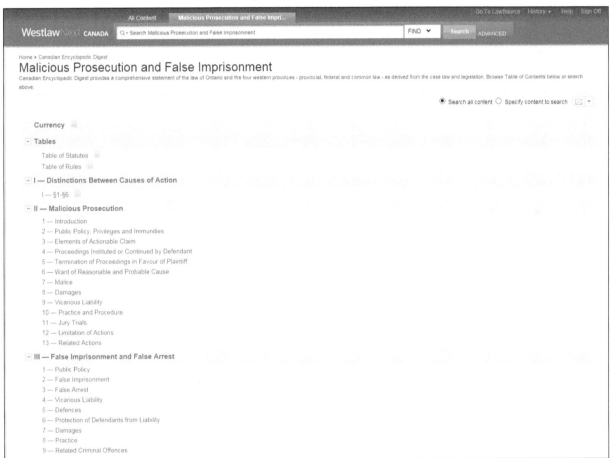

We select "III—False Imprisonment and False Arrest" to get the results shown in Figure 14.5.

Figure 14.5   CED Online Listing Under Part III of Subject Title ("False Imprisonment and False Arrest")

As with the paper version of the CED, we have to read the paragraphs under subheadings 1 ("Public Policy"), 2 ("False Imprisonment"), and 3 ("False Arrest"), which are under the main heading ("III — False Imprisonment and False Arrest"), and we need to pay particular attention to the paragraph referred to in subheading 3: "(c) Arrest by Private Citizen." That paragraph is reproduced in Figure 14.6, with the corresponding footnotes shown in Figure 14.7.

Note that the text and footnotes are identical to those in the paper version of the CED.

Figure 14.6   General Statement of Law in Online CED ("Arrest by Private Citizen")

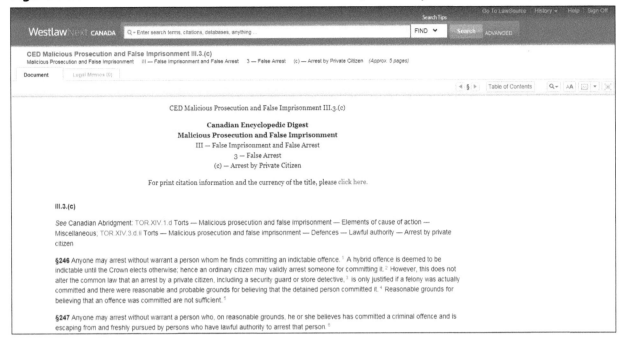

Figure 14.7   Footnotes for Statement of Law in Online CED ("Arrest by Private Citizen")

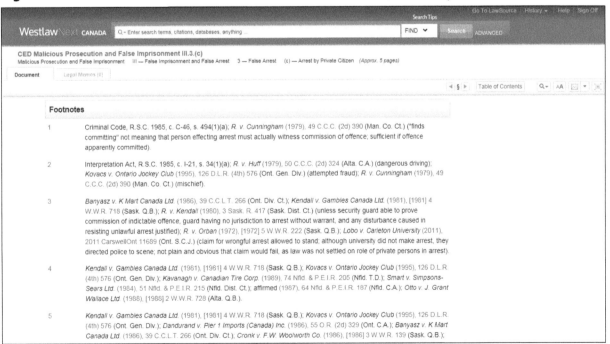

Searching the CED by Keyword

We can also use some of the keywords identified in our analysis of the fact situation to construct a terms and connectors (Boolean) search, as set out in Figure 14.8. As you can see, the first result shows the same subheading we arrived at using the table of contents.

Figure 14.8   Searching the Online CED by Keyword

Reading the Results

By different routes we arrived each time at paragraph 246 (see Figure 14.3 or Figures 14.6 and 14.7). The first and third sentences in the statement of the law address our fact situation directly:

> Anyone may arrest without warrant a person whom he finds committing an indictable offence. … However, this does not alter the common law that an arrest by a private citizen, including a security guard or store detective, is only justified if a felony was actually committed and there were reasonable and probable grounds for believing that the detained person committed it.

Footnote 1 refers us to s 494(1)(a) of the *Criminal Code*, RSC 1985, c C-46. Footnote 3 refers us to several cases, including the case of *Banyasz v K Mart Canada Ltd* (1986), 39 CCLT 266 (Ont Div Ct).

Finding the Primary Sources of Law

Next, we have to look at the statutes and cases to which the secondary sources have referred us.

Statute Law

In the CED, s 494(1)(a) of the *Criminal Code* is cited as the source for the following statement: "Anyone may arrest without warrant a person whom he finds committing an indictable offence."

Finding the Text of the Statute

We find the text of s 494(1)(a) of the *Criminal Code* by using the citation: RSC 1985, c C-46. Recall that "RSC" is an abbreviation for the *Revised Statutes of Canada*, which tells us that the statute is a federal statute, so we go to the federal Justice Laws website. Because we know the name of the statute, we can browse by title by selecting the link "Consolidated Acts" under the heading Laws and then the letter "C." Selecting "Criminal Code" takes us to the statute's table of contents. Scroll down to s 494 and select it to get the text of the section (Figure 14.9).

Figure 14.9   Text of Section 494 of the Criminal Code

Arrest without warrant by any person

494. (1) Any one may arrest without warrant

(*a*) a person whom he finds committing an indictable offence; or

(*b*) a person who, on reasonable grounds, he believes

(i) has committed a criminal offence, and

(ii) is escaping from and freshly pursued by persons who have lawful authority to arrest that person.

Reading the Statute

Having found the text of the statute, we must read and understand it by breaking it down into its elements (as discussed in Chapter 2). Broken down into its separate elements, s 494(1)(a) looks like this

> Any one
> may arrest without warrant
> a person whom he finds committing
> an indictable offence

The store clerk in Elwood's case accused Elwood of shoplifting, which is a form of theft, so we need to find out whether theft is an indictable offence. If we search the *Criminal Code* for the terms "theft" and "indictable offence," we get a number of results, one of which is s 334, shown in Figure 14.10.

Figure 14.10   Section 334 of the Criminal Code

Punishment for theft

334. Except where otherwise provided by law, every one who commits theft

(*a*) is guilty of an indictable offence and liable to imprisonment for a term not exceeding ten years, where the property stolen is a testamentary instrument or the value of what is stolen exceeds five thousand dollars; or

(*b*) is guilty

(i) of an indictable offence and is liable to imprisonment for a term not exceeding two years, or

(ii) of an offence punishable on summary conviction,

where the value of what is stolen does not exceed five thousand dollars.

A store clerk may *suspect* Elwood of having committed an indictable offence, but that is insufficient grounds for a citizen's arrest; the statute clearly states that the person must actually be *found committing* the offence. In Elwood's case, although the store clerk suspected that Elwood had shoplifted, he had not in fact done so.

Case Law

Paragraph 246 of the CED, shown in Figures 14.3 and 14.6, states that s 494(1)(a) "does not alter the common law that an arrest by a private citizen, including a security guard or store detective, is only justified if a felony was actually committed." The CED cites the case of *Banyasz v K Mart Canada Ltd*, among others, as the source for that statement.

Finding a Case Digest

Before looking for the full text of the *Banyasz* case, we decide to read a digest of the case in the *Canadian Abridgment* to confirm that it's relevant to Elwood's fact situation. The digest also provides parallel citations for the case, which will make it easier to locate the text of the case if we have to use print sources to obtain it.

Referring to Figure 14.6, you can see that the online CED entry gives us the corresponding *Canadian Abridgment* Key classification number: TOR.XIV.3.d.ii. Selecting the hyperlink takes us to the online *Canadian Abridgment Digests* and the page shown in Figure 14.11.

Figure 14.11   CAD Online Text Under TOR.XIV.3.d Lawful Authority

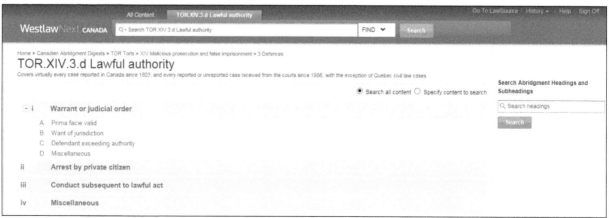

Selecting "Arrest by private citizen" brings up 19 cases, number 9 of which is *Banyasz v K-Mart Canada Ltd.* See Figure 14.12.

Figure 14.12   CAD Online Case Digest for *Banyasz v K-Mart Canada Ltd*

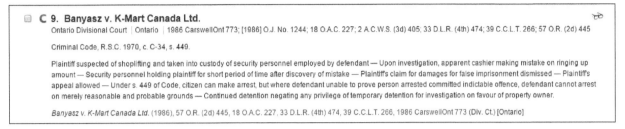

Finding the Text of the Case

There are a number of ways to locate the text of a case. We discussed them in Chapter 13.

Using the citations in Figure 14.12, we could locate a print version of the *Banyasz* case at the library. The citations contain all the information we need to find the case: the name and volume number of the law report series, and the page number within the volume. We could start by finding the law report series (making sure to look in the correct series number), in this case one of the *Ontario Reports, Ontario Appeal Cases, Dominion Law Reports,* or *Canadian Cases on the Law of Torts.* Then we would find the correct volume number and turn to the page number set out in the citation.

Or we could locate the text of the case using one of the computerized sources discussed in Chapter 13. In this instance, the simplest way is to link to the text of the case from the *Canadian Abridgment Digests* entry in Figure 14.12. That will take us to the page shown in Figure 14.13.

Figure 14.13   Text of *Banyasz v K-Mart Canada Ltd*

We can read the text of the case on the web page or we can view the version of the case published in the *Dominion Law Reports* or in the *All-Canada Weekly Summaries* by selecting either of those links under "Case Views" on the right-hand side of the page. The *Dominion Law Reports* version is reproduced below.

Reading the Case

Banyasz v. K-Mart Canada Ltd.

(1986), 33 D.L.R. (4th) 474

Ontario High Court of Justice, Divisional Court, Callaghan A.C.J.H.C.

S. Pasternak, for appellant.

G. Will, for respondent.

[1]   CALLAGHAN A.C.J.H.C. (orally):—This is an appeal by the plaintiff from the judgment of the Provincial Court (Civil Division) of North York, Ontario, dated February 12, 1985, wherein the plaintiff's claim for damages for false imprisonment was dismissed.

[2]   The plaintiff was suspected of shoplifting and was taken into custody by the security personnel employed by the defendant store. It was suspected that the plaintiff had stolen a battery for a walkie-talkie and had left the store without paying for the same. Upon investigation it became immediately apparent that the cashier had made a mistake in ringing up the amount chargeable to the plaintiff. Notwithstanding the admitted mistake, the security personnel continued to hold the plaintiff for a short period of time thereafter.

[3]   The learned trial judge considered the pertinent elements of the cause of action and concluded on the evidence that the plaintiff in fact was detained by the security personnel and that there was a constructive imprisonment (transcript, p. 24, line 2). As there was evidence to support such a finding this court will not interfere therewith on this appeal. The trial judge further concluded that while the plaintiff left the store with a battery he had not paid for there was no evidence of any intent on the plaintiff's part to commit theft or fraud (*ibid.* p. 76, line 15). The aforesaid conclusion was consistent with the finding that the mistake was that of the cashier in failing to charge the plaintiff the cost of the battery which was not included in the walkie-talkie. The effect of the trial judge's finding was that a criminal offence in the circumstances of this case had not been committed.

[4]   In considering a disposition of the matter, the trial judge stated the applicable test as follows:

> If there is reasonable and probable grounds. If the defendant objectively had reasonable and probable grounds for believing that fraud had been committed, then the actions of the defendant were justified.

(*Ibid.* p. 75, line 29).

[5] The trial judge concluded that in the circumstances the security personnel had reasonable and probable grounds for believing that theft had been committed and accordingly dismissed the plaintiff's action. In so doing he erred.

[6] At the outset it must be noted that "security personnel" employed to guard against theft of merchandise have no higher rights of arrest than those conferred on citizens generally: *Dendekker v. F.W. Woolworth Co.*, [1975] 3 W.W.R. 429 [Alta SC]. The appropriate rule is that established in the case of *Williams v. Laing* (1923), 55 O.L.R. 26 at p. 28 [CA], wherein Mr. Justice Hodgins stated:

> The law is quite clear that in order to succeed in establishing this defence the appellants must prove first that the crime they suspected had actually been committed, not necessarily by the person detained, but by someone, and that they had reasonable ground for suspecting the person detained.

[7] Mere suspicion that an offence has been committed is not sufficient when arrest is effected by a citizen. The person alleging justification for arrest must be prepared to establish that the crime was in fact committed: see also *McKenzie v. Gibson* (1852), 8 U.C.Q.B. 100 at p. 101-2, *per* Sir John Robinson C.J.

[8] Under s. 449 of the *Criminal Code*, a citizen can make an arrest where he or she finds another committing an indictable offence. Where the defendant is unable to prove that the person arrested has committed an indictable offence, the defendant cannot arrest merely on reasonable and probable grounds: see *Hayward v. F.W. Woolworth Co. Ltd. et al.* (1979), 98 D.L.R. (3d) 345, 23 Nfld. & P.E.I.R. 17, 8 C.C.L.T. 157 [Nfld SC]; *Kendall et al. v. Gambles Canada Ltd. et al.*, [1981] 4 W.W.R. 718, 11 Sask. R. 361 [QB].

[9] The defendant/respondent herein relied on the judgment in *Karogiannis v. Poulus et al.* (1976), 72 D.L.R. (3d) 253, [1976] 6 W.W.R. 197 [BCSC]. In that case it was held that it was not necessary that the defendant show that the plaintiff had actually committed theft but only that he had reasonable grounds for believing and did believe that a theft had been committed. The court therein held that s. 449(1)(a) of the *Criminal Code* is to be read as if it included the word "apparently" so that it would read "whom he finds (apparently) committing an indictable offence" and thereby affords justification for a defendant who arrested a person who in fact did not commit an offence. With respect, I cannot agree with that decision. I am in agreement with the reasoning of Mr. Justice Goodridge in *Hayward v. F.W. Woolworth Co. Ltd.*, *supra*, and Mr. Justice Cameron in *Kendall et al. v. Gambles Canada Ltd.*, *supra*, wherein that interpretation of s. 449 is rejected.

[10] The problem of shoplifting is a serious one for storekeepers notwithstanding that the law of tort favours the interest in individual freedom over that of protection of property. While there may be a developing privilege of temporary detention for investigation in favour of a property owner (see Prosser, *Handbook of the Law of Torts*, 4th ed. (1971), p. 121), this is not a case where such a privilege should prevail. The continued detention after the

cashier admitted her mistake negatives any consideration of such a privilege in this case.

[11] In result, therefore, the appeal must be allowed, a verdict entered for the plaintiff, and the matter referred back to the trial judge for an assessment of damages. The plaintiff will have its costs of this appeal and the costs of the first trial in the court below. The costs of this assessment will be reserved to the trial judge.

Appeal allowed.

Understanding the Case

Using the approach to reading a case set out in Chapter 4, we now break down the *Banyasz* case into its constituent elements and summarize each one.

PURPOSE

This is an appeal by the plaintiff from a judgment of the Provincial Court dismissing his claim for damages for false imprisonment.

FACTS

The facts of the case are as follows:

- The plaintiff was shopping at K-Mart, where he bought a walkie-talkie.
- The cashier made a mistake in failing to charge the plaintiff for the cost of the battery, which was not included in the walkie-talkie.
- As the plaintiff was leaving the store, he was taken into custody by security personnel employed by the defendant, on suspicion of stealing a battery.
- The cashier's mistake was immediately apparent on investigation; nevertheless, security personnel continued to hold the plaintiff for a short time.
- At trial, the judge concluded on the evidence that the plaintiff was detained by security personnel and that there was constructive imprisonment.
- At trial, the judge concluded that, although the plaintiff left the store with a battery he had not paid for, there was no evidence of intent to commit theft or fraud—therefore, no criminal offence had been committed.
- At trial, the judge concluded that security personnel had reasonable and probable grounds for believing that theft had been committed and therefore dismissed the plaintiff's action.

ISSUES

The two main issues are as follows:

1. Whether the plaintiff was falsely imprisoned—was there lawful justification for detention of the plaintiff?
2. Whether a reasonable belief that an offence has been committed constitutes lawful justification for detention of the plaintiff.

LAW

The key points of law discussed by the judge in *Banyasz* are as follows:

- Security personnel employed to guard against theft of merchandise have no higher rights of arrest than those conferred on citizens generally (*Dendekker v FW Woolworth Co*, [1975] 3 WWR 429 (Alta SC)).

- A citizen can make an arrest where he or she finds another committing an indictable offence (*Criminal Code*, RSC 1970, c C-34, s 449).

- Where the defendant is unable to prove that the person arrested has committed an indictable offence, the defendant cannot arrest merely on reasonable and probable grounds (*Hayward v FW Woolworth Co Ltd et al* (1979), 98 DLR (3d) 345 (Nfld SC); *Kendall et al v Gambles Canada Ltd et al*, [1981] 4 WWR 718 (Sask QB)).

- Mere suspicion that an offence has been committed is not sufficient when arrest is effected by a citizen. The person alleging justification for arrest must be prepared to establish that the crime was in fact committed (*McKenzie v Gibson* (1852), 8 UCQB 100 at 101-2, Robinson CJ).

- To succeed in establishing the defence of lawful justification, the appellants must prove first that the crime they suspected had actually been committed, not necessarily by the person detained but by someone, and that they had reasonable grounds for suspecting the person detained (*Williams v Laing* (1923), 55 OLR 26 at 28 (CA), Hodgins J).

- It is not necessary that the defendant show that the plaintiff had actually committed theft but only that he had reasonable grounds for believing and did believe a theft had been committed (*Karogiannis v Poulus et al* (1976), 72 DLR (3d) 253 (BCSC)).

  This interpretation of s 449 (now s 494) of the *Criminal Code* was rejected by the judge.

- There may be a developing privilege of temporary detention for investigation in favour of a property owner (WL Prosser, *Handbook of the Law of Torts*, 4th ed (St Paul, Minn: West, 1971) at 121).

RATIO

The appeal judge was in agreement with the reasoning in *Hayward v FW Woolworth*, wherein the *Karogiannis* interpretation of s 449 was rejected.

While there may be a developing privilege of temporary detention for investigation in favour of a property owner, this is not a case where such a privilege should prevail. The continued detention after the cashier admitted her mistake negates any consideration of such a privilege in this case.

DECISION

The appeal must be allowed, a verdict entered for the plaintiff, and the matter referred back to the trial judge for an assessment of damages.

DISPOSITION

Appeal allowed.

Applying the Case to Our Issue

As we can see, the facts in the *Banyasz* case are very similar to ours. In both cases, the person making the arrest was a citizen, not a peace officer, and, while the person detained was suspected of having committed a theft, no offence was in fact committed. The issues in the *Banyasz* case are identical to ours: whether there was false imprisonment and, in particular, whether a store clerk (a citizen, not a peace officer) has legal justification to arrest a customer whom he suspects has committed a crime but who has not in fact committed a crime.

Therefore, the ratio in the *Banyasz* case is relevant to our fact situation. It can be summarized as follows:

- A citizen can make an arrest where he or she finds another committing an indictable offence.
- Where the defendant is unable to prove that the person arrested has committed an indictable offence, the defendant cannot arrest merely on reasonable and probable grounds.
- Mere suspicion that an offence has been committed is not sufficient when arrest is effected by a citizen. The person alleging justification for arrest must be prepared to establish that the crime was in fact committed.

Before we move on from this case, it is important to note that the case refers to and interprets s 449(1)(a) of the *Criminal Code*, not s 494(1)(a), which is the section of the *Criminal Code* that we encountered in our preliminary research. To ensure that the case is still relevant to the statute law today, we have to check whether s 494 is the same or at least sufficiently similar to s 449. If we go back to the section on the federal Justice Laws website, there is a link to the previous version at the bottom of the section. See Figure 14.14.

We select the link, and it takes us to Figure 14.15, an earlier version of s 494. At the bottom it sets out the citation of the pre-consolidated version of the section: "R.S., c. C-34, s. 449; R.S., c. 2 (2nd Supp.), s. 5." In other words, the s 449 discussed in the case is the same as the current s 494.

Figure 14.14   Section 494 of the Criminal Code on the Justice Laws Website, Showing Link to Previous Version

Arrest without warrant by any person

494. (1) Any one may arrest without warrant

(*a*) a person whom he finds committing an indictable offence; or

(*b*) a person who, on reasonable grounds, he believes

(i) has committed a criminal offence, and

(ii) is escaping from and freshly pursued by persons who have lawful authority to arrest that person.

Arrest by owner, etc., of property

(2) The owner or a person in lawful possession of property, or a person authorized by the owner or by a person in lawful possession of property, may arrest a person without a warrant if they find them committing a criminal offence on or in relation to that property and

(*a*) they make the arrest at that time; or

(*b*) they make the arrest within a reasonable time after the offence is committed and they believe on reasonable grounds that it is not feasible in the circumstances for a peace officer to make the arrest.

Delivery to peace officer

(3) Any one other than a peace officer who arrests a person without warrant shall forthwith deliver the person to a peace officer.

For greater certainty

(4) For greater certainty, a person who is authorized to make an arrest under this section is a person who is authorized by law to do so for the purposes of section 25.

R.S., 1985, c. C-46, s. 494; 2012, c. 9, s. 3.

Previous Version

Figure 14.15   Earlier Version of Section 494 of the Criminal Code

Arrest without warrant by any person

494. (1) Any one may arrest without warrant

(*a*) a person whom he finds committing an indictable offence; or

(*b*) a person who, on reasonable grounds, he believes

(i) has committed a criminal offence, and

(ii) is escaping from and freshly pursued by persons who have lawful authority to arrest that person.

Arrest by owner, etc., of property

(2) Any one who is

(*a*) the owner or a person in lawful possession of property, or

(*b*) a person authorized by the owner or by a person in lawful possession of property,

may arrest without warrant a person whom he finds committing a criminal offence on or in relation to that property.

Delivery to peace officer

(3) Any one other than a peace officer who arrests a person without warrant shall forthwith deliver the person to a peace officer.

R.S., c. C-34, s. 449; R.S., c. 2(2nd Supp.), s. 5.

Updating the Primary Sources

We must update any statute, regulation, or case we find to make sure it is still good law.

Statute Law

There is no need to update the *Criminal Code* because we found the text on the Justice Laws website, which is generally updated every two weeks.

Case Law

There are a number of ways to update a case, using print and computer sources. In our case, it is easiest to update the case using WestlawNext Canada, because we found the text of the case by linking from the digest in the *Canadian Abridgment Digests* (see Figure 14.13).

Note the tabs at the top of the screen. The number (0) on the History tab tells us that the case was not appealed. The number (12) on the Citing References tab tells us that the case has been cited 12 times. Choosing this tab takes us to the screen shown in Figure 14.16.

Looking under the Type column, we see that the *Banyasz* case has been judicially considered nine times. The Treatment column tells us that the case has been followed twice, considered four times, and referred to three times. Its decision has never been reversed.

Figure 14.16   Results from Choosing the Citing References Tab: Westlaw

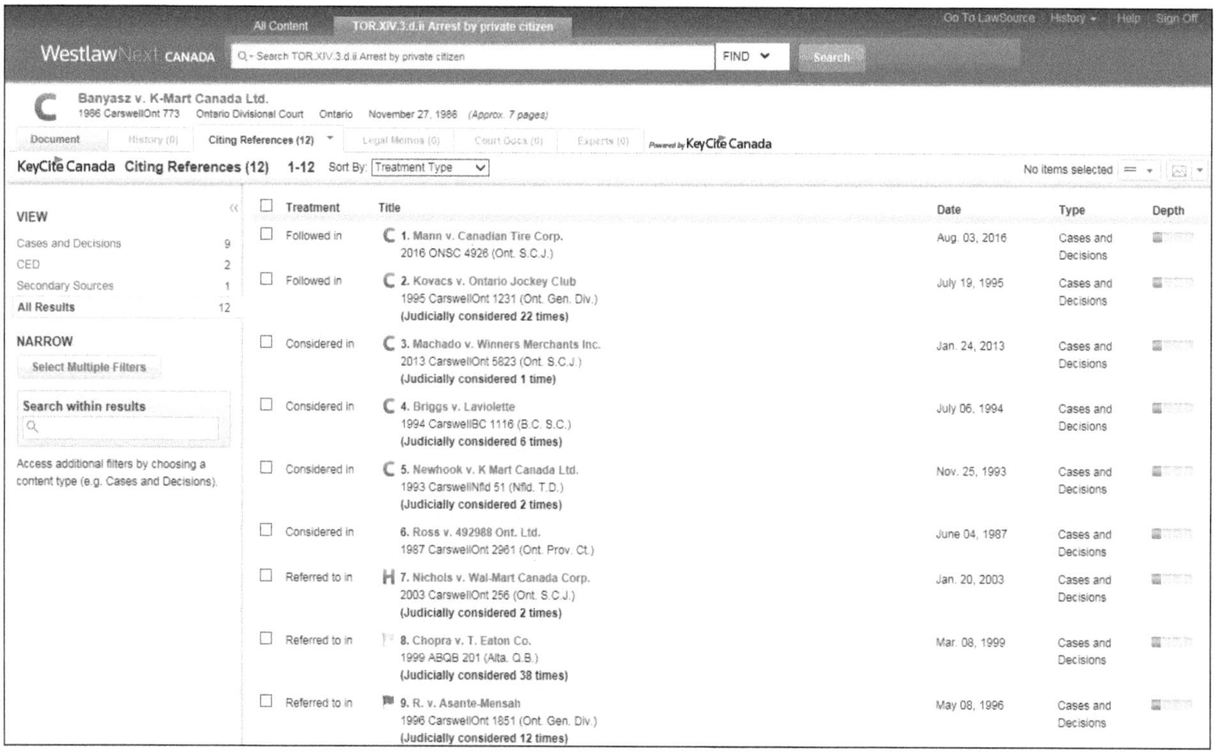

Our Conclusion

On the basis of our review of the facts and the law, we can reach the following conclusions:

- Because Elwood had not in fact stolen anything, he had not committed an indictable (or any) offence.
- Because Elwood had not committed an indictable offence, the store clerk could not justify the arrest under the right granted to an individual who is not a peace officer under s 494(1)(a) of the *Criminal Code.*
- The case law does not change the clear meaning of s 494(1)(a).
- Because there was no right to arrest, there was no right to detain. Therefore, there was false imprisonment.
- Therefore, the client has a cause of action.

Memo of Law

We don't want all our valuable research to be lost or forgotten, so instead of just sticking a copy of s 494 and the *Banyasz* case into the file, we will write our research up in a memo of law that will stay with the file. Having a memo in the file also means that we (or anyone else in the firm) can quickly get up to date on the facts and law, and won't have to waste time searching for a statement of the facts and rereading *Banyasz* to remember what it's about. For our memo on Elwood Blues and Kwik-e-Mart, see Appendix 14.1.

Opinion Letter

Finally, it's time to tell the clients what our research demonstrated. We will inform them by way of an opinion letter. We did most of the work involved in preparing an opinion letter when we wrote up the memo of law. Now we just need to put it in letter form, and make sure that it can be understood by someone without legal training. The opinion letter is shown in Appendix 14.2.

Appendix 14.1

Memo

To: File
From: Perry Legal
Re: Elwood Blues and Kwik-e-Mart
File No.:12345
Date: *Day/Month/Year*

I met with Elwood Blues and his family on *day/month/year*. They retained our firm to advise them whether they have a cause of action. After getting the facts from them, I have researched this matter and the results of that research are set out in this memo.

Facts

Sixteen-year-old Elwood Blues went into the Kwik-e-Mart, a convenience store close to his home. He walked all around the store looking for his favourite brand of cookies. He didn't find what he was looking for and was about to leave the store when he found his way blocked by the clerk, a husky man named Steve Barnes. Barnes said, "You put something into your pocket!" Elwood replied, "No, I didn't." "We'll see about that!" Barnes said. Barnes then told Elwood that he was making a citizen's arrest, called the police, and told Elwood that he couldn't leave the store until the police got there. Barnes stayed in front of the door until the police arrived, blocking the store's only exit. When the police arrived, Barnes told the officer, "I think this boy shoplifted something from my store and put it into his pocket." The police officer asked Elwood for his side of the story. Elwood said, "I didn't take anything. See?" and emptied his pockets. There was nothing belonging to the store in his pockets, so the police officer told Elwood he was free to go. Elwood then left.

Issues

- Whether there was false imprisonment
- Whether a store clerk (a citizen, not a peace officer) can arrest a customer whom he suspects has committed a crime but who has not in fact committed a crime

Note to file: The following issues have yet to be researched and will not be pursued until we have instructions from the client to proceed further with a lawsuit:

- Whether substantial damages will be awarded where a wrongful detention was of short duration and the detainee was not treated abusively
- Whether a 16-year-old can start a lawsuit

- What is Steve Barnes's relationship to Kwik-e-Mart? Is he the owner, or an employee, or even just a friend helping out?
- Is Kwik-e-Mart a sole proprietorship? A partnership? A corporation?

Law

STATUTE

Criminal Code, RSC 1985, c C-46

Section 494
494(1) Any one may arrest without warrant
(a) a person whom he finds committing an indictable offence

Section 334
334. Except where otherwise provided by law, everyone who commits theft
(a) is guilty of an indictable offence and liable to imprisonment for a term not exceeding ten years, where the property stolen is a testamentary instrument or the value of what is stolen exceeds five thousand dollars; or
(b) is guilty
(i) of an indictable offence and is liable to imprisonment for a term not exceeding two years, or
(ii) of an offence punishable on summary conviction,
where the value of what is stolen does not exceed five thousand dollars.

CASE LAW

Banyasz v K Mart Canada Ltd (1986), 57 OR (2d) 445, 18 OAC 227, 33 DLR (4th) 474, 39 CCLT 266, 1986 CarswellOnt 773 (Div Ct)

- Security personnel employed to guard against theft of merchandise have no higher rights of arrest than those conferred on citizens generally.

  > *Dendekker v FW Woolworth Co*, [1975] 3 WWR 429 (Alta SC)

- A citizen can make an arrest where he or she finds another committing an indictable offence.

  > *Criminal Code*, RSC 1970, c C-34, s 449

- Where the defendant is unable to prove that the person arrested has committed an indictable offence, the defendant cannot arrest merely on reasonable and probable grounds.

  > *Hayward v FW Woolworth Co Ltd et al* (1979), 98 DLR (3d) 345 (Nfld SC);
  > *Kendall et al v Gambles Canada Ltd et al*, [1981] 4 WWR 718 (Sask QB)

- Mere suspicion that an offence has been committed is not sufficient when arrest is effected by a citizen. The person alleging justification for arrest must be prepared to establish that the crime was in fact committed.

  > *McKenzie v Gibson* (1852), 8 UCQB 100 at 101-2, Robinson CJ

- To succeed in establishing the defence of lawful justification, the appellants must prove first that the crime they suspected had actually been committed, not necessarily by the person detained but by someone, and that they had reasonable grounds for suspecting the person detained.

Williams v Laing (1923), 55 OLR 26 at 28 (CA), Hodgins J

The *Banyasz* case has been judicially considered nine times: followed twice, considered four times, and referred to three times. Its decision has never been reversed.

Discussion

As we can see, the facts in the *Banyasz* case are similar to ours. In both cases, the person making the arrest was a citizen, not a peace officer, and, although the person detained was suspected of having committed a theft, no offence was in fact committed. The issues in the *Banyasz* case are identical to ours: whether there was false imprisonment, and in particular whether a store clerk (a citizen, not a peace officer) can arrest a customer whom he suspects has committed a crime but who has not in fact committed a crime.

1. Whether there was false imprisonment

   Elwood was certainly prevented from leaving the store, but it was not false imprisonment if the store clerk had a right to arrest him in the first place. Therefore, we'll proceed to issue 2.

2. Whether a store clerk (a citizen, not a peace officer) can arrest a customer whom he suspects has committed a crime but who has not in fact committed a crime

   A citizen can make an arrest where he or she finds another committing an indictable offence.

   Where the defendant is unable to prove that the person arrested has committed an indictable offence, the defendant cannot arrest merely on reasonable and probable grounds.

   Mere suspicion that an offence has been committed is not sufficient when arrest is effected by a citizen. The person alleging justification for arrest must be prepared to establish that the crime was in fact committed.

Conclusions

- Because Elwood had not in fact stolen anything, he had not committed an indictable (or any) offence.
- Because Elwood had not committed an indictable offence, the store clerk could not justify the arrest under the right granted under s 494(1)(a) of the *Criminal Code*.
- The case law does not change the clear meaning of s 494(1)(a).
- Since there was no right to arrest, there was no right to detain. Therefore, there was false imprisonment.
- Therefore, there is a cause of action.

Appendix 14.2

Opinion Letter for Client

Dear Mr. and Mrs. Blues and Elwood:

Re: Elwood Blues and Kwik-e-Mart

Thank you for meeting with me on *day/month/year* and retaining me to look into this matter for you.

Facts

When we met, you told me the following story. Elwood went into the Kwik-e-Mart, a convenience store close to your home. He walked all around the store looking for his favourite brand of cookies. He didn't find what he was looking for and was about to leave the store when he found his way blocked by the clerk, a husky man named Steve Barnes. Barnes said, "You put something into your pocket!" Elwood replied, "No, I didn't." "We'll see about that!" Barnes said. Barnes then told Elwood that he was making a citizen's arrest, called the police, and told Elwood that he couldn't leave the store until the police got there. Barnes stayed in front of the door until the police arrived, blocking the store's only exit. When the police arrived, Barnes told the officer, "I think this boy shoplifted something from my store and put it into his pocket." The police officer asked Elwood for his side of the story. Elwood said, "I didn't take anything. See?" and emptied his pockets. There was nothing belonging to the store in his pockets, so the police officer told Elwood he was free to go. Elwood then left.

You asked me to determine whether Elwood has a right to sue Kwik-e-Mart for damages as a result of being detained by the store clerk.

Issues

The facts that you told me raise the following legal issues:

1. Whether there was false imprisonment. False imprisonment is the intentional confinement by one person of another person within fixed boundaries without lawful justification. The word "false" means wrongful or without lawful justification. No prison is necessary. A person can be confined anywhere.

2. Whether a store clerk (a citizen, not a peace officer) can arrest an individual in his store whom he suspects has committed a crime but who has not in fact committed a crime.

Discussion of the Issues

1. Whether there was false imprisonment

   Elwood was certainly prevented from leaving the store, but it was not false imprisonment if the store clerk had a right to arrest him in the first place. Therefore, we'll proceed to issue 2.

2. Whether a store clerk (a citizen, not a peace officer) can arrest an individual in his store whom he suspects has committed a crime but who has not in fact committed a crime

   A citizen can make an arrest where he or she finds a person committing an indictable offence. Shoplifting can be an indictable offence. However, mere suspicion that an offence has been committed is not sufficient to justify an arrest by a citizen. The person claiming justification for an arrest must establish that an indictable offence was in fact committed.

   Because Elwood had not in fact stolen anything, he had not committed an indictable (or any) offence. Because Elwood had not committed an indictable offence, the store clerk could not justify arresting or detaining him. Because there was no right to arrest, there was no right to detain. Therefore, there was false imprisonment. Therefore, you have a cause of action and can start a lawsuit if you want.

Next Steps

Before you decide whether to start a lawsuit, a number of additional issues need to be considered: whether a lawsuit would be financially worthwhile; who should bring the lawsuit, since Elwood is only 16; and who the defendant(s) should be (the clerk, the convenience store, or both). If you decide to proceed, we can discuss these issues at our next meeting.

I will need your instructions before I can do anything further in this matter.

Please do not hesitate to contact me if you have any questions or if I can be of any further assistance.

Yours truly,

Perry Legal

Legal Writing

LEARNING OUTCOMES

After reading this chapter, you will understand:

- The format of a memo of law

- The format of an opinion letter

- The practical steps involved in writing a memo of law

- The practical steps involved in writing an opinion letter

- Some principles of good legal writing

Introduction

When you complete your legal research, you will most likely have to record and/or communicate your research findings in writing. It is important that you be able to do this in a clear and concise manner. This chapter discusses two forms of legal writing: memos of law and opinion letters. As a bonus, the chapter ends with some general guidance on how to write well (see Appendix 15.1).

In both opinion letters and memos of law, the writer sets out a question or a fact situation that the client has presented, and then sets out the law that relates to (and if possible determines) that question or fact situation. An opinion letter will always, in addition, suggest possible courses of action and the legal consequences of each course of action. A memo may also do this.

Writing a Memo of Law

The results of legal research that are intended for internal use in the firm are often recorded in a memorandum (or memo) of law, often a "memo to file" rather than a memo to another legal professional. Writing a memo of law after performing your research ensures that the research won't be wasted; it will be available the next time it's needed, in an easily comprehended form. A memo of law may form the basis of an opinion letter written either by the researcher or by another member of the firm.

Before you prepare the final version of a memo of law according to the format set out below, use a list of steps to work through the form systematically. These steps are described below, under the heading "Steps in Creating a Memo of Law." You will find a sample memo of law in Chapter 14 (see Appendix 14.1). Reread it now before we start working through the process, and keep it handy as a reference point.

Format of a Memo of Law

Most memos of law include the following elements:

- heading,
- introduction,
- facts,
- issue(s),
- law,
- discussion,
- conclusions,
- references, and
- attachments.

Heading

The memo's heading appears as follows:

Memo

To:

From:

Re:

File No.:

Date:

Introduction

In the introduction, briefly state what you have been asked to do and why. State the question(s) that the client or lawyer has asked, or set out the fact situation that he or she has described. If the person asking the question is familiar with the field, the question asked may turn out to be the issue as well. If the person asking the question knows little about the field, the question may not be the same as the legal issue that you have actually had to research.

Facts

These are the facts that are relevant to the issue(s), and you present them in chronological order.

Issue(s)

What is the issue of law that must be examined here—that is, what problem must be solved in order to reach a solution? Issues are usually introduced by the word "whether." There may be just one issue, or there may be several.

Law

For legislation, set out the relevant statutory or regulatory provisions as they appear in the statute or regulation, with a full citation of the statute or regulation and section.

For cases, set out the relevant passages from them, with a full citation of each case. If there is more than one issue in a case, restate each issue exactly as it appeared in the issue section before setting out the law on that issue.

Do not set out diverging lines of authority that you find in a case. You are quoting the case to show the law the judge followed and the decision that the judge reached, not to show the law the judge decided not to follow. If you think the law the judge did *not* follow is useful to you, get the cases and quote the judge's words directly.

Discussion

Discuss or analyze the statute, regulation, and/or case law in light of the given fact situation. This is the appropriate place to discuss

1. whether the facts in the cases you have found are sufficiently similar to your client's situation for the law in those cases to be applicable to your fact situation;

2. the state of the law—for example, whether it is changing, or whether there are conflicting cases or conflicting statutory or regulatory provisions;

3. whether existing statutes, regulations, and cases in fact address the problem in your fact situation (Is yours a new or unusual point of law? If so, can you use existing law to suggest a likely solution to the problem?); and

4. whether previously unforeseen problems for the client arise out of your study of the law.

Be objective. A client will be helped neither by a memo that ignores problems that arise in the law nor by a memo that—when the law generally seems to go against the client—ignores possible solutions.

Conclusion

Draw together the facts and the law. State what you have concluded from applying the law to the facts in your situation. There should be one paragraph or section in the conclusion for each issue. Also point out any further information that is required or any problems that need further research.

References

Make sure to reference any law that you cite. Include the name and citation of the case or statute in the body of your memo. Alternatively, provide only the name of the case or statute in the body of the memo, and then provide the citation in a footnote.

Attachments

Attach any cases and statutory and regulatory provisions that you refer to in your memo.

Steps in Creating a Memo of Law

1. Analyze the fact situation.

2. Research the law.

3. Prepare a draft memo of law. At this point, as you prepare the draft memo, you need to see the problem as a whole. A draft memo of law gives you a chance to try out different ideas about what you think is going on from a legal

point of view. This way, you can settle on the true issues, the important facts, and the relevant law. You may have to rework your draft once or twice before you're satisfied that you've approached the problem from the correct angle.

- In your draft memo, you should NOT start with the *facts* and work down. Start with the *question* asked by the client or lawyer.

- Then set out the legal *issues* that arise out of the question, out of the facts, and out of the law you have found in your research.

- Then set out the *law*.

- When you have done all this, you will be able to look at the facts and decide which ones are relevant to the principles of law involved. Delete irrelevant facts. Emphasize essential facts.

- Discuss the law as it relates to the facts in your particular case.

- Finally, reach a conclusion. Suggest possible action and potential consequences of such action.

4. Prepare a final memo of law in the format above. Remember that a memo of law is not a 5,000-word term paper; keep it short and to the point. Anyone who later reads the memo is also going to read the attached statute law, regulatory provisions, and case law, and may draw his or her own conclusions.

Writing an Opinion Letter

The results of legal research are often communicated to the client by way of an opinion letter. An opinion letter is just what it sounds like: a letter expressing an opinion about the problem that the client has brought to the lawyer. The opinion might be that the client has a good case; on that basis, the letter might set out a path for proceeding with the matter (such as bringing a lawsuit). Or it may be that the client has no case. In that event, the careful legal professional may want to suggest alternative ways for the client to proceed. (For example, if the client wants to sue her previously retained lawyer or paralegal but does not have a cause of action, the opinion letter might suggest sending a letter of complaint to the Law Society of Upper Canada.)

An opinion letter is more than just your opinion, however. The opinion itself can't be whatever pops into your head on hearing the client's story. It must be

- complete with respect to the relevant facts presented by the client and with respect to the law applicable to those facts, so that anyone (not just you and your client) can read it and understand the situation and the available course(s) of action;
- well informed and well reasoned; and
- neutral and fair.

And the opinion letter must, in addition to providing the opinion,

- set out the client's options in the circumstances, and
- request the client's instructions.

You will find a sample opinion letter in Chapter 14 (see Appendix 14.2). We suggest that you reread it now, before you proceed to the next topic, which concerns the format of an opinion letter. Keep the sample opinion letter in mind as we go through the steps of producing one.

When you write an opinion letter, we suggest the following steps:

1. Introduce the subject of the letter, usually by setting out the question(s) the client has asked you.

2. State in summary form the facts that the client has told you—but only the ones that are relevant to the legal issues you identified in your research. (Clients often leaven their statement of the facts with irrelevant comments about things like a similar situation that happened ten years ago, or their brother-in-law's thoughts about the chances of winning a lawsuit. You will eventually learn to tune these out and concentrate on essential facts.) Make sure you include *all* the relevant facts, however, because your opinion will be based only on the facts stated.

3. List the issues that you have identified as arising out of the client's question(s). Be brief, because this list will provide the headings for your discussion of the issues.

4. Under the heading for each issue, discuss the issue. In your discussion, you want to include the following (preferably, in this order):

   - The major legal principle you have identified as relevant to the issue. We are assuming that your client is a layperson, and so we generally counsel against quoting directly from statutes or judgments or giving case citations. State the law in your own words, but make sure it's a correct statement of the law.

   - How (if applicable) recent court decisions have dealt with the major legal principle (for example, have they narrowed or expanded it?). It's not necessary to cover this if your research has shown that the major legal principle is firm as bedrock.

   - The conclusion that arises from your applying the legal principle(s) to the client's fact situation.

   - The courses of action that lie open to the client in these circumstances.

   - The possible arguments that could be made for and against each course of action.

   - A request for the client's instructions.

   - An offer to respond to any questions the client may have after reading the letter.

EXERCISES

A. Prepare a memo of law from the information and materials provided below.

> Memo
> To: You
> From: Lawyer
> Re: *Giller and Keaton Estate*
> Date: December 12, Year Zero
>
> Elizabeth Giller is our 58-year-old client.
>
>   Elizabeth met Jack Keaton in Year Minus Six and they became involved with each other. Elizabeth had been separated from her husband for 12 years at that time (she is still not divorced from him). Jack was a widower and had two adult daughters from his marriage. For two years, she and Jack spent much time together, slept over at each other's residences, and went on vacations together, but did not live together. She decided to leave her apartment and move into his house in January, Year Minus Four, because his health was beginning to fail and they agreed that he shouldn't live alone. By early Year Minus Two, he was so ill that she quit her job to be with him full time. They were able to live fairly comfortably on his pension and investments, although Elizabeth ended up spending money looking after him and she now has debts. In August Year Zero, Jack died. In his will (which he never changed after meeting Elizabeth), he left everything to his two adult daughters.
>
>   Elizabeth was a senior secretary at an investment firm before she stopped working to look after Jack. She is starting to suffer from arthritis in her hands and finds it difficult to use a keyboard. She began looking for work after Jack's death but quickly realized that she would have a lot of trouble re-entering the workforce at her age. She has saved a little money on which she is now living, and she will receive a pension, but not until she turns 65. Elizabeth believes that she would not be in financial trouble if she had not looked after Jack, of whom she was very fond. In addition, she was shocked and hurt that he left her nothing at all in his will.
>
>   Elizabeth wants to know whether there is anything in law that can be done to help her. She would like an income, if possible—at least until she starts receiving pension benefits—and money to pay her debts that relate to looking after Jack.
>
>   Further information: The law of Ontario applies.

NOTE: Don't forget to consider in your memo

- whether the client has the legal status to make an application under the *Succession Law Reform Act*,
- what factors the court is likely to look at *in this case* to determine whether to order support, and
- whether the Act provides for what Elizabeth wants (an income and money to pay off debts).

Selected provisions of the *Succession Law Reform Act*, RSO 1990, c S.26:

PART V
SUPPORT OF DEPENDANTS

Definitions, Part V

57. In this Part,

"child" means a child as defined in subsection 1(1) and includes a grandchild and a person whom the deceased has demonstrated a settled intention to treat as a child of his or her family, except under an arrangement where the child is placed for valuable consideration in a foster home by a person having lawful custody;

"cohabit" means to live together in a conjugal relationship, whether within or outside marriage;

"court" means the Superior Court of Justice;

"dependant" means,

   (a) the spouse of the deceased,
   (b) a parent of the deceased,
   (c) a child of the deceased, or
   (d) a brother or sister of the deceased,

to whom the deceased was providing support or was under a legal obligation to provide support immediately before his or her death;

"letters probate" and "letters of administration" include letters probate, letters of administration or other legal documents purporting to be of the same legal nature granted by a court in another jurisdiction and resealed in this province;

"parent" includes a grandparent and a person who has demonstrated a settled intention to treat the deceased as a child of his or her family, except under an arrangement where the deceased was placed for valuable consideration in a foster home by a person having lawful custody;

"spouse" means a spouse as defined in subsection 1(1) and in addition includes either of two persons who,

   (a) were married to each other by a marriage that was terminated or declared a nullity, or
   (b) are not married to each other and have cohabited,
      (i) continuously for a period of not less than three years, or
      (ii) in a relationship of some permanence, if they are the natural or adoptive parents of a child.

Order for support

58.(1) Where a deceased, whether testate or intestate, has not made adequate provision for the proper support of his dependants or any of them, the court, on application, may order that such provision as it considers adequate be made out of the estate of the deceased for the proper support of the dependants or any of them.

Applicants

(2) An application for an order for the support of a dependant may be made by the dependant or the dependant's parent.

Same

(3) An application for an order for the support of a dependant may also be made by one of the following agencies,

(a) the Ministry of Community and Social Services in the name of the Minister;

(b) a municipality, excluding a lower-tier municipality in a regional municipality;

(c) a district social services administration board under the *District Social Services Administration Boards Act*;

(d) a band approved under section 15 of the *General Welfare Assistance Act*; or,

(e) a delivery agent under the *Ontario Works Act, 1997*,

if the agency is providing or has provided a benefit under the *Family Benefits Act*, assistance under the *General Welfare Assistance Act* or the *Ontario Works Act, 1997* or income support under the *Ontario Disability Support Program Act, 1997* in respect of the dependant's support, or if an application for such a benefit, assistance or income support has been made to the agency by or on behalf of the dependant.

Idem

(4) The adequacy of provision for support under subsection (1) shall be determined as of the date of the hearing of the application.

Suspensory order

59. On an application by or on behalf of the dependants or any of them, the court may make an order suspending in whole or in part the administration of the deceased's estate, for such time and to such extent as the court may decide.

Application for support order

60.(1) An application under this Part may be made to the court by notice of application in accordance with the practice of the court.

Idem

(2) Where an application for an order under section 58 is made by or on behalf of any dependant,

(a) it may be dealt with by the court as; and

(b) in so far as the question of limitation is concerned, it shall be deemed to be,

an application on behalf of all persons who might apply.

Limitation period

61.(1) Subject to subsection (2), no application for an order under section 58 may be made after six months from the grant of letters probate of the will or of letters of administration.

Exception

(2) The court, if it considers it proper, may allow an application to be made at any time as to any portion of the estate remaining undistributed at the date of the application.

Determination of amount

62.(1) In determining the amount and duration, if any, of support, the court shall consider all the circumstances of the application, including,

(a) the dependant's current assets and means;

(b) the assets and means that the dependant is likely to have in the future;

(c) the dependant's capacity to contribute to his or her own support;

(d) the dependant's age and physical and mental health;

(e) the dependant's needs, in determining which the court shall have regard to the dependant's accustomed standard of living;

(f) the measures available for the dependant to become able to provide for his or her own support and the length of time and cost involved to enable the dependant to take those measures;

(g) the proximity and duration of the dependant's relationship with the deceased;

(h) the contributions made by the dependant to the deceased's welfare, including indirect and non-financial contributions;

(i) the contributions made by the dependant to the acquisition, maintenance and improvement of the deceased's property or business;

(j) a contribution by the dependant to the realization of the deceased's career potential;

(k) whether the dependant has a legal obligation to provide support for another person;

(l) the circumstances of the deceased at the time of death;

(m) any agreement between the deceased and the dependant;

(n) any previous distribution or division of property made by the deceased in favour of the dependant by gift or agreement or under court order;

(o) the claims that any other person may have as a dependant;

(p) if the dependant is a child,

(i) the child's aptitude for and reasonable prospects of obtaining an education, and

(ii) the child's need for a stable environment;

(q) if the dependant is a child of the age of sixteen years or more, whether the child has withdrawn from parental control;

(r) if the dependant is a spouse,

(i) a course of conduct by the spouse during the deceased's lifetime that is so unconscionable as to constitute an obvious and gross repudiation of the relationship,

(ii) the length of time the spouses cohabited,

(iii) the effect on the spouse's earning capacity of the responsibilities assumed during cohabitation,

(iv) whether the spouse has undertaken the care of a child who is of the age of eighteen years or over and unable by reason of illness, disability or other cause to withdraw from the charge of his or her parents,

(v) whether the spouse has undertaken to assist in the continuation of a program of education for a child eighteen years of age or over who is unable for that reason to withdraw from the charge of his or her parents,

(vi) any housekeeping, child care or other domestic service performed by the spouse for the family, as if the spouse had devoted the
time spent in performing that service in remunerative employment and
had contributed the earnings to the family's support,

(vi.1) Repealed.

(vii) the effect on the spouse's earnings and career development of
the responsibility of caring for a child,

(viii) the desirability of the spouse remaining at home to care for a
child; and

(s) any other legal right of the dependant to support, other than out of
public money.

Evidence

(2) In addition to the evidence presented by the parties, the court may direct other evidence to be given as the court considers necessary or proper.

Idem

(3) The court may accept such evidence as it considers proper of the deceased's reasons, so far as ascertainable, for making the dispositions in his or
her will, or for not making adequate provision for a dependant, as the case may
be, including any statement in writing signed by the deceased.

Idem

(4) In estimating the weight to be given to a statement referred to in subsection (3), the court shall have regard to all the circumstances from which an
inference can reasonably be drawn as to the accuracy of the statement.

Conditions and restrictions

63.(1) In any order making provision for support of a dependant, the court
may impose such conditions and restrictions as the court considers
appropriate.

Contents of order

(2) Provision may be made out of income or capital or both and an order
may provide for one or more of the following, as the court considers
appropriate,

(a) an amount payable annually or otherwise whether for an indefinite
or limited period or until the happening of a specified event;

(b) a lump sum to be paid or held in trust;

(c) any specified property to be transferred or assigned to or in trust for
the benefit of the dependant, whether absolutely, for life or for a term of
years;

(d) the possession or use of any specified property by the dependant for
life or such period as the court considers appropriate;

(e) a lump sum payment to supplement or replace periodic payments;

(f) the securing of payment under an order by a charge on property or
otherwise;

(g) the payment of a lump sum or of increased periodic payments to
enable a dependant spouse or child to meet debts reasonably incurred for
his or her own support prior to an application under this Part;

(h) that all or any of the money payable under the order be paid to an
appropriate person or agency for the benefit of the dependant;

(i) the payment to an agency referred to in subsection 58(3) of any amount in reimbursement for an allowance or benefit granted in respect of the support of the dependant, including an amount in reimbursement for an allowance paid or benefit provided before the date of the order.

Idem

(3) Where a transfer or assignment of property is ordered, the court may,

(a) give all necessary directions for the execution of the transfer or assignment by the executor or administrator or such other person as the court may direct; or

(b) grant a vesting order.

Agreement or waiver

(4) An order under this section may be made despite any agreement or waiver to the contrary.

Notice to parties before order

(5) The court shall not make any order under this section until it is satisfied upon oath that all persons who are or may be interested in or affected by the order have been served with notice of the application as provided by the rules of court, and every such person is entitled to be present and to be heard in person or by counsel at the hearing.

Exception

(6) Despite subsection (5), where, in the opinion of the court,

(a) every reasonable effort has been made to serve those entitled to notice; or

(b) after every reasonable effort has been made, it is not possible to identify one or more of the persons entitled to notice,

the court may dispense with the requirement of notice in respect of any person who has not been served.

1. Prepare a draft memo of law.

   a. What are the questions being asked?

   b. What are the legal issues that you have identified? (Hint: Look at the note on page 279.)

   c. What are the sections in the statute that are relevant to the issues?

   d. What are the facts that are relevant to the law?

   e. Discuss the law as it relates to the facts in this case.

   f. What is your conclusion? What action can be taken for your client?

2. Prepare a formal memo of law.

3. Prepare a draft opinion letter to the client based on the formal memo of law.

B. Prepare a memo of law from the information and materials provided below.

Memo
To: You
From: Lawyer
Re: *Brown v Litoff*
Date: December 23, Year Zero

As you know, this action for arrears of rent under a commercial lease has been dragging on for years, partly because of the client's unreasonable behaviour.

Mr. Brown came in to see me yesterday to instruct me to add a tort claim—an action for assault and false imprisonment—to the claim for arrears. He says he's been thinking about the last time he talked to the defendant, Litoff, in Year Minus Two, when he demanded that Litoff pay the rent. He says that Litoff threatened him with violence and prevented him from leaving a room. He says that because Litoff is making him go all the way to trial on this action, he wants to put some heat on Litoff.

See if you can find out whether we can amend or not.

Further information: The law of Ontario applies.

A. The pleadings in the *Brown v Litoff* action:

Assault and false imprisonment were not specifically pleaded. One paragraph of the pleadings states:

8. On or about the 14th day of March, Year Minus Two, the plaintiff attended at the defendant's office to discuss with him the payment of outstanding rent. The plaintiff states that the defendant refused to discuss payment or settlement. The plaintiff further states that the defendant shook his fist at him and told him not to come asking for the outstanding rent again.

B. Discoveries in the *Brown v Litoff* action:

Discoveries were held in Year Minus One. The following appears in the transcript of the discovery of the defendant:

197. Q. Did the plaintiff come to your office on March 14, Year Minus Two to ask you about paying the outstanding rent?
     A. Maybe. I think so.

198. Q. Can you tell me what happened at that meeting?
     A. I told him I had no money to pay the rent.

199. Q. Did the two of you argue?
     A. Yeah. He called me an S.O.B. and said he'd put me out of business.

200. Q. Did you say anything in reply?
     A. Yeah, I think I told him if he didn't leave me alone I'd give him a good punch in the nose. Or maybe I took a swing at him. I don't remember.

201. Q. Did you hit him?
     A. Nah, the pipsqueak. He took off as fast as he could.

202. Q. Did you try to prevent him from leaving?
     A. Why would I? I was glad to see the back of him.

C. *Rules of Civil Procedure*, RRO 1990, Reg 194, r 26.01

> 26.01 On motion at any stage of an action the court shall grant leave to amend a pleading on such terms as are just, unless prejudice would result that could not be compensated for by costs or an adjournment.

D. *Limitations Act, 2002*, SO 2002, c 24, Schedule B, s 4

Basic limitation period

> 4. Unless this Act provides otherwise, a proceeding shall not be commenced in respect of a claim after the second anniversary of the day on which the claim was discovered.

E. *Denton v Jones et al (No 2)* (1976), 14 OR (2d) 382 (H Ct J)

APPEAL from an order of the Senior Master refusing plaintiff's application to amend the statement of claim.

R.E. Anka, for defendant, R.W. Marshall.

J.S. McNeil, for plaintiff.

GRANGE, J.:—This is an appeal from the order of the Senior Master refusing the plaintiff's application to amend her statement of claim. The appeal has a sad history. When it originally came on before me a preliminary objection was taken that the order appealed from was a final order and the appeal therefore lay to the Divisional Court. I reserved judgment on the objection and heard the appeal on its merits. I then decided that the preliminary objection was well taken and adjourned the motion to the Divisional Court under Rule 225(3) [rep. and sub. O. Reg. 115/72, s. 5].

Unfortunately at the time of making the latter order I did not appreciate that the writ in the action had been issued prior to April 17, 1972, when the *Judicature Amendment Act, 1970 (No. 4)*, 1970 (Ont.), c. 97, which gave the Divisional Court jurisdiction, was proclaimed. Accordingly, *A.J. Freiman Ltd. v. M.W. Kosub Ltd. et al.*, [1973] 2 O.R. 608, applied and this appeal lay to a Judge in Chambers regardless of whether the order was final or interlocutory. It has therefore been referred back to me for disposition.

The action is one for dental malpractice and in the claim as originally delivered the plaintiff alleged negligence on the part of the defendant Marshall in that he was instructed to extract certain upper teeth and had, in fact, extracted not only those upper teeth but all of the lower teeth as well.

Upon the publication of *Schweizer v. Central Hospital et al.* (1974), 6 O.R. (2d) 606, 53 D.L.R. (3d) 494, the plaintiff brought application to amend the statement of claim to allege trespass to the person based upon the same facts. The application came on before the Senior Master in December, 1975, and was dismissed. From that decision this appeal, after its many vicissitudes comes on for determination.

The main reason advanced in opposition to the amendment is, of course, that the dental operation took place on October 7, 1969, and that in the interval the limitation period, be it for dental malpractice (six months under the *Dentistry Act*, R.S.O. 1970, c. 108, s. 28, or one year under the *Health Disciplines Act*, 1974 (Ont.), c. 47, s. 17), for assault (four years under the *Limitations Act*, R.S.O. 1970, c. 246, s. 45(1)(j)), or upon the case (six years, *Limitations Act*, s. 45(1)(g)), had expired.

The defendant relies upon the principle stemming from the dicta of Lord Esher, M.R., in *Weldon v. Neal* (1887), 19 Q.B.D. 394 at p. 395, as follows:

> We must act on the settled rule of practice, which is that amendments are not admissible when they prejudice the right of the opposite party as existing at the date of such amendments. If an amendment were allowed setting up a cause of action, which, if the writ were issued in respect thereof at the date of the amendment, would be barred by the Statute of Limitations, it would be allowing the plaintiff to take advantage of her former writ to defeat the statute and taking away an existing right from the defendant, a proceeding which, as a general rule, would be, in my opinion, improper and unjust. Under very peculiar circumstances the Court might perhaps have power to allow such an amendment, but certainly as a general rule it will not do so.

This principle was acknowledged in *Radigan v. Canadian Indemnity Co. et al.*, [1953] O.W.N. 788, [1953] 3 D.L.R. 653, [1951-55] I.L.R. 488; where the Court of Appeal held it inapplicable to a situation where the insured sought to add an alternative claim under the same policy and was applied in *Pitt v. Bank of Nova Scotia et al.*, [1956] O.W.N. 872, where the Senior Master refused an amendment to claim recovery in nuisance against a municipality where the original claim was in negligence. Many other instances are given in Professor Garry Watson's learned discussion on the matter to be found in "Amendment of Proceedings After Limitation Periods." 53 *Can. Bar Rev.* 237 (1975), particularly at pp. 242-3.

I am not sure that the mere pleading of an alternative ground for relief arising out of the same facts constitutes the raising of a new cause of action—see *Canadian Industries Ltd. v. Canadian National R. Co.*, [1940] O.W.N. 452, [1940] 4 D.L.R. 629, 52 C.R.T.C. 31 [affirmed [1941] S.C.R. 591, [1941] 4 D.L.R. 561, 53 C.R.T.C. 162], where an amendment in a contract action was permitted to claim relief in negligence based upon the same facts upon the ground that such new claim did not create a new cause of action, but merely an alternative claim with respect to the same cause. We must always bear in mind the distinction between "forms of action" and "causes of action." …

But even if the amendment here asked does constitute a new cause of action, I consider that there are circumstances justifying a departure from the general rule. In *Basarsky v. Quinlan et al.*, [1972] S.C.R. 380, 24 D.L.R. (3d) 720, [1972] 1 W.W.R. 303, Hall, J., equated the word "peculiar" in Lord Esher, M.R.'s exception with "special" in current usage and found that circumstances existed to justify an amendment, after the expiration of the limitation period, setting up a claim under the *Fatal Accidents Act* of Alberta where the original claim had been under the *Trustee Act* of that province. Among those circumstances were many that apply equally here. There as here, all the facts upon which the later claim could be based were already pleaded. There as here, there was no need to reopen discoveries and most important there as here, there was no possibility of prejudice to the defendants other than the inevitable prejudice of what might turn out to be the successful plea. To me this amendment comes within the spirit and intent of our Rules, particularly Rule 185 which is as follows:

> 185. A proceeding shall not be defeated by any formal objection, but all necessary amendments shall be made, upon proper terms as to costs and otherwise, to secure the advancement of justice, the determining of the real

matter in dispute, and the giving of judgment according to the very right and justice of the case.

Moreover, the amendment seems to me to be precisely in line with the decision of Reid, J., in *Royal v. Municipality of Metropolitan Toronto et al.* (1975), 9 O.R. (2d) 522, which is almost the converse of the case at bar. There an amendment to include a claim for negligence was permitted after the limitation period had expired when the original claim was one for assault.

I would therefore allow the appeal and permit the amendment sought. Costs of the appeal should be in the cause.

Appeal allowed.

1. Prepare a memo of law to file.

    a. What are the questions being asked?

    b. What are the legal issues that you have identified?

    c. i. What are the sections in the legislation that are relevant to the issues?

        ii. What are the passages in the case law that are relevant to the issues?

    d. What are the facts that are relevant to the law?

    e. Discuss the law as it relates to the facts in this case.

    f. What is your conclusion? What action can be taken for your client?

2. Prepare a formal memo of law.

3. Prepare a draft opinion letter to the client based on the formal memo of law.

Appendix 15.1

What Is Legal Writing?

The term "legal writing" is used to describe the drafting of any type of law-related document, not just the two kinds of writing we have discussed above. Legal writing may include

- court pleadings, such as statements of claim, statements of defence, or third-party claims;
- affidavits;
- contracts;
- wills;
- applications to government programs; and
- letters of all kinds to clients, to other legal professionals, and to government departments.

What Is Good Legal Writing?

Good legal writing does not require complex language and a lot of "legalese." In fact, it avoids both. It simply requires writing that is well-organized, concise, understandable, accurate, and free of grammatical and spelling errors. In other words, good legal writing isn't very different from ordinary good writing.

To write well, you must pay attention to your

- audience,
- purpose,
- tone,
- constraints,
- grammar,
- spelling, and
- presentation.

You must also pay attention to the general rules of good writing.

Audience

The audience for your writing is the intended reader. Ask yourself who will be reading your document, and then write for that reader. Your audience may be a legal professional, such as a law clerk, articling student, lawyer, or judge; or a layperson, such as a client or someone you are contacting on behalf of the client—a business or a neighbour, for example. A legal professional will be more familiar and comfortable with legal terms and concepts than a layperson. Therefore, when you write for a legal professional, you can use legal terms and concepts without having to define, explain, or translate them as you would for a layperson. But, in either case, your writing should be as clear, simple, and straightforward as possible.

Whoever your intended reader is, you should always keep in mind that you are writing for a business purpose. You should therefore maintain a level of formality in your writing, avoiding slang and colloquial language (such as "cops" for "police officers") and limiting the use of contractions (such as "isn't" for "is not").

Purpose

The purpose of the document you are writing could be, for example, one of the following: to record the results of your research in the form of a memo to file or to another legal professional; to write a letter to a client requesting information; or to use your research to give the correct structure to an affidavit that your client will sign. Whatever your purpose, you have to make sure that the content and organization of the document achieve that purpose.

Tone

The choice of tone for your document is largely determined by your purpose. For example, a letter requesting information from a client requires a cordial tone, while a demand letter requires a neutral or even a stern tone.

Constraints

Make sure you are clear about any limitations or restrictions on your writing. Take time to find out exactly what information the document is required to contain. You might need to look up the applicable rules of court, contact a court office for advice, or read online instructions about filling out a government application. Determine whether there is a limit on the length of the document, or whether there are any formatting or style requirements that you must follow, such as font type, font size, spacing, and page numbering. These constraints may be dictated by a variety of guidelines such as court rules or program requirements, or by your law firm's policies or standard operating procedures.

Don't forget that there may be a deadline you need to meet for completing and/or sending off your document. If your document must be written and sent within one hour, for example, adjust your writing plan accordingly.

Grammar

Grammar is the proper treatment of connected words in a sentence in order to express thoughts without confusion or error. Good writing requires good grammar—properly constructed sentences using proper punctuation. Grammatically incorrect writing not only annoys people who know something about grammar (count among them judges, lawyers, and, not infrequently, clients), but is often unclear. Clarity is very important in legal documents. This means that good grammar is also very important.

We can't give you a grammar course in this book, but here are some tips to help you avoid a few of the most common and most glaring grammatical mistakes.

1. USE APOSTROPHES CORRECTLY

The apostrophe (') is used for two different purposes: to form a possessive and to create a contraction.

To form the possessive of a noun, add "'s" after the end of the noun, unless it is a plural noun ending in "s." In that case, add the apostrophe only. Examples: "the plaintiff's claim" (for a single plaintiff); the "plaintiffs' claim" (for more than one plaintiff).

To form a contraction, place an apostrophe where the missing letter(s) would go. Examples: "do not" becomes "don't"; "cannot" becomes "can't"; "you are" becomes "you're"; "it is" becomes "it's."

"It's" is a contraction for "it is" or "it has" and is NEVER a possessive. Examples: "It's time to go"; "It's been two weeks since the case began." "Its" is the possessive form of "it." Example: "The corporation? I've got its address here."

The apostrophe should never be used to form the plural of a noun: "The plaintiff's will be in court today" is WRONG! If you are only forming the plural of a noun and not a possessive, there is no apostrophe: "The plaintiffs will be in court today."

2. USE "I" AND "ME" CORRECTLY

"I" is a subject and "me" is a direct or indirect object. Writers get tangled up especially when there is more than one individual populating the sentence. "Please respond to John and I" is INCORRECT; "Please respond to John and me" is correct. An easy way to decide whether to use "I" or "me" is to remove the other individual(s). The correct choice is then usually clear.

- He ordered John and (I or me?) to pay costs.

"He ordered *I* to pay costs"? ✗	"He ordered *me* to pay costs"? ✓

- If Nancy, Fred, and (I or me?) are sued, we will hire a lawyer.

"If *me* am sued"? ✗	"If *I* am sued"? ✓

Don't use "myself" as a way to get around deciding whether the correct answer is "I" or "me"!

3. USE SINGULAR AND PLURAL PRONOUNS CORRECTLY

Use a singular pronoun to refer to an individual person. It has become common for writers to try to avoid specifying the gender of an individual by using plural pronouns instead. For example, "If your pet has been sprayed by a skunk, do not bring them into the clinic!" This should read, "If your pet has been sprayed by a skunk, do not bring him or her into the clinic!" But if you don't want to get into the gender question, you can still write gracefully in the plural: "Pets that have been sprayed by a skunk should not be brought into the clinic!"

4. USE "THERE," "THEIR," AND "THEY'RE" CORRECTLY

- "There" is an adverb indicating place. ("The pleadings are over there on the table.") It can also introduce a sentence or clause. ("There is a hearing scheduled for 10 a.m.")
- "Their" is a possessive pronoun. ("Their briefcases are on the counsel table.")
- "They're" is a contraction for "they are." ("They're meeting with the judge this afternoon.")

5. USE "BETWEEN" CORRECTLY

Between assumes there are only two things connecting with each other. ("This is a matter between him and me.") If there are more than two things connecting, use *among.* ("A fight broke out among a dozen of the first-class passengers.")

Between is completed by "and" (and not by "to"). "The judge will be in her chambers between one and three o'clock," NOT "between one to three o'clock." "Between ten and twenty police officers attended the hearing," NOT "between ten to twenty."

6. MAKE SURE THE VERB AGREES WITH THE SUBJECT

A singular subject requires a singular verb. If there is more than one subject in the sentence, the form of the verb must be plural. Examples are as follows:

- The court <u>is</u> in session.
- The judge and the bailiff <u>are</u> conferring about the next case on the docket.
- The lawyer for the defendant, accompanied by the lawyer for the plaintiff, <u>is</u> approaching the bench.

Collective nouns may take a singular or plural verb, depending on the sentence. Examples are as follows:

- The jury <u>has</u> reached its verdict. [One group working together]
- The jury <u>are</u> going home. [The group does not share a home. However, you can avoid the issue of whether "jury" is a collective noun by saying, "The jurors are going home."]

The pronouns "everyone" and "each" require a singular verb. Other frequently used words that require a singular verb are the following: "anyone," "neither," and "either."

7. TRY TO AVOID SPLITTING INFINITIVES

An infinitive is made up of "to" plus a verb. "To argue" and "to ignore," for example, are infinitive forms. When you put an adverb between "to" and the verb, you "split" the infinitive. Although some grammar experts think there's nothing wrong with splitting an infinitive ("to boldly go where no man has gone before" would sound strange now if the infinitive were *not* split), others are horrified by the practice.

To be on the safe side, don't split an infinitive if you can avoid doing so. It is usually possible to find a reasonably graceful spot in the sentence for the adverb other than between "to" and the verb. For example, you can avoid saying, "It was difficult to completely ignore her argument," which involves a split infinitive. You can say, instead, "It was difficult to ignore her argument completely." This option is both natural-sounding and grammatically unassailable.

8. PUT "ONLY" IN ITS PROPER PLACE

In most cases, the word "only" should be placed directly before the word or phrase you are emphasizing. The meaning of a sentence changes depending on the placement of the word "only." Consider the following sentences and their meanings:

- You only have to interview one witness. [This is the sole thing you have to do.]
- You have to interview only one witness. [You do not have to interview more than one witness.]
- Only you have to interview one witness. [You are the person who has to interview one witness—presumably others have to interview more than one.]

Think about what you mean, and then make sure you place the word "only" only where it belongs!

If you are not sure about where to place "only," consider omitting it. Most often, the easiest way to fix the problem with "only" is to remove it.

9. USE "PRINCIPAL" AND "PRINCIPLE" CORRECTLY

"Principal" can be used as an adjective or as a noun. When used as an adjective, it means "most important" or "highest in rank." When used as a noun, it refers to the head or director of a school ("The principal is leading the school assembly"), or to an amount of money that has been lent or borrowed ("The investor is earning 4 percent interest on the principal"). As a legal term, it may refer to an individual who gives authority to another to act on his or her behalf. ("The principal gives authority to the agent.")

"Principle" is a noun and means "law," "rule," or "general truth." ("The principle of solicitor–client confidentiality is well established.")

10. USE "LAY" AND "LIE" CORRECTLY

Many people (including Bob Dylan) have trouble with "lay" and "lie." "Lay" is a transitive verb, which means that it has to have an object. "Lie" is an intransitive verb, which means that it must not have an object. Examples: "I'm going to lie down on the sand and get some sun"; "I'm going to lay a towel on the sand, lie down, and get some sun." So when Bob Dylan wrote "Lay, lady, lay, lay across my big brass bed," he was being ungrammatical (but he still wrote a very popular song). For a more commercial example of "lay," consider this sentence: "Lay out the terms of the deal and we'll take a look at them."

In the past tense, the trouble continues. The past tense of the intransitive verb "lie" is "lay." Example: "I lay down last night and got some sleep." The past tense of the transitive verb "lay" is "laid." Example: "The client laid down her money and laid out her expectations."

So when you use the transitive verb "to lay" (past tense "laid"), make sure you put an object in the sentence. "He is laying on the floor" is always wrong. "He is lying on the floor" is correct (although it's not good behaviour, in a law office or a court-room). "He is laying tiles on the floor" is also correct.

Spelling

Good writing also requires correct spelling. Improper spelling, just like incorrect grammar, not only makes the writer look unprofessional, but can change the meaning of what you have written, even if the grammar, content, and organization of your document are otherwise flawless.

You probably noticed that several of the grammar tips above involve making sure you choose the correct spelling of certain words that sound alike but are spelled differently. You'll need to correctly spell not only general words such as these, but also specific legal terms, such as "waive" and "enure," which are *never* to be confused with "wave" and "ensure." Check your documents for spelling errors by proofreading them thoroughly. Use the spell-check feature of your word-processing software, but do not rely on the spell-check alone; it will not pick up words that are improperly spelled only in the context in which they are used (for example, "your" and "you're"), and it will probably not tell you the correct spelling of unusual words like "enure." In fact, what it may do is change "enure" to "ensure."

Be aware of spelling variations for some Canadian and American words. Choose Canadian spelling—but keep in mind that your spell-checker may use American spelling. You may want to set your computer's language to English (Canada) rather than to English (United States) when running a spell-check.

Presentation

Your writing must be not only well organized but well presented. Consider what font style and size you want to use (or are required to use), as well as line spacing, headings, and paragraph numbering. Your formatting should be consistent throughout your document. For example, if you choose to italicize and underline your headings, make sure all the headings in your document are formatted this way. If your document is more than one page long, include page numbers.

When you have finished your writing, take the extra time to proofread and, if necessary, edit or revise. Make sure your writing

- achieves your purpose,
- is clear and easy to read,

- is well organized and in the correct format, and
- contains relevant and necessary information only.

Proofread slowly and check that all words are spelled correctly. You should also check for other typing errors, such as extra spaces or repeated words.

Some Rules of Good Writing

Here are some basic rules of good writing:

- *Use proper sentence structure.* The simplest structure usually works best: subject–verb–object. For example: "The judge handed down her decision."

- *Use the active voice and the passive voice appropriately.* With sentences framed in the active voice, the subject performs the action. ("The plaintiff delivered the statement of claim.") With the passive voice, what was the object of the verb in the active voice becomes the subject of the verb, and the subject receives the action. ("The statement of claim was delivered by the plaintiff" or "The statement of claim was delivered.") The active voice is usually clearer, simpler, and more direct, as the above examples show; it almost always uses fewer words. However, you should use the passive voice when

  - you want to "hide" the actor who is performing the action (see the second example above);

  - the actor is unimportant, unknown, or obvious (see the second example above); or

  - you want to emphasize the receiver of the action.

  But a good rule of thumb is to use the active voice unless you have identified a good reason not to.

- *Omit needless words and phrases.* Very often, when it comes to good writing, less is more. Revise wordy sentences by omitting extra words and phrases that do not add to the meaning of your writing. For example, instead of writing "because of the fact that," or "due to the fact that," write "because." Instead of writing "a sufficient number of," write "enough." Instead of writing "it is true and correct," write either "it is true" or "it is correct"; both words are not needed. Omit from your writing any needless phrases such as "What I want to say is" or "The point is that."

- *Use transitional phrases to help the reader follow your writing.* For example: "There are three issues. The first issue is …"; or "The relevant law is set out in …" Such phrases tell the reader where you are heading.

- *Avoid turning verbs into nouns.* Verbs that have been turned into nouns are "nominalizations." For example: "He will make a suggestion that … ." Nominalizations often make sentences too wordy and passive. Use their base verbs instead. For example, instead of writing "he will make a suggestion that," use the more direct "he will suggest."

- *Use paragraphs effectively*. Each paragraph should focus on only one matter. The paragraph should start with a "topic sentence" that introduces the main point of the paragraph.

- *Use parallel construction*. In other words, present all similar elements (words, phrases, or clauses) of a sentence in the same form.

    Examples of non-parallel construction:

    The witness took the stand, was testifying, and then he leaves the courtroom.

    The lawyer needs to interview the client, the witness should be contacted, and there has to be some legal research done.

    Examples of parallel construction:

    The witness took the stand, testified, and then left the courtroom.

    The lawyer needs to interview the client, contact the witness, and research the law.

- *Use quotations and quotation marks correctly*. Quotation marks are used to show borrowed words. If you quote a sentence from a case (assuming it's not a paragraph-length sentence), enclose it in quotation marks. If you want to quote a longer passage from a book or case, set it off from the main text and do not put quotation marks around it.

    Examples:

    As Lord Atkin asked in *Donoghue v Stevenson*, "Who, then, in law is my neighbour?"

    Lord Atkin wrote in *Donoghue v Stevenson*:

    Who, then, in law is my neighbour? The answer seems to be—persons who are so closely and directly affected by my act that I ought reasonably to have them in contemplation as being so affected when I am directing my mind to the acts or omissions which are called in question.

- *Avoid "legalese."* Even though you are doing "legal writing," it's best to avoid using little-known legal terms and expressions when you can. Use plain English instead. Using legalese will not make your writing sound more intelligent or more "legal."

  Examples:

DON'T USE	USE
the party of the first part	the first party
endeavour	try
heretofore	before
inasmuch as	because
in the event that	if
execute the contract	sign the contract
per annum	a year, yearly
utilize	use
verbiage	language

- *Use positive forms to make your writing easier to understand.* Instead of writing "he was not uncooperative," write "he was cooperative."

Standard Abbreviations for Commonly Used Report Series and Statutes

A

AC	Law Reports, Appeal Cases (England)
ACWS	All Canada Weekly Summaries
AR	Alberta Reports
Admin LR	Administrative Law Reports
All ER	All England Reports
Alta LR	Alberta Law Reports
App Cas	Law Reports, Appeal Cases (England)

B

BCLR	British Columbia Law Reports
BLR	Business Law Reports

C

CBR	Canadian Bankruptcy Reports
CBR (NS)	Canadian Bankruptcy Reports (New Series)
CCC	Canadian Criminal Cases
CCEL	Canadian Cases on Employment Law
CCLI	Canadian Cases on the Law of Insurance
CCLT	Canadian Cases on the Law of Torts
CCSM	Continuing Consolidation of the Statutes of Manitoba
CED (Ont 3rd)	Canadian Encyclopedic Digest (Ontario Third Edition)
CELR	Canadian Environmental Law Reports
CLR	Construction Law Reports
CPR	Canadian Patent Reporter
CPR (NS)	Canadian Patent Reporter (New Series)
CR	Criminal Reports
CRR	Canadian Rights Reporter
CTC	Canada Tax Cases
CTR	Canada Tax Reports
Can Abr (2d)	Canadian Abridgment (Second Edition)

D–E

DLR	Dominion Law Reports
ER	English Reports
ETR	Estates and Trust Reports

F–K

FTR	Federal Trial Reports
Imm LR	Immigration Law Reporter
KB	Law Reports, King's Bench (England)

L

LAC (3d)	Labour Arbitration Cases (Third Series)
LR	Law Reports (England)
LR Ch	Law Reports Chancery Cases (England)
LRCP	Law Reports Common Pleas (England)
LR Eq	Law Reports Equity (England)
LR Ex	Law Reports Exchequer (England)
LRHL	Law Reports House of Lords (England)
LTR	Law Times Reports (England)

M

MPLR	Municipal and Planning Law Reports
MVR	Motor Vehicle Reports
Man LR	Manitoba Law Reports
Man R	Manitoba Reports

N

NBR	New Brunswick Reports
NR	National Reporter
NSR	Nova Scotia Reports
Nfld & PEIR	Newfoundland and Prince Edward Island Reports

O–Q

OAC	Ontario Appeal Cases
OMBR	Ontario Municipal Board Reports
OR	Ontario Reports
OWN	Ontario Weekly Notes
QAC	Quebec Appeal Cases

R

RFL	Reports of Family Law
RPR	Real Property Reports
RSA	Revised Statutes of Alberta
RSBC	Revised Statutes of British Columbia
RSC	Revised Statutes of Canada
RSM	Revised Statutes of Manitoba
RSN	Revised Statutes of Newfoundland
RSNB	Revised Statutes of New Brunswick
RSNWT	Revised Statutes of Northwest Territories
RSO	Revised Statutes of Ontario
RSPEI	Revised Statutes of Prince Edward Island
RSQ	Revised Statutes of Quebec
RSS	Revised Statutes of Saskatchewan
RSYT	Revised Statutes of Yukon Territory

S

SA	Statutes of Alberta
SCR	Supreme Court Reports
SBC	Statutes of British Columbia
SC	Statutes of Canada
SM	Statutes of Manitoba
SN	Statutes of Newfoundland
SNB	Statutes of New Brunswick
SNWT	Statutes of Northwest Territories
SO	Statutes of Ontario
SPEI	Statutes of Prince Edward Island
SQ	Statutes of Quebec
SS	Statutes of Saskatchewan
SYT	Statutes of Yukon Territory
Sask LR	Saskatchewan Law Reports

T–V

TLR	Times Law Reports (England)
UCCP	Upper Canada Common Pleas Reports
UCQB	Upper Canada Queen's Bench Reports

W–Z

WCB	Weekly Criminal Bulletin
WDCP	Weekly Digest of Civil Procedure
WLR	Weekly Law Reports (England)
WWR	Western Weekly Reports
WWR (NS)	Western Weekly Reports (New Series)
YR	Yukon Reports

For abbreviations not found here, consult the front pages of any volume of *Canadian Case Citations* or *Canadian Statute Citations* or *Cardiff Index to Legal Abbreviations* at <http://www.legalabbrevs.cardiff.ac.uk>.

Law-Related Internet Sites*

B

Sites That Provide Access to Primary Sources

Statutes

- Ontario statutes: <http://www.ontario.ca/laws>
- Federal statutes: <http://laws-lois.justice.gc.ca>

Cases

- Supreme Court of Canada: <http://scc-csc.gc.ca>
- Ontario Court of Appeal: <http://www.ontariocourts.on.ca/coa/en/> (cases back to 1998)
- Ontario Superior Court of Justice: <http://www.ontariocourts.ca/scj/> (cases back to 1987)
- Links to statutes and cases of other jurisdictions are available through the Canadian Legal Information Institute website at <http://www.canlii.org>

Government Sites

- Government of Canada: <http://www.canada.ca>
  - information about government services
  - links to
    - departments and agencies—alphabetical listing of government of Canada departments and agencies with links to their sites
    - structure of the government of Canada—including information on the Canadian ministries, members of the House of Commons, and Senate
    - provincial and territorial governments
    - municipalities by provinces and territories

---

* Sites may be moved, altered, or closed at any time.

- Specific Government of Canada sites:
  - Statistics Canada: <http://www.statcan.gc.ca> (for statistics on things such as the consumer price index, population rates and unemployment rates)
  - Canada Revenue Agency: <http://www.cra-arc.gc.ca> (for information and forms regarding income tax, GST, customs)
  - Industry Canada: <http://www.ic.gc.ca> (for information relating to business)
- Government of Ontario: <http://www.ontario.ca>
  - government propaganda
  - links to
    - specific ministries
    - a complete services and offices directory—included in the list are tribunals, boards, and agencies
    - a Government of Ontario telephone directory
    - information about contacting MPPs
    - site map is very helpful for finding the location of information
- Specific Government of Ontario sites:
  - Attorney General: <http://www.attorneygeneral.jus.gov.on.ca> for information about
    - going to court
    - getting a lawyer
    - family law matters
    - small claims court
  - Guide to the Ontario Courts: <http://www.ontariocourts.ca> (with links to the Court of Appeal, Superior Court of Justice, and Ontario Court of Justice)
- Law Society of Upper Canada: <http://www.lsuc.on.ca>—for information about:
  - the legal profession
  - finding a lawyer
  - the legal profession's opinions of paralegals
  - research tools

General Legal Sites

- Access to Justice Network: <http://www.acjnet.org>
  - a project of the legal studies program of the University of Alberta
  - provides access to public legal education articles

- Canadian Legal FAQs: <http://www.law-faqs.org> (also a project of the legal studies program of the University of Alberta)
  - information about law, studying law, and legal research
- Cardiff Index to Legal Abbreviations: <http://www.legalabbrevs.cardiff.ac.uk>
  - provides the meaning of abbreviations for legal publications
- Your Legal Rights: <http://yourlegalrights.on.ca>
  - provides resources on topics affecting low-income and disadvantaged communities
- Best Guide to Canadian Legal Research: <http://www.legalresearch.org>
  - site run by Catherine Best, professor at UBC Faculty of Law, and former director of legal research and writing
  - excellent source of information about legal research
  - also has links to legal sources
- Bora Laskin Law Library (University of Toronto Faculty of Law): <http://library.law.utoronto.ca>
  - contains guides to legal research
  - provides community legal information
  - also has links to legal resources
- William R. Lederman Law Library: <http://library.queensu.ca/law> (run by the Queen's University Faculty of Law)
  - contains a comprehensive legal research manual—<http://library.queensu.ca/law/lederman/index>
- Toronto Lawyers Association Free Legal Research Websites: <http://www.tlaonline.ca/?page=HelpfulWebsites1>
- Canadian Legislation and Case Law Research Guide: <http://uottawa.ca.libguides.com/content.php?pid=90739&sid=677805> (run by the University of Ottawa Library)
- Isthatlegal.ca: Guides to Ontario and Canadian Law: <http://www.isthatlegal.ca> (summaries of selected recent Supreme Court of Canada and Ontario Court of Appeal cases)
- Legalline.ca: <http://legalline.ca> (website of easy-to-understand answers to legal questions)
- FindLaw: <http://www.findlaw.com> (American site that provides free legal information and includes a directory of lawyers and law firms)
- PublicLegal: <http://www.ilrg.com> (American site run by the Internet Legal Research Group that can find law-related sites in 238 countries, islands, and territories, including Canada, but its emphasis is on the United States)

Glossary

advanced search template template containing pre-defined fields that help to develop a Boolean search

appeal history history of a case—for example, whether the case has been confirmed or overturned on appeal and the name of the highest court that reviewed the decision

bills proposed statutes that are before Parliament or a provincial/territorial legislature but have not yet been passed

binding decision existing decision that a judge or master must follow if the facts and/or issues in that case and in the case before the court are sufficiently similar

binding law law that must be followed by a court

Boolean search method of searching that is based on principles of logic and that requires the use of keywords together with specific syntax

Boolean terms and connectors search Boolean search—method of searching that is based on principles of logic and that requires the use of keywords together with specific syntax

bylaw law made by a body (here, a municipal government) that is granted the power to do so by a legislature

case citator tool that updates a case and lists other cases that have considered or mentioned the case

case digests summaries of how legal issues were decided in particular cases

CED Index separate volume of the CED that contains the List of Titles in the CED and the Index Key

chain of appeal path through the court system that an appeal must follow in accordance with the statutes governing the applicable courts

disposition judge's orders set out at the end of a case

dissenting opinion opinion written by an appeal court judge who did not agree with the majority opinion

enabling statute statute that delegates the power to make regulations

finding tools secondary sources that refer you to primary sources of law

framework legislation legislation that provides an outline of the intended law and leaves the details to be worked out in the regulations

General Index one of two finding tools used to locate digested cases in the *Canadian Abridgment Case Digests*; locates the relevant case digests by volume number(s) and case digest numbers

headnote editor's explanation of the case, appearing at the head of the case

housekeeping provisions sections that cover the details of statutes, such as the date of coming into force

index alphabetical, detailed list of names, places, and subjects discussed in a source and the pages on which each entry appears

Index Key combines the individual indexes from all the titles and contains an alphabetical list of keywords, together with extensive cross-references within and among subject titles in the CED

interlocutory orders orders that relate to the process rather than to the substance of the matter under litigation

issue the specific problem that you must solve in order to provide a client with a solution to a problem posed by the entire fact situation

issues specific problems that the judge or adjudicator must resolve to reach a decision

judicially considered term describing a decision that has been discussed or interpreted by other courts

Key and Research Guide one of two finding tools used to locate digested cases in the *Canadian Abridgment Case Digests*; uses the key classification system

key classification system multi-level classification system used in the hardcover and supplement volumes of the *Canadian Abridgment Case Digests*

keywords words with which researchers search computerized sources for information stored randomly in databases

law of evidence sets out the manner in which facts are introduced and proved in a trial or a proceeding

leave permission from the court

legislative history a citation to the previous revision of a provision followed by a citation to any statute that amended the provision; given at the end of each provision in a statute

lines of authority sets of cases that share the same or similar viewpoint over a period of time

long title full, unabbreviated title of a statute

majority opinion the opinion agreed upon by a majority of the appeal court judges

master judge-like officer who decides certain procedural matters in the superior courts of some provinces

minority opinion see *dissenting opinion*

noting up updating a case to determine whether it has been followed, not followed, overturned, distinguished, or not applied

obiter dicta statements made by a court in its reasons for judgment that may be of interest but that are inessential to the decision and therefore have no binding authority; Latin for "words by the way"

persuasive law law that a court is not required to follow, but may follow if it wishes (usually case law)

plain language search method of searching a computerized source by means of a question, a sentence, or descriptive words, without using special syntax such as connectors and truncation symbols

plain or natural language search method of searching a computerized source by means of a question, a sentence, or descriptive words, without using special syntax such as connectors and truncation symbols

preamble part of a statute that outlines its purpose and main principles

primary sources the statutes, regulations, bylaws, and case decisions that create the law

private law governs the relationship between legal persons, and includes such areas as contracts, family law, property law, real estate, torts, wills and estates, and commercial law

procedural law sets out the process that a party must follow to enforce his/her/its rights in a court proceeding or to defend a proceeding

provision section or subsection

public law governs the relationship between legal persons (individuals, partnerships, and corporations) and the state (federal, provincial, or municipal government), and includes such areas of law as municipal law, immigration and refugee law, environmental law, constitutional law, criminal law, tax law, and child welfare

purpose the nature of the proceedings

ratio decidendi often simply called the ratio, a combined statement of the pre-existing principle of law on which the judge based the decision on an issue and its application to the facts of the particular case; Latin for "reason for deciding"

regulations rules made under the authority of a statute

reported case judge's decision and reasons about a case published in a law report series or a legal database

search engine website with a computer program that searches a database of Web documents or websites to match supplied keywords

secondary sources sources that summarize, discuss, or explain primary sources, and include legal encyclopedias, digests of cases, indexes to statutes, textbooks, and articles

short title abbreviated title of a statute

stare decisis principle that similar cases should be decided in a similar fashion; Latin for "to stand by things decided"

statute law created by Parliament or a provincial legislature

statute citator tool that updates a statute and lists cases that consider the statute generally or a particular section of the statute

statutory instrument general term that includes federal regulations

style of cause portion of the citation that sets out the names of the parties; also called a case name

substantive law defines legal rights and obligations; legal rights may be enforced by way of legal proceedings, so substantive law also includes defences to legal proceedings

substitution symbol symbol that replaces a single variable letter in keywords that may be spelled more than one way

table of cases list of all cases that are cited in a book

table of contents listing of chapters or article titles in a source together with the page numbers where each chapter or article starts

Table of Regulations alphabetical list of the regulations referred to in the subject titles in the CED

Table of Rules alphabetical list of the rules of court referred to in the subject titles in the CED

Table of Statutes alphabetical list of all current federal and provincial statutes referred to in the various subject titles in the CED

terms and connectors (Boolean) search method of searching that is based on principles of logic and that requires the use of keywords together with specific syntax

tribunals agencies, boards, and commissions that make decisions under regulatory or legislative schemes

truncation symbol symbol used in a computerized search to find all possible endings of a root word

unreported case case not published in a law report series

update determine whether the statute, regulation, or case is still good law (has not been repealed or overruled), and determine how the statute or regulation has been interpreted by the courts or how the case has been treated by other judges

updating tools sources that update primary sources of law

user's guide information in a research source about how to use that source

Index

Credits

Page and screen reproductions from the *Canadian Encyclopedic Digest, Halsbury's*, and WestlawNext® Canada are reproduced by permission of Thomson Reuters Canada Limited.

Screen reproductions from the Justice Laws website (http://laws-lois.justice.gc.ca) are reproduced with the permission of the Department of Justice Canada, 2016.

Screen reproductions from the Ontario e-Laws website (https://www.ontario.ca/laws) are reproduced with permission. © Queen's Printer for Ontario, 2015.

Screen reproductions from Quicklaw and QuickCITE are reproduced with permission of LexisNexis Canada Inc. All Rights Reserved.